Bloom's Modern Critical Interpretations

Bloom's Modern Critical Interpretations

Tennessee Williams's
The Glass Menagerie
Updated Edition

Edited and with an introduction by
Harold Bloom
Sterling Professor of the Humanities
Yale University

BLOOM'S
LITERARY CRITICISM
An imprint of Infobase Publishing

Bloom's Modern Critical Interpretations: The Glass Menagerie, Updated Edition

Copyright © 2007 Infobase Publishing
Introduction © 2007 by Harold Bloom

Bloom's Literary Criticism
An imprint of Infobase Publishing
132 West 31st Street
New York NY 10001

ISBN-10: 0-7910-9349-2
ISBN-13: 978-0-7910-9349-8

Library of Congress Cataloging-in-Publication Data
Tennessee Williams's The glass menagerie / Harold Bloom, editor. — Updated ed.
    p. cm. — (Bloom's modern critical interpretations)
  Includes bibliographical references and index.
  ISBN 0-7910-9349-2
  1. Williams, Tennessee, 1911-1983. Glass menagerie.
I. Bloom, Harold. II. Title. III. Series.
  PS3545.I5365G5383 2007
  812'.54—dc22   2006034132

Contributing Editor: Janyce Marson
Cover designed by Ben Peterson
Cover photo © Hulton Archive / Getty Images
Printed in the United States of America
Bang EJB 10 9 8 7 6 5 4 3 2 1

This book is printed on acid-free paper.

Contents

Editor's Note

My Introduction traces the barely evaded identification of Tom Wingfield with Williams himself, and of both with Hart Crane and *his* precursors, Shelley and Walt Whitman.

Nancy M. Tischler chronicles the public fortunes of *The Glass Menagerie*, after which Frank Durham finds in the play a full advent of Williams's poetic stance.

Menagerie is judged as deliberate avoidance of the tragic mode by Thomas E. Scheye, while Brian Parker attempts to restore multiplicity to the play.

For Roger Boxill, *Menagerie* is Tom's drama, though most performances emphasize his mother's role, after which Chekhov's *The Sea Gull* is seen by Drewey Wayne Gunn as Williams's prime source for the play.

A shrewd reading of *Menagerie* by C. W. E. Bigsby emphasizes the skilled employment of theatrical metaphors, while Gilbert Debusscher illuminates the play by studying its early drafts.

Bert Cardullo meditates on Laura's Romanticism in *Menagerie*, after which William Fordyce contrasts Tom Wingfield with Georg Kaiser's Cashier in *From Morn to Midnight*, a major Expressionist work of modern German drama.

This volume concludes with Lori Leathers Single's study of *Menagerie*'s images of the self.

HAROLD BLOOM

Introduction

In Hart Crane's last great Pindaric ode, "The Broken Tower," the poet cries aloud, in a lament that is also a high celebration, the destruction of his battered self by his overwhelming creative gift:

> The bells, I say, the bells break down their tower;
> And swing I know not where. Their tongues engrave
> Membrane through marrow, my long-scattered score
> Of broken intervals ... And I, their sexton slave!

This Shelleyan and Whitmanian catastrophe creation, or death by inspiration, was cited once by Williams as an omen of Crane's self-immolation. "By the bells breaking down their tower," in Williams's interpretation, Crane meant "the romantic and lyric intensity of his vocation." Gilbert Debusscher has traced the intensity of Crane's effect upon Williams's Romantic and lyric vocation, with particular reference to Tom Wingfield's emergent vocation in *The Glass Menagerie*. More than forty years after its first publication, the play provides an absorbing yet partly disappointing experience of rereading.

A professed "memory play," *The Glass Menagerie* seems to derive its continued if wavering force from its partly repressed representation of the quasi-incestuous and doomed love between Tom Wingfield and his crippled, "exquisitely fragile," ultimately schizophrenic sister Laura. Incest, subtly termed the most poetical of circumstances by Shelley, is the dynamic of the erotic drive throughout Williams's more vital writings. Powerfully displaced, it is the secret dynamic of what is surely Williams's masterwork, *A Streetcar Named Desire*.

The Glass Menagerie scarcely bothers at such a displacement, and the transparency of the incest motif is at once the play's lyrical strength and, alas, its dramatic weakness. Consider the moment when Williams chooses to end the play, which times Tom's closing speech with Laura's gesture of blowing out the candles:

> TOM: I didn't go to the moon, I went much further—for time is the longest distance between two places. Not long after that I was fired for writing a poem on the lid of a shoebox. I left St. Louis. I descended the steps of this fire escape for a last time and followed, from then on, in my father's footsteps, attempting to find in motion what was lost in space. I traveled around a great deal. The cities swept about me like dead leaves, leaves that were brightly colored but torn away from the branches. I would have stopped, but I was pursued by something. It always came upon me unawares, taking me altogether by surprise. Perhaps it was a familiar bit of music. Perhaps it was only a piece of transparent glass. Perhaps I am walking along a street at night, in some strange city, before I have found companions. I pass the lighted window of a shop where perfume is sold. The window is filled with pieces of colored glass, tiny transparent bottles in delicate colors, like bits of a shattered rainbow. Then all at once my sister touches my shoulder. I turn around and look into her eyes. Oh, Laura, Laura, I tried to leave you behind me, but I am more faithful than I intended to be! I reach for a cigarette, I cross the street, I run into the movies or a bar, I buy a drink, I speak to the nearest stranger—anything that can blow your candles out!
>
> [*Laura bends over the candles.*]
>
> For nowadays the world is lit by lightning! Blow out your candles, Laura—and so goodbye....
>
> [*She blows the candles out.*]

The many parallels between the lives and careers of Williams and Crane stand behind this poignant passage, though it is fascinating that the actual allusions and echoes here are to Shelley's poetry, but then Shelley increasingly appears to be Crane's heroic archetype, and one remembers Robert Lowell's poem where Crane speaks and identifies himself as the Shelley of his age. The cities of aesthetic exile sweep about Wingfield/Williams like the dead, brightly colored leaves of the "Ode to the West Wind," dead leaves that are at once the words of the poet and lost human souls, like the beloved sister Laura.

What pursues Tom is what pursues the Shelleyan Poet of *Alastor*, an avenging daimon or shadow of rejected, sisterly eros that manifests itself in a further Shelleyan metaphor, the shattered, colored transparencies of Shelley's dome of many-colored glass in *Adonais*, the sublime, lyrical elegy for Keats. That dome, Shelley says, is a similitude for life, and its many colors stain the white radiance of Eternity until death tramples the dome into fragments. Williams beautifully revises Shelley's magnificent trope. For Williams, life itself, through memory as its agent, shatters itself and scatters the colored transparencies of the rainbow, which ought to be, but is not, a covenant of hope.

As lyrical prose, this closing speech has its glory, but whether the dramatic effect is legitimate seems questionable. The key sentence, dramatically, is: "Oh, Laura, Laura, I tried to leave you behind me, but I am more faithful than I intended to be!" In his descriptive list of the characters, Williams says of his surrogate, Wingfield: "His nature is not remorseless, but to escape from a trap he has to act without pity." What would pity have been? And in what sense is Wingfield more faithful, after all, than he attempted to be?

Williams chooses to end the play as though its dramatic center had been Laura, but every reader and every playgoer knows that every dramatic element in the play emanates out from the mother, Amanda. Dream and its repressions, guilt and desire, have remarkably little to do with the representation of Amanda in the play, and everything to do with her children. The split between dramatist and lyrist in Williams is manifested in the play as a generative divide. Williams's true subject, like Crane's, is the absolute identity between his artistic vocation and his homosexuality. What is lacking in *The Glass Menagerie* is that Williams could not have said of Amanda, what, Flaubert-like, he did say of the heroine of *Streetcar*: "I am Blanche DuBois." There, and there only, Williams could fuse Chekhov and Hart Crane into one.

NANCY M. TISCHLER

The Glass Menagerie

The six-months contract Audrey Wood had wangled for her client with M.G.M. on the basis of his one-actors and *Battle of Angels*, proved to be considerably more profitable for Williams than for his boss and the studio. Although the author had expected to work on the best-selling novel *The Sun Is My Undoing*, the studio immediately set him to work on the scenario for *Marriage Is a Private Affair*, a bit of fluff that eventually starred Lana Turner. Williams has since established a mental block about the picture, refusing to remember its title. "I always thought of it as *The Celluloid Brassière*," he says. The dialogue he wrote was brilliant, he recalls, but not suitable for the story or the star. When his scenario was rejected, he was assigned to another picture starring Margaret O'Brien. His refusal to perform this chore was prefaced by a violently candid evaluation of child actors. He said such prodigies made him vomit.

In the meantime, he had once again entrusted Miss Wood with his money, which he admitted was "peanuts compared to what the names are getting, but it was riches to me," and he had asked her to dole it out to him fifty or seventy-five dollars at a time. He purchased a motor-scooter and a narrow-brim Tyrolean hat adorned with a bright little feather. He must have seemed an eccentric addition to Hollywood society as he roared into the studio lot behind huge, black, shiny Cadillacs and Rolls-Royces. But he was

From *Tennessee Williams: Rebellious Puritan*: pp. 91–116. © 1961 by The Citadel Press little concerned with the opinion of Hollywood, which he located on the "periphery" of his existence.

After his abortive attempts at writing movie scripts, he offered the film industry an idea of his own which he felt worthy of development. He had worked out the synopsis for a film he referred to as *The Gentleman Caller*. In introducing the outline to his superior at M.G.M., he announced, "This will run three times as long as *Gone With the Wind*. Shortly thereafter, his boss advised him to draw his pay-check quietly each week for the remainder of his contract—three and a half months—and to stay away from the office. Delighted, Williams sat out the remaining period of his $250-a-week contract on the beach at Santa Monica writing *The Gentleman Caller*, which he renamed *The Glass Menagerie*.

His life was happier now than it had been in some years. He had a good salary, a good idea for a play, and as good health as he ever allows himself to admit. Since he is never happier than when working, the arrangement was ideal. A short story that grew out of this period, "The Mattress in the Tomato Patch," describes his solidly contented landlady, the tanned athletes who roamed the beach and the house, and the richness of the sun-worshipping life—symbolized by the lushness of a bowlful of ripe tomatoes on his desk. Seldom have characters received such benevolent treatment at the hands of Tennessee Williams as in the work of that Santa Monica period—this earthy short story and the gentle play about his frightened sister.

When his contract was up he moved to Provincetown where he finished the play and sent it to his agent. Rather apologetically, he spoke of it to friends as "another of those old uncommercial plays of mine." Paul Moor records that "Miss Wood, much affected by the delicate story, tried to think of a producer who would be sympathetic to it and not botch it. For three weeks it did not leave her office; the fact that Williams never murmured about this apparent inactivity is a sample of his regard for Miss Wood.... Finally she remembered Eddie Dowling's touching production of Paul Vincent Carroll's *Shadow and Substance*, and sent it to him. No other producer ever had a chance at it. Dowling bought it, literally overnight."

Never a good critic of his own work, Williams later looked back at both *Battle of Angels* and *The Glass Menagerie* and said of the first, "That play was, of course, a much better play than this one. The thing is, you can't mix up sex and religion, as I did in *Battle of Angels*, but you can always write safely about mothers." He had worked so hard on the complex plot for his first Broadway play that the simple story of the second made it appear inferior. Authors seldom perceive that difficulty in composition bears little relation to the merit of the finished product. The troublesome play is like a maimed or difficult child that one loves all the more for the trouble he causes. To anyone but the writer himself, the fact that *The Glass Menagerie* was so easy to write suggests something of its truth, its naturalness, and its artistry.

The mother Williams had chosen to write about in *The Glass Menagerie* was, naturally, his own. The story is that of his last years in St. Louis—the Depression, "when the huge middle class of America was matriculating in a school for the blind. Their eyes had failed them, or they had failed their eyes, and so they were having their fingers pressed forcibly down on the fiery Braille alphabet of a dissolving economy." Tom, the hero, is working days at the shoe factory and writing nights in his stuffy room or going to the movies. The father of the play, who deserted the family some years earlier, having been a telephone man who fell in love with long distances, haunts the scene pleasantly in the form of an ineluctably smiling photograph. The mother, Amanda Wingfield, is trying to hold the family together and to steer her children into more practical paths than those she has followed herself, for she is a disillusioned romantic turned evangelical realist.

She lectures Tom on the merits of tending to business. By soliciting magazine subscriptions over the phone she finances a secretarial course in business school for Laura, her daughter. When Amanda finds that Laura is too nervous to learn to type, she decides that the girl must marry. This requires exposing her to an eligible bachelor, whom, to his consternation, Tom is to provide. Tom finally approaches Jim O'Connor, a fellow employee at the shoe factory, and invites him to dinner. Overdoing it, as usual, Amanda sets about redecorating the house and revising her daughter's dress and personality. Her frenzy makes the trio increasingly tense as they await the approach of Jim, the gentleman caller.

Jim had known Laura in high school and has been her idol for years. His nice manners appeal to Amanda. The dinner, consequently, proceeds beautifully, with only one slight interruption: the lights go off because Tom has spent the electric-bill money. Candlelight, however, suffices.

After dinner, Amanda hauls her son to the kitchen to provide privacy to the young couple whom this obvious maneuver reduces to painful embarrassment. Very shortly, though, Jim's good nature melts Laura's shyness, and she finds herself sitting on the floor with him chatting cozily by candlelight, sipping dandelion wine. They talk of Jim's ambitions in electro-dynamics and of his night-school courses. Then they turn to a discussion of Laura's collection of tiny glass animals and of her prize, a little unicorn. When, a few minutes later, they start to dance, Jim stumbles and breaks the horn off the little animal. Laura cradles her pet in her palm, musing that he is better off without his horn, for now he can be normal, like the other animals of the menagerie.

In this glimpse, we realize that sweet, simple Laura believes in these little creatures with the same eagerness that Jim believes in electro-dynamics. Finally, in a clumsy effort to apply his half-digested understanding of psychology, Jim decides that Laura has an inferiority complex and that he can cure it with a kiss. Then, horrified at what his action might suggest to this fuzzily romantic girl, he blurts out the secret that he is engaged. Laura, strangely enough, seems to be no more hurt by this clumsiness than by the breaking of the unicorn. Rather, on learning that her gentleman caller is not an eligible bachelor, she smiles stoically and gives him her now-hornless unicorn as a souvenir.

The tender mood is broken by the gay entrance of Amanda, bearing a pitcher of lemonade and singing a cruelly appropriate song about lemonade and old maids. Jim, finally understanding why he was invited, takes this moment to explain to Amanda that he plans to marry soon. Then he beats a hasty retreat. Amanda turns spittingly upon her son, who in turn stalks off to the movies. She screams after him that he can "go to the moon" since he is nothing but a selfish dreamer anyway. The final scene is a *tableau vivant* of Amanda, looking dignified and beautiful, comforting her daughter while Tom explains that he eventually escaped from the women to follow the pattern of his roving father. This simple story, turning on a dinner party given by a Southern family for an outsider whom they hope to match with their unmarried daughter and the character revelations that occur in its course, constitutes Tennessee Williams' most fragile and lovely play.

In some ways, *The Glass Menagerie* is a variation of the battle-of-angels theme. Tom expresses the same need to escape the nailed-up coffin of his restricted existence that Val expresses in the earlier play; but Tom seems to be more conscious of a corresponding loss that such freedom implies. He rejects the possessive love of his family because he can accept it only by shouldering the responsibility and accepting the imprisonment that go with it. The rejection of this relationship gives him pain, however, as his proposed desertion of Myra apparently did not give Val. This is a more realistic evaluation of human needs and yearnings. The characters also are more realistic. Although Tom and the others in *The Glass Menagerie* may represent attitudes toward life, none are personified abstractions. There is no Jabe to represent death. A subtler type of characterization combined with a simpler, less melodramatic story yields a far more artistic product.

One of the chief characters is sketched only by implication. The father of the Wingfield family hovers over the scene, although he never appears on stage at all. An enlarged photograph of him, which the spotlight occasionally illuminates, reminds us of his part in the formation of the dramatic situation. It is the picture of a handsome young man in a doughboy's cap. Though deeply hurt by his desertion, Amanda considers her erstwhile husband the embodiment of romance, associating him with that time in her life when the house in Blue Mountain was filled with gentleman callers and jonquils. (Blue Mountain is Mr. Williams' poetic name for Clarksdale, the standard symbol in his plays for romantic, happy youth.) Not having seen her husband growing old and ugly enables her to preserve her romantic image of him. That the father does not appear directly in the play suggests that Tennessee Williams could not view him with sufficient objectivity to portray him. The photograph apparently represents the standard view the outside world caught of the gay, soldierly C. C. Williams, whom his son hated so much that the sweetness would have gone out of the play if he had been included.

To Tom Wingfield, on the other hand, his father represents escape. He says of him, in the narrator's preface to the story, "He was a telephone man who fell in love with long distances; he gave up his job with the telephone company and skipped the light fantastic out of town." Then follows a hinted admiration of his romantic disappearance: "The last we heard of him was a picture post-card from Mazatlan, on the Pacific coast of Mexico, containing a message of two words—'Hello—Good-bye!' and no address." Tom's interest in his father's wanderlust, at the beginning of the play, prepares us for Tom's departure at its end. The picture itself, an enlarged photograph of Tom's own face, further emphasizes the similarities of their natures. Thus, while the father still personifies love to the romantic memory of the middle-aged Amanda, he symbolizes another kind of romance to his son—the romance of escape and adventure.

In discarding the real father's part, Tennessee Williams found it necessary to endow the mother with some masculine practicality, thus giving Amanda Wingfield an exceedingly complex personality. Like Myra of *Battle of Angels*, she has her past to recall and her present to endure. One had Moon Lake and love in the vineyard, the other Blue Mountain and gentleman callers. Amanda is, obviously, far more the lady, the Southern aristocrat, than the more voluptuous Myra. The only way Amanda can live with ugly reality is to retreat into her memories; there is no sexual solution for her. Her clothes, her speech, and her ideals for her children declare her belief in the past and her rejection of the present. As the author says of Amanda, "She is not paranoiac, but her life is paranoia."

The feature of this woman, which makes her a more admirable character than the later Blanche of *Streetcar* is the anomalous element of practicality encased in her romantic girlishness. Although she has approached much of her life unrealistically, her plans for her children and her understanding of their shortcomings are grimly realistic. Even when refusing to admit it, she knows Laura will never marry. She then tries to find Laura a protective corner of the business world. When this fails, she rallies for the valiant but hopeless attempt to marry the girl off. This second failure, we feel, is less tragic[1] for the daughter than for the mother.

Here we see the quality that Williams suggests from the beginning as the key to her character—her heroism. This, rather than her romantic turn, is her attraction. At the end of the play, when Tom has left, Amanda bends over Laura, huddled upon the sofa, to comfort her. By then, the audience realizes that Amanda herself is in greater need of this sympathy than the quietly resigned Laura. "Now that we cannot hear the mother's speech," says Williams, "her silliness is gone and she has dignity and tragic beauty."

We see this heroism in Amanda in her relations with Tom as well as with the more delicate and more romantic Laura. Although Tom understands the personality of his mother better than any other character in the story, he is more visionary and irresponsible than she is. He cannot see or accept the necessities of their life. Because of this and her previous experience with a romantic husband, she discourages Tom's attempts at a poetic or a nautical career. She returns the D. H. Lawrence novel to the library and nags at him whenever he escapes to a movie. She prods him to take an interest in practical things, like Jim's night classes in electro-dynamics. Here, as with her daughter, she is doomed to failure. Consequently, her final line is, "Go, then! Then go to the moon—you selfish dreamer!" Amanda is better able to speak these words with understanding because she shares his yearnings. Her dream has been smashed by reality, but has not been forgotten.

Tom is a poet who is desperately unhappy in his warehouse job, and, as yet, frustrated in his poetry. Since Tennessee William knows something of this not-very-tender trap, he speaks with feeling about the afflictions of the machine age. Believing that many, like himself, are poetic rather than mechanistic, he considers surrender to the machine a perversion of man's nature. His escape, heartless though it may seem, is a "necessary and wholesome measure of self-preservation" (as John Gassner expresses it).

Laura, like Rose, obviously can't escape into movies, alcohol, or literature; she simply isn't that violent or decisive. Her retreat is into a world of glass and music. Her father's old phonograph records provide her with escape that the unfamiliar new tunes can't provide. In the short story out of which the play grew, "Portrait of a Girl in Glass," Tom occasionally brings new records to his sister, but she seldom cares for them because they remind her too much of "the noisy tragedies in Death Valley or the speed-drills at the business college." Her collection of glass absorbs her time. She spends hours polishing the tiny animals that are as delicate and fragile as she.

Unable to adapt to the modern scene of electro-dynamics, she lives in a world of candlelight and fantasy. The encounter with the machine age is brief and useless. Laura could no more learn to type than Tom could ever come to like his job. Yet, unlike Tom, Laura seems not to feel the ugliness and entombment of their lives. Incapable of his violence, she never steps into the world for fear it would be impossible to bear. She merely stands at the brink and catches what she can of its beauty without becoming a part of it—a lovely picture of the simple Rose, who all through her brother's life has represented to him everything good and beautiful, soft and gentle.

Laura's early surrender is explained at the opening of the play by an allusion to an illness in childhood which left her crippled, one leg slightly shorter than the other and held in a brace (a physical parallel to Rose's mental affliction). The author explains, "Stemming from this, Laura's separation increases till she is like a piece of her own glass collection, too exquisitely fragile to move from the shelf."

Her mother is both Laura's disease and her brace. It is Amanda's forcefulness that allows Laura to walk at all, but it is also Amanda's example that discourages Laura from walking naturally. At one point, Laura puts on her mother's old coat, which of course is a poor fit for her, an action symbolic of her vague efforts at imitating a personality so alien to her powers and her own nature. She knows that she is like the unicorn or the blue rose, wrong for real life. Laura cannot see that Amanda exaggerates this wrongness by her impossibly romantic dreams. When Laura entered her high-school classes late, the sound of the brace on her leg seemed to her like claps of thunder. She thinks her affliction is dreadful because Amanda thinks it is. This flaw, a symbol of the crippling of a sensitive person thrust into a world unwilling to make allowances for sensitivity, becomes the cause of her separation from reality.

For Tennessee Williams, his sister became a symbol of the sensitive and the outcast, for their sensitivity invariably subjects them to mutilation. It is no accident that Laura's story appears in the collection of early fiction, eventually published under the title *One Arm*. Every important character in the book—the college students, the vagrant poet, the sallow little masochist, the perverted artist, the consumptive factory worker, the one-armed male prostitute, and the girl with her glass menagerie—can be destroyed at a touch. All, like Laura, are crippled in some way. The radiance of such people is like a "piece of translucent glass touched by light, given a momentary radiance, not actual, not lasting."

Laura contrasts with the normal, middle-class, realistic Jim, with whom she falls dreamily in love. Their views show their complete diversity. For example, when they discuss her favorite animal, the unicorn, Laura thinks of him as intrinsically different from his companions, while Jim sees him simply as a horse with a horn. In the same way, Jim sees the defect in Laura's leg as only unfortunately incidental to her normal body, while Laura feels that the flaw transforms her whole being. Jim can sympathize with Laura's world of glass and candlelight for this evening, but his real interests are in the modern mechanical world of self-improvement. He is the only character in the play who goes out of the house into a normal world of "reality." Tom emphasizes this in the opening and closing lines of the play; he is an emissary from another world; he does not belong to the Wingfield world of dreams and fears and unexpressed desires.

Jim is not an especially effective character study because Williams can feel little sympathy with such a substantial and placid citizen. Yet he is a kindly reminder of the reasonable, normal human pattern, like the men Williams had met at the shoe factory—clean-living, honest, sweet-natured, materialistic, eager American businessmen. The gently satirical portrait bears no relationship to the later, bitter portraits of C. C. Williams.

Since it is characteristic of Amanda, more than of the others, to long for everything Jim represents, he is for her an archetype of the "long delayed but always expected something we live for." Unintentionally, Jim breaks up the Wingfield dreams. We suspect that his entrance into the household is part of a recurring pattern. Every contact with the real world has shattered Amanda's unrealistic hopes over the years.

The setting of *The Glass Menagerie* was interesting in its symbolism and technical experimentation. Moving from the deep South to St. Louis for his story, Williams retains the memory of the South, as a haunting presence under the superimposed Midwestern setting. The audience, never seeing the gracious mansion that was the scene of Amanda's girlhood, feels its remembered glory and its contrast to the mean present. Awareness of the past is always an element in Williams' plays. His characters live beyond the fleeting moments of the drama—back into a glowing past and shrinking from a terrifying future. For both Amanda and the later Blanche of *Streetcar*, the South forms an image of youth, love, purity, all of the ideals that have crumbled along with the mansions and the family fortunes.

Since the setting in *Menagerie* is that of a memory play, Tennessee Williams could feel free in its staging. His theory of expressionism is propounded in the introductory production notes, which are, in fact, directly applied in the play. His concept of the "new, plastic theatre" was probably influenced by Erwin Piscator, a German director who had helped him at the New School Seminar. He suggests that in *The Glass Menagerie*'s "considerably delicate or tenuous material, atmospheric touches and subtleties of direction play a particularly important part." Williams justifies such unconventional techniques as expressionism or impressionism on the basis that their subjectivity provides a "closer approach to truth." No playwright should use such devices in an effort to avoid the "responsibility of dealing with reality, or interpreting experience." But he believes that the new drama has followed the other arts in recognizing that realism is not the key to reality.

"The straight realistic play with its genuine frigidaire and authentic ice-cubes, its characters that speak exactly as its audience speaks," he says, "corresponds to the academic landscape and has the same virtue of photographic likeness." Then, with unique optimism regarding current artistic tastes, he continues, "Everyone should know nowadays the unimportance of the photographic in art: that truth, life, or reality is an organic thing which the poetic imagination can represent or suggest, in essence, only through transformation, through changing into other forms than those which were merely present in appearance." The philosophy expressed here is in accord with the nineteenth century romantics and their followers in this century. The expressionistic concepts propounded in this preface have proved so effective in Tennessee Williams' work that set-designers have usually chosen to use expressionistic even when realistic settings are called for in Williams' manuscripts. Williams has a poet's weakness for symbols, and this modern technique frees his hand for scattering them about the stage. Their use to reflect, emphasize, and contrast with the meanings of the actions and the words has become a trademark of the Williams play.

The Glass Menagerie projected symbolic elements in line with Williams' newly enunciated theory. To reinforce the spoken word the author recommends the use of a screen device. A legend or image projected on the screen for the duration of the scene emphasizes the most important phrase. For example, in the scene where Jim remembers that Laura is the girl who was stricken with pleurosis, whom he mistakenly nicknamed "Blue Roses," the legend on the screen accents the peculiarity of the name, and the audience, along with Laura, is made more keenly aware that although blue is beautiful, it is wrong for roses. Eddie Dowling considered this device superfluous and omitted it from the stage production, and wisely so. Mr. Gassner also considered the screen device "redundant and rather precious." Williams is "straining for effect not knowing that his simple tale, so hauntingly self-sufficient, needs no adornments."

Williams' expressionist theory also leads him to another variation from strictly realistic drama. The lighting changes with the mood. The stage is as dim as the participants' lives. Shafts of light flicker onto selected areas or actors, "sometimes in contradiction to what is the apparent center." When Tom and Amanda are quarreling, the light on them is low red, while Laura stands in a pool of light of that "peculiar pristine clarity such as light used in early religious portraits of saints or madonnas." The tone, strength, and occurrence of the lights have the power of emotional emphasis. In a technique reminiscent of Chekhov's, Williams heightens the emotional truths of the scenes and the reality of the internal action through unusual external effects.

The musical accompaniment of *The Glass Menagerie* is another element of Tennessee Williams' expressionism that characterizes his dramas. The theme is a tune called "The Glass Menagerie," composed by Paul Bowles. It is "like circus music, not when you are on the grounds or in the immediate vicinity of the parade, but when you are at some distance and very likely thinking of something else.... It expresses the surface vivacity of life and the underlying strain of immutable and inexpressible sorrow." The music becomes Laura's symbol: of this world which is like a circus for her—heard from a safe distance; and of her retreat into a world of music as well as of glass.

The depiction of the Wingfields' apartment also follows the dicta of expressionism. The ugly uniformity of the tenements depresses Tom and makes him frantic to escape. The place is described as "one of those vast hive-like conglomerations of cellular living-units that flower as warty growths in overcrowded urban centers of lower middle-class populations." They are, says the temporarily socially conscious author, "symptomatic of the impulse of this largest and fundamentally enslaved section of American society to avoid fluidity and differentiation and to exist and function as one interfused mass of automatism." Of the characters in the play, only Tom seems aware of this grotesque uniformity; and since the whole story takes place in his memory, he would naturally exaggerate the dismal reality he sees.

On both sides of the building, dark, narrow alleys run into "murky canyons of tangled clotheslines, garbage cans and sinister lattice-work of neighboring fire escapes." The meaning of these alleys is clear if the reader recalls Tom's picture of "Death Valley," where cats were trapped and killed by a vicious dog. The predicament becomes a symbol of his factory work, murderous to his creative imagination. For Laura, the alley represents the ugly world from which she retreats to gaze into her tiny glass figures. For Amanda, too, the alley is the world of her present hopeless poverty and confusion from which she retreats into her make-believe world of memory and pretence. Inside the apartment, where she tries to create an illusion of gentility, her husband's portrait grins at her futile efforts.

The apartment is entered by a fire escape, "a structure whose name is a touch of accidental poetic truth, for all those huge buildings are always burning with the slow and implacable fires of human desperation." On this fire escape, Tom Wingfield seeks liberation from his private hell. It is no mere coincidence that this play's solution (like those of *Battle of Angels* and *Stairs to the Roof*) centers around the stairway. Stairs are the tangible sign of man's change in levels of reality.

It would seem that every item of the setting is symbolic—even the Paradise Dance Hall, across the alley. There sexual gratification provides the cliff-dwellers of the neighborhood a temporary paradise. In their moments of closeness, they achieve the escape that Tom finds in his movies and poetry.

The story, characterization, and setting of this play combine to form a "static" drama, a technique Williams has used in other plays, including the rewrite of *Battle of Angels*. Action is softened by this "patina" of time and distance; framed in memory, it becomes more artistic. The interest of this play depends on neither incident nor situation. Unlike most of Williams' other works that are charged with sensationalism and sex, this story holds the audience by the revelation of quiet and ordinary truths. This play, unique among Williams' dramas, combines poetic and unrealistic techniques with grim naturalism to achieve a gossamer effect of compassion, fragility, and frustration, typical of Tennessee Williams at his most sensitive and natural best. The play is his most effective poetic work.

As soon as Eddie Dowling saw the play, he was interested. He already had a play with "commercial possibilities" ready to put on when he read *The Glass Menagerie*. Delighted with its artistic but probably uncommercial possibilities, he asked his backer, Louis J. Singer, to release him from their arrangement. "I've found a play I love," he told the newcomer to the ranks of Broadway producers. I don't think it will earn a dime but it will make me very happy to do it."

Mr. Singer asked, "Have you arranged for backing?"

"Not yet," replied Dowling. "You've got a partner."

Dowling then showed the script to George Jean Nathan, who was immediately interested in the part of Laura for Julie Haydon. He also thought the role of Amanda ideal for the woman considered by many to be America's greatest living actress, Laurette Taylor.

As soon as Miss Taylor saw the script, she called her closest friend. "I've found it, Eloise!" she said. "I've found the play I've been waiting for." The aging actress had, in recent years, starred in only a few plays. Her greatest success had been years earlier, when she had one of Broadway's longest runs as *Peg o' My Heart*. Since her husband's death, she had become an alcoholic, and her theatrical opportunities had steadily declined. Producers were afraid to trust her. Recently, however, she had recovered her control and had been looking for a good part. She recognized in the Amanda created by this unknown playwright a flesh-and-blood character who would challenge all the resources of an experienced actress. She accepted the part with enthusiasm.

When Williams heard that Laurette Taylor was to play Amanda, he was astonished. He thought she had died. The only memory of her he could dredge up was of walking by a St. Louis movie theatre and reading the advertisements for the silent film *Peg o' My Heart*, starring Laurette Taylor. He had not gone in.

Before going to Chicago to join the company at rehearsals, Williams went to St. Louis to see his mother. Since *The Glass Menagerie* was on its way to Broadway with big-name stars in its cast, the St. Louis press welcomed the visiting playwright whom it could claim as its own. To the discomfiture of the reporters, he replied to their inquiries with brutally candid recollections of his miserable youth there and his impressions of its ugliness and unfriendliness, thereby alienating many civic-minded St. Louisans. But one of the interviewers, the man sent by the *Star-Times*, happened to be William Inge, then its amusement-page editor. Inge called Williams to discuss the interview and to suggest some entertainment, since anyone so long away from St. Louis would probably find few of his old friends still there. Williams went to Inge's apartment, located in a housing project. "When he opened the door, I saw over his shoulder a reproduction of my favorite Picasso," wrote Williams of this visit, "I knew that the interview would be as painless as it turned out to be." The two became friends, swimming together at the "Y" every day while Williams was in St. Louis. Since the editor had passes to plays and movies he was to cover for his paper, he took the penniless visitor along with him.

From St. Louis, Williams met the troupe and went on to Chicago for rehearsals. Later, recalling the loneliness of his arrival at Chicago's Union Station, he remembered his delight on seeing a familiar face and figure. "It was a short and nearly square figure in a peculiar costume, like something rooted from the bottom of an old wardrobe trunk." This costume consisted of a grey muskrat coat, the pelts of which were "not enjoying the most pacific relation," and a broad-brimmed hat "of the type that is worn by cinema buccaneers." Staring out from between the turned-up collar and turned-down brim were eyes "much too bright to be described as brown." The face was framed by a "cloudy profusion of hair that is lighter than auburn." This small woman looked as lost and frightened as the young author himself. His heart went out to her.

"Laurette!" he called. She turned and called out his name. "Then and there," he remembers, "we joined forces. The station diminished to a comfortable size; the bitter cold thawed a little, we moved off together with a feeling of union deeper than physical, more than accidental, to find a taxi."

Laurette Taylor was a legend in the theatre long before Tennessee Williams wrote his first play. She brought to the role of Amanda, which proved to be her last, all her genius for characterization. She worked feverishly to catch the essence of the woman. Her technique was to study the part, learning rather than memorizing, and she drove Eddie Dowling almost out of his mind. From time to time he would murmur, "That woman is crucifying me!" It didn't occur to her that other actors didn't appreciate the changes she made and resented her unreadiness during rehearsals. Everyone else knew his part before she.

However, her interest in the play far outstripped theirs. She actually directed many of the scenes in which she and Julie Haydon appeared, and Williams estimates her directing as "a top-notch job." This continued even after the play was in production. "Almost every night in Chicago," Williams recalls, "there was something new but she never disturbed the central characterization. Everything she did was absolutely in character." She and the author were not always in perfect accord about suggested changes. She tried to talk him into changing one speech, of which he was especially enamoured, the one in which Amanda reminisces about the house full of flowers and suitors. She insisted, "It's just too many jonquils, Tennessee. Can't you cut a few?"

His reply was, "Laurette, it's got rhythm. Ah need all those jonquils!"

One of her major problems was the acquisition of a Southern accent. When they first started rehearsals, the author came up to Miss Taylor and said quietly, as she remembered, "Miss Taylor, Ah hopes yo' don't mahn mah sayin' so but yo' Southe'n accent is a little thick."

"All right," she answered. "How would you like it if I copied you?"

He agreed. At rehearsals after that, she would say, "Talk to me, Tennessee, just talk to me. Don't explain how to pronounce the words, just keep talking."

Their friendship grew, despite the barrier which separates the shy Williams from the rest of the world. Miss Taylor used to say of him, "Tennessee is a *very* sensitive fellow." She couldn't quite understand his kind of sensitivity but she could sympathize with it.

Miss Taylor was never happy with Eddie Dowling in the role of her son, thinking him too old and too mannered in the part. However, they, Julie Haydon, and Anthony Ross formed a highly-skilled team. With such a collection of talent, and with the additional boost of Margo Jones as assistant-director with Eddie Dowling, the outlook seemed good.

Nevertheless, ill luck at first pursued *The Glass Menagerie*. When the company arrived in Chicago, the set-erector was too drunk to work, and without him, it took twenty-four hours of steady work to set up a single scene. Then Jo Mielziner found that Julie Haydon's costume for the second act showed up poorly in the light. Louis Singer, the coproducer, was dubious about the play's chances for success and wanted to back out. He refused to put another dollar into the production. When twenty dollars were needed for another costume, Eddie Dowling, Miss Haydon, and Williams chipped in to buy it. Then Laurette Taylor, who had become almost paralyzed with fear by opening night, was discovered in her dressing room, a few hours before the opening curtain, dyeing a bathrobe which she was to wear in the second act; she was frantic.

But somehow, everything mysteriously fitted together by opening night. The excited audience cried, "Author! Author!" and the red-faced young playwright took a happy bow.

Though tempered with some adverse critical comment on the unevenness of the writing, the intrusion of the narrator, and the poeticizing, the reviews were mostly raves. The critics loved the play and adored Miss Taylor in it. The Chicago journalist and writer, Lloyd Lewis, reported that Miss Taylor had not been the center of so much discussion since *Peg o' My Heart*, exactly thirty years before. Analyzing her remarkable style, he noted, "When Miss Taylor mumbles in magnificent realism she is still enough of a vocal wizard to be intelligible to her audience, and when she pouts, nags or struts in pathetic bursts of romantic memory she is superb at pantomime. Her descents into hysteria are masterpieces of understatement, dramatic enough that they force the audience to do the acting for her."

Ashton Stevens, the critic for the *Herald-American*, was so entranced he saw *The Glass Menagerie* six more times after opening night. He closed his review by saying, "From neighboring seats I heard William Saroyan mentioned, and Paul Vincent Carroll and Sean O'Casey, and even a playwright named Barrie. But the only author's name I could think of was Tennessee Williams, whose magic was his own." However, the public did not respond at first, and there were many empty seats.

William Inge, who went up to Chicago to see his new friend's play that December, reports that "Williams was in a state of gloom. The reviews had been favorable, but the audiences weren't coming yet. They did, a few weeks later, lashed into it by a steady stream of propaganda from the critics." Inge himself was delighted with the play: "I've been really inspired very few times in the theater. What the play did for me was show me for the first time the dynamic relationship between art and life. After seeing it I seemed to know where to look for material in myself." The two of them spent a dreary New Year's Eve together that year. "We went around to bars and watched others celebrate."

Williams' mother also came to Chicago to see the play that December. Her son had not told her that Amanda was a portrait of herself. He still remembers her reactions with fond humor. As she listened to Laurette Taylor uttering her favorite comments about the family and life in general, "Mother began to sit up stiffer and stiffer. She looked like a horse eating briars. She was touching her throat and clasping her hands and quite unable to look at me…. What made it particularly hard for Mother to bear is that she is a tiny, delicate woman with great dignity and always managing to be extremely chic in dress, while Laurette Taylor invested the part with that blowsy, powerful quality of hers—and thank God she did, for it made the play."

When the performance was over, he asked his mother to go backstage and meet Miss Taylor. "She was somewhat constrained," he says in obvious understatement, "but she went." The meeting was one to remember. Laurette Taylor, oblivious of her feelings, promptly said, "And how do you like yourself on the stage?" Mrs. Williams could not quite bring herself to answer that question. She expressed polite surprise that Miss Taylor should consider it her portrait. "Laurette had another tactless idea. 'I have a very intellectual forehead,' she confided in Mother. 'However, the woman in this play is a fool. That's why I wear bangs.'" Williams reports with barely suppressed amusement, "Mother kept her composure but it was a severe test. Later she came to see that to have been portrayed by Laurette Taylor was the greatest tribute she could have and her visit backstage became her favorite story."

Plaudits for the play and the performers continued, and gradually the audiences began to crowd out the returning critics. *The Glass Menagerie* lost its reputation for "preciousness" and became a full-fledged success.

By the time the company had reached New York, its critical reputation had preceded it and stirred up a healthy anticipation. On opening night the audience again called "Author! Author!" and the author, overcome with delight at his newly achieved success and his appreciation of the cast, stepped into the aisle from his fourth-row seat and bowed first to the stage, thereby presenting the first-night audience with an unexpected view of his rear.

Robert Rice calls this opening night a "memorable evening in the theatre." The enthusiasm of the audience was reflected at the box-office. *The Glass Menagerie* ran for nearly two years on Broadway.

When the critics gathered to vote on the coveted Critics' Award, on April 10, 1945, at the Algonquin, it took them only fifteen minutes to choose *The Glass Menagerie* by nine out of fourteen votes. *Harvey* was the runner-up.

Although *The Glass Menagerie* had proved a winner, Williams doubted needlessly that critics would like future plays of his as well. "In this play I said all the nice things I have to say about people," he confessed. "The future things will be harsher." And indeed they were! But harsh or no, Tennessee Williams was to continue to be the "awards man of the younger generation."

His pleasure in his success was marred by something that was to plague the playwright through the rest of his career. Miss Taylor's powerful handling of her part and Eddie Dowling's effective direction evoked comments that the triumph was that of the company rather than of the playwright. Rumor exaggerated Eddie Dowling's suggestions, that the screen device be omitted and that a drunk scene be added, into conclusions that the success was the result of skillful rewriting by talented play doctors. Williams' readiness to listen to those more experienced than he looked like a weakness rather than a virtue to outsiders. For that reason the published version of the play has italicized: "There is *only one important difference between the original and acting version of the play* and that is the *omission* in the latter which I tentatively included in my *original* script." The italics are his; the effect of the statement was to squelch a few of these rumors—but they were to reappear with each of his successes.

Since Tennessee Williams has owed much of his success to the designers, directors, and actors who have caught the fire of his conception and conveyed it vividly and artistically to the audience, these belittling rumors are partially justified. The reader, however, has only to see how fully he conceives the scenery and the people of his dramas to realize that the greatest credit for the final product belongs to the writer. His parts are exciting to play, a fact to which one actor after another has testified; and his dramas are challenging to stage, lending themselves to the impressionistic or expressionistic devices of imaginative designers or directors.

Laurette Taylor was one of many who tried to make the modest Williams see that the talent was his. No actor or actress was indispensable to him. Everyone had worried about Miss Taylor's dependability from the beginning; after her phenomenal success in the part, speculation grew that the play would collapse without her. Her throat began to give her trouble in Chicago, but because she knew the rumors about her alcoholism, she refused to take a rest. She continued in the demanding part—frequently vomiting after a performance, looking white and weak—obviously a sick woman. Williams later recalled how few people sympathized with her in her ordeal. He said that she was keenly aware of the reservation in so many minds about her. She was "determined to beat it. She did. She was neither a well nor a strong person at any time during the run of the play and often continued her performance when a person of ordinary spirit would not have dared to."

No one seemed to realize the sacrifice of personal comfort and health involved in her remaining a year and a half with *The Glass Menagerie*. "She remained in the part that long because of a heroic perseverance I find as magnificent as her art itself." The term which best fits Williams' view of this fine actress as she battled ill health and ugly rumors is *gallantry*. Amanda proved to be her last part. She died in 1946.

Tennessee Williams joined the host of her mourners, insisting that she was "the greatest artist of her profession that I have known. I loved her as a person. I'm afraid it is the only close friendship I have ever had with a player." In her, he experienced a rare glimpse of "something that lies outside the flesh and its mortality.... There was a radiance about her art which I can compare only to the greatest lines of poetry, and which gave me the same shock of revelation as if the air about us had been momentarily broken through, by light from some clear space beyond us.... Having created a part for Laurette Taylor is a reward I find sufficient for all the effort that went before and any that may come after."

Just before she died, Laurette Taylor had retired from her role. When the road company opened in Pittsburgh, with Pauline Lord as Amanda, the notices spoke warmly of Pauline Lord's performance in the part of Amanda. "I have just read the Pittsburgh notices," Miss Taylor wired the adoring author, then adding, "What did I tell you, my boy? You don't need me." These are the last words that Tennessee Williams was ever to hear from Laurette Taylor, but they summarize much of the generous, warm, human understanding of this fine actress.

Shortly after *The Glass Menagerie* had settled into the Playhouse for its long run, Robert van Gelder interviewed Tennessee Williams for *The New York Times*. He found his subject a clean-shaven, individualistic, befuddled young man in his early thirties. He said of him that, when he went to shake hands, he put out both hands as if confused as to which one to use. A man of "quiet candor," Tennessee Williams seemed a "composed, confident dreamer, observant, self-centered, sympathetic, remote." He still disliked New York, as he had on that first visit and as he does to this day, bluntly stating, "I have no interest in the intellectuals or pseudo-intellectuals that I find here.... They mean nothing to me creatively." Assuming a pose of disinterest, he disclaimed being impressed by applause, desiring only to write for the "creative theatre."

As his income began to rise, Williams signed 50 per cent of his earnings over to his mother. His friends insisted that his shabbiness was now uncalled-for and was therefore faintly pretentious. So he moved into a suite at a good hotel that had a swimming pool, bought some expensive clothes, and even replaced his old faithful phonograph with a new electric model.

But with increased fame and income came unexpected difficulties. His Bohemian existence left him unprotected from self-seekers. (He even thought it was required by law to put a name card on the door wherever he lived.) So leeches and pack rats appeared in droves. Not so cynical as most who reach this position, he was appalled at the insincerity of the people who came to cadge his time and money. Old friends started complaining that he was high-hatting them because he couldn't spend so much time with them as in the past. Perplexed, he tried to reason out the difficulty he felt: "There is a kind of problem in personal integrity," he decided. "The real fact is that no one means a great deal to me, anyway, but almost anybody will do. I'm rather selfish in picking my friends, anyway; that is, I prefer people who can help me in some way or another, and most of my friendships are accidental.... I don't want to be like most people. And I do think there is a problem of personal integrity involved." One of those who especially disgusted him and whom he avoided was his father. After years of trying to discourage his writing, old C. C. Williams suddenly took pride in his hitherto worthless son.

Another touch of ironic satisfaction accompanied the success of *The Glass Menagerie*. The last word Tennessee Williams had had from M.G.M. studios was in answer to a question he had asked while still working for them. He had requested permission to go to the opening of one of his plays in Cleveland, and his boss had answered that he could go on one condition— that he never come back. Now here was the rejected manuscript, née *The Gentleman Caller*, a Broadway success and the subject of heated bargaining by several Hollywood producers, among them, to Williams' immense satisfaction, M.G.M. The play written on M.G.M. time went to Warner Brothers.

For a while the plan was to use Ethel Barrymore for Amanda, but then Feldman of Warner Brothers decided on Gertrude Lawrence. Miss Lawrence wasn't especially interested at first, fearing that she would become typed for mother roles. Finally, though, she agreed, and Feldman was willing to wait two years for her to become available for the part. He managed to satisfy her pride by including some flashbacks of the young Amanda. "Otherwise," said Miss Lawrence, "she [Amanda] would have been only a character study of a middle-aged woman, and I don't want to get mother roles, and unglamorous ones at that. I'd be afraid if I succeeded I'd never do any thing else."

So *The Glass Menagerie* headed for Hollywood, settled in for a long New York run, began road company tours, opened in London (Helen Hayes, the London Amanda, like Miss Taylor gained credit for "making" the show), and finally toured the Continent. Tennessee Williams found that he had finally embraced the "Bitch Goddess" Success.

NOTES

1. My use of the term *tragic* corresponds with Mr. Williams'. I do not see most of his people as having the stature of the classical or neo-classical tragic heroes, but to their symbolic value they do express heroism. Their status and their values are not so exalted as in the older plays. They are more realistic and pathetic than the traditional hero was allowed to be.

FRANK DURHAM

Tennessee Williams, Theatre Poet in Prose

Modern American attempts at verse drama have, on the whole, produced a harvest of respectable failures—*vide* the ambitious but incongruously rhetorical and ornate plays of Maxwell Anderson and the mannered and rather coldly calculated pieces by T. S. Eliot. Anderson bravely called for a return to poetry in the theatre and ground out a kind of blank verse that wore the label "Poetry"—in red paint;[1] while Eliot, likewise, wrote on the need for poetry in drama but staunchly maintained that the verse of the poet-dramatist should be so subtly disguised as, for the most part, not to sound like verse at all.[2] One of the difficulties regarding the use of verse in the modern theatre, as Eliot and MacLeish point out,[3] is the belief that the audience demands to see life as it is and that to such an audience poetry (or is it merely verse?) sounds "artificial." Eliot does say that there is a "peculiar range of sensibility [which] can be expressed by dramatic poetry, at its moments of greatest intensity," "a fringe of indefinite extent," beyond the capabilities of prose drama to express.[4] However, it is the contention of this paper that, while American drama has increasingly sought to portray this "peculiar range of sensibility," the most successful means of doing so has not been verse. It has, instead, been best portrayed by a new, or seemingly new, poetic drama which eschews verse for an eclectic but organic union of both verbal and non-verbal elements of the theatre, which many critics have

From *South Atlantic Bulletin*, vol. XXXVI, no. 2 (March 1971): pp. 3–16. © 1971 by the South Atlantic Modern Language Association.

recognized and which Tennessee Williams, one of its major practitioners, calls "plastic theatre." *The Glass Menagerie* will serve as a prime example of the form.

It is, of course, no longer necessary to argue that verse need not be metrical, but certainly the comparative failures of both Anderson and Eliot can be attributed largely to their clinging to the idea that metre is an essential of poetic drama. In fact, Anderson employed a somewhat modified blank verse, which in itself throws up a barrier between the contemporary play and the contemporary audience's acceptance of it; for blank verse is firmly fixed in the theatre-going mind with Shakespeare and the raft of pallid pseudo-Shakespeareans. To use it on stage today is somewhat analogous to employing the Dickensian chronicle for a modern psychological novel. It reeks of the past—and of fustian. And Eliot's adherence to a three-stressed line with a caesura is somewhat reminiscent of Anglo-Saxon verse.

What we have developed in twentieth-century America is a type of poetic drama peculiarly relevant to our own time, a drama which maintains a speaking acquaintance with surface reality but which, through all the means at its disposal, probes into and bodies forth what Eliot calls that "peculiar range of sensibility," the inner truth, the often unutterable essences of human action and human emotion. As Alan Downer says:

> Thus the true poet of the theater is not necessarily concerned in the least with the traditional forms and language of poetry, but with making all the elements at his disposal—plot, actor, action, stage, lighting, setting, music, speech—unite to serve as a vehicle for his theme, his vision, or his interpretation of man's fate.[5]

And again:

> Properly handled, organically related to the action and purpose of the whole work, the devices of expressionism have permitted playwrights to penetrate beneath the surface of their situations, to reveal truths which realism by its nature tends to disguise. This penetration, this revelation of inner truth, brings the contemporary drama once more into a close relationship with the great repertory of the poetic drama of the past.[6]

O'Neill was one of the first American playwrights to move thus beyond realism toward a new poetry of the theatre, but today its chief figure is Tennessee Williams.

In his "Author's Production Notes" to *The Glass Menagerie*, in which he discusses at length such "extra-literary" elements as music and lighting, Williams makes clear that he is consciously striving to write this new type of poetic drama. Calling the piece "a memory play" and saying that it is therefore to be produced "with unusual freedom of convention," he says:

> Because of its considerably delicate or tenuous material, atmospheric touches and subtleties of direction play a particularly important part. Expressionism and all other unconventional techniques in drama have only one valid aim, and that is a closer approach to truth. When a play employs unconventional techniques, it is not, or certainly shouldn't be, trying to escape its responsibility of dealing with reality, or interpreting experience, but is actually or should be attempting to find a closer approach, a more penetrating and vivid expression of things as they are. The straight realistic play with its genuine frigidaire and authentic ice-cubes, its characters that speak exactly as its audience speaks, corresponds to the academic landscape and has the same virtue of photographic likeness. Everyone should know nowadays the unimportance of the photographic in art: that truth, life, or reality is an organic thing which the poetic imagination can represent or suggest, in essence, only through transformation, through changing into other forms than those which merely present an appearance.
>
> These remarks are not meant as a preface only to this particular play. They have to do with a conception of a new, plastic theatre which must take the place of the exhausted theatre of realistic conventions if the theatre is to resume vitality as a part of our culture.[7]

Thus Williams is consciously ushering in a new period in drama and a form, as Esther Merle Jackson says, distinctively and consciously American, a popular art form embodying all levels of American culture and life and in its intentions definitely poetic: "The search for a concrete expressive form—a shape congruent with poetic vision—is a motif that appears throughout the work of Williams."[8]

His realization of the need for "transformation" suggests Frost's idea: "... it is the height of poetry, the height of all thinking, the height of all poetic thinking, that attempts to say matter in terms of spirit and spirit in terms of matter." And, Frost continues, poetry (and thinking) is simply "saying one thing in terms of another."[9] Elsewhere Frost maintains that "every poem is a new metaphor inside or it is nothing," and every poem is a symbol.[10] Certainly in *The Glass Menagerie*, often called a "lyric play," Williams is employing this concept of "transformation," of the dominant metaphor and symbol. Tom, his narrator-character, begins by telling us: "I give you truth in the pleasant guise of illusion" (p. 3).

In *The Glass Menagerie* there are two dominant metaphors or symbols. The more obvious is, of course, glass, as the title itself implies. Laura's glass animals, especially the unicorn, which is broken, symbolize the tenuousness of her hold on reality, the ease with which her illusion may be shattered. Of her, Williams says, "... the lovely fragility of glass which is her image" (p. vii). This symbol is relevant to the other characters also, for their ability to exist at all in the world rests on illusions as easily destroyed as the unicorn. Without her belief in her romantic past and in Laura's ultimate wooing by the non-existent Gentleman Caller, Amanda, who is the strongest, would be unable to face the harsh struggle for survival, would lose that fierce strength which in her is both comic and tragically admirable. At the touch of truth, her world will shatter into a thousand irretrievable fragments. The Gentleman Caller, Jim O'Connor, is also sustained by two illusions, that of his great success and promise in high school and that of his future triumph based on the empty slogans of his television night course: "Because I believe in the future of television! I want to be ready to go right rip along with it.... I'm planning to get in on the ground floor. Oh, I've already made the right connections. All that remains now is for the industry itself to get under way—full steam! You know, *knowledge*—ZSZZppp! Money—ZZZZZZpp! POWER! Wham! That's the cycle democracy is built on!" (p. 54) Jim himself, as Tom tells us, is the momentary and disappointing embodiment of Laura and Amanda's illusion—"But having a poet's weakness for symbols, I am using this character as a symbol—as the long-delayed but always expected something we live for" (p. 3). Tom, despising his job in the warehouse, escaping temporarily into the fantasy world of the movies, cherishes the ideal of the absconded father ("He was a telephone man who fell in love with long distance....") and envies Malvolio the Magician, who, nailed inside a coffin, "got out without removing one nail" (p. 19). But in Tom's case glass is both fragile and everlasting, for his physical escape brings no real liberation. Though he travels widely, the trap still holds him:

> Perhaps it was a familiar bit of music. Perhaps it was only a piece of transparent glass.... Perhaps I am walking along a street at night, in some strange city, before I have found companions, and I pass the lighted window of a shop where perfume is sold. The window is filled with pieces of colored glass, tiny transparent

bottles in delicate colors, like bits of a shattered rainbow. Then all at once my sister touches my shoulder. I turn around and look into her eyes. (p. 62)

While glass is the more obvious of the metaphors or symbols which govern the play—and it is, to me, the symbol of the theme—the motion picture serves as the symbol determining the over-all form of the play. Tom, the narrator, through whose consciousness we see the entire action, tells us at the start, "The play is memory.... Being a memory play, it is dimly lighted, it is sentimental, it is not realistic" (p. 3). Since it is Tom's memory and since Tom's escape from reality is the motion picture, Williams logically portrays Tom's memories in terms of the motion picture, the silent film even though dialogue is used. The structure and rhythmic flow of the scenes are like those of the motion picture. The screen device, generally omitted in production, resembles closely the use of subtitles on the silent screen, and Williams even employs simulated close-ups on several occasions, focusing his spotlight on individuals or objects, such as the father's photograph, much in the manner of the camera.

Once Tom's initial address to the audience establishes the entire play as memory, the action begins. The opening scene, that of Amanda and Laura in the dining room at the rear of the living room, commences as if it were what in motion pictures is called a long shot, for the two women are seen through a pair of scrim curtains which achieve the effect of both unreality and distance. First, the scrim representing the outside wall is raised, and Tom joins the women. Then Williams calls for the raising of the inner scrim, and the whole effect is like that of a camera dollying in for a closer shot. In the most widely published version, though not in the acting edition, Williams calls for subtitles and images to be projected "on a section of wall between the front-room and the dining-room," like those of the silent film. In such films a subtitle was often used at the beginning of a scene to tell the audience what to expect, sometimes to give the mood or thematic significance of the images to follow. When Laura and Amanda are revealed the subtitle is "OU SONT LES NEIGES." Williams says that the screen device was originally intended

to give accent to certain values in each scene. Each scene contains a particular point (or several) which is structurally most important. In an episodic play, such as this, the basic structure or narrative line may be obscured from the audience; the effect may seem fragmentary rather than architectural.... The legend or image upon the screen will strengthen the effect of what is merely allusion in the writing and allow the primary point to be made more simply and lightly than if the entire responsibility were on the spoken lines.[11]

In short, Williams is describing a structure remarkably close to that of the silent film—a series of short scenes, each making one or more points, with little or no transition between. The cumulative effect of these scenes, the relationships achieved by their juxtaposition and flow—these resemble what is in film called montage, originally associated with the work of Griffith and Eisenstein. Several critics have likened Williams' technique to that of the cinema and have used the term *montage* in their analyses of his structure.

In his comments on lighting and in his use of it in the play, Williams frequently suggests cinematic camera shots. He employs light, for example, for reaction close-ups. He says,

> Shafts of light are focused on selected areas or actors, sometimes in contradistinction to what is the apparent center. For instance, in the quarrel scene between Tom and Amanda, in which Laura has no active part, the clearest pool of light is on her figure. This is also true of the supper scene, when her silent figure on the sofa should remain the visual center. (p. vii)

In this way, the emphasis is not on the action itself but on a character's reaction to that action, the character highlighted as if in a close-up. And somewhat reminiscent of the diffused lighting Griffith used to employ to heighten the fragility of the young Lillian Gish or Mae Marsh, Williams calls for a special lighting of Laura: "The light upon Laura should be distinct from the others, having a peculiar pristine clarity such as the light used in early religious portraits of female saints or madonnas" (p. vii). He further says that throughout the production the light should suggest that in religious art, notably the work of El Greco, and that such lighting will make the use of the screen device more effective. The highlighting of the father's photograph has already been cited, and yet another outstanding example of the use of the cinematic close-up comes in Act I, Scene III, when Amanda tries to sell magazine subscriptions on the telephone. The light in the alley where Tom is fades out, "*and a head-spot falls on AMANDA, at phone in living-room*" (p. 13). The rest of the stage is dark, and Amanda stands alone in a circle of light revealing only her face. At the conclusion of her scene, "*Dining-room and living-room lights dim in. Reading lamp lights up at same time*" (p. 14). The close-up gives way to a longer shot of the whole room. Speaking generally of the lighting, Williams says: "A free, imaginative use of light can be of enormous value in giving a mobile, plastic quality to plays of a more or less static nature" (p. vii).

In the motion picture, both silent and sound, music has been a key element. For silent films whole scores were sometimes composed, for example, that played by the full orchestra which accompanied the initial road-showing of *The Big Parade* and *Ben Hur*; and for lesser films there was usually a music cue-sheet to guide the organist or pianist in his underlining of the mood or action of various scenes. Throughout the Acting Edition of *The Glass Menagerie* there are many music cues, and Williams stresses the importance of music as an "extra-literary accent" in the production. He calls for a "single recurring tune, 'The Glass Menagerie,'" to supply "emotional emphasis to suitable passages" (p. vi), and the mood of memory is established at the outset by "*dance-hall music ... Old popular music of, say, 1915–1920 period*" (p. 1). The music, in general, is dim, like music far away. "It seems ... to continue almost interminably and it weaves in and out of your preoccupied consciousness." It should be both gay and sad, expressing the beauty and the fragility of glass. "Both of these ideas should be woven into the recurring tune, which dips in and out of the play as if it were carried on wind that changes." It serves, too, as a link between the narrator and his story and helps to join the episodic, cinematic scenes: "Between each episode it returns as reference to the emotion, nostalgia, which is the condition of the play. It is primarily Laura's music and therefore comes out most clearly when the play focuses upon her and the lovely fragility of glass which is her image" (pp. vi–vii). Thus, as in the film, music is employed for both mood and transition, evoking the atmosphere of memory and establishing relationships between the individual scenes, stressing the fluidity of the progress of an otherwise static plot. It is significant that the first dramatic version of the story Williams did was a motion picture script for Metro-Goldwyn-Mayer.[12]

Other elements of the new non-verse poetic drama are also integral parts of the play. One of the most commented upon in the work of Williams is the symbol. In his preface to *Camino Real* Williams writes:

> I can't deny that I use a lot of those things called symbols, but being a self-defensive creature, I say that symbols are nothing but the natural speech of drama.
>
> We all have in our conscious and unconscious minds a great vocabulary of images, and I think all human communication is based on these images as are our dreams; and a symbol in a play has only one legitimate purpose, which is to say a thing more directly and simply and beautifully than it could be said in words.[13]

Sometimes, it is true, Williams tends to overwhelm us with symbols, apparently for their own sake, but in *The Glass Menagerie* the symbols are employed effectively as organic elements in his poetic concept. A simple listing of them would include such obvious ones as the Paradise Dance Hall, the fire escape, the father's photograph, "Blue Roses," the idea of the Gentleman Caller, and many others. But the one most often discussed is the glass unicorn from Laura's little menagerie. Williams' use of it reveals him at his poetic best, for the unicorn not only stands for something else (or for several something elses) but is used dramatically to symbolize a change in relationships between two of the characters. Generally, the glass menagerie, including the unicorn, portrays Laura, her fragility, her delicacy, her beauty, her unworldliness, and at the same time the unicorn in particular symbolizes her life-maintaining illusion, her idealized concept of Jim, the high school hero. When Jim appears in person, and the audience sees him as a sadly commonplace and frustrated human being, Laura still retains her illusions about him. But when she entrusts the unicorn in his hands, she says, "Oh, be careful—if you breathe, it breaks!" (p. 55) And Jim says, "Unicorns, aren't they extinct in the modern world?" (p. 55). Then in the ecstasy of the dance he knocks the unicorn from the table and it breaks—loses its horn, the thing that made it different from the others. And Laura, foreshadowing her coming disillusionment with the discovery of Jim's engagement, says, "The horn was removed to make him feel less-freakish! ... Now he will feel more at home with the other horses, the ones who don't have horns ..." (p. 57). Thus Jim, the unicorn, the unique hero, subsides into the normal, the ordinary, himself destroying the aura of distinctiveness which Laura gave him, destroying her illusion—and yet she seems to accept this catastrophe with resignation. The unicorn has vanished, yes; but she still has her glass menagerie and the escape offered by her ancient phonograph records. One illusion is gone, but her other means of escape, her other illusions, still offer protection from life's harsh realities. Here the use of the symbol is not static but dynamic, embodying and underlining a major alteration in relationships.

While Eliot clung to the idea that poetic drama should be in verse, his concept of the effect which dramatic verse should create is relevant to Williams' use of language. Eliot says that audiences at a poetic, to him verse, drama

> expect poetry to be in rhythms which have lost touch with col-
> loquial speech. What we have to do is to bring poetry into the
> world in which the audience lives and to which it returns when
> it leaves the theatre; not to transport the audience into some
> imaginary world totally unlike its own, an unreal world in which

poetry is tolerated. What I should hope might be achieved, by a generation of dramatists having the benefit of our experience, is that the audience should find, at the moment of awareness that it is hearing poetry, that it is saying to itself: "*I could talk poetry too!*" Then we should not be transported into an artificial world; on the contrary, our own sordid, dreary daily world would be suddenly illuminated and transfigured.[14]

It is just this, I believe, that Williams is able to accomplish and to do so without resorting to the dangerous artificialities of verse. He takes colloquial speech, often the colloquial speech of the South, and through a keen ear for its rhythms and patterns, its imagery and symbolism, lifts it to the level of poetry. It is *real* speech, but real speech intensified and heightened so that it not only evokes the pleasure of recognition but communicates the inexpressible, the very essence of character, emotion, and situation in a way traditionally associated with poetry.

The Glass Menagerie is filled with such passages, expressing a broad spectrum of the emotions—Tom's hilariously pathetic parodies of motion pictures and stage shows, Amanda's tragi-comic magazine sales talk, and many others. The oft-cited jonquil speech is perhaps the best known. It has the patterned construction of a poem, its rhythms capture the emotions of its speaker, it embodies the comic-pathetic ideal of the gracious past, and it relies on floral imagery to enhance its resonance as poetry. Awaiting the arrival of the Gentleman Caller, Amanda dresses herself in the old gown of her youthful triumphs in the lost Never-Never Land of the Delta:

> This is the dress in which I led the cotillion. Won the cakewalk twice at Sunset Hill, wore one spring to the Governor's ball in Jackson!
>
> See how I sashayed around the ballroom, Laura? [*She raises her skirt and does a mincing step around the room.*]
>
> I wore it on Sundays for my gentlemen callers! I had it on the day I met your father—
>
> I had malaria fever all that spring. The change of climate from East Tennessee to the Delta—weakened resistance—I had a little temperature all the time—not enough to be serious—just enough to make me restless and giddy!—Invitations poured in—parties all over the Delta!—"Stay in bed," said Mother, "you have fever!"—but I just wouldn't.—I took quinine but kept on going, going!—Evenings, dances!—Afternoons, long, long rides! Picnics—lovely!—So lovely, that country in May.—All lacy with

dogwood, literally flooded with jonquils!—That was the spring I
had the craze for jonquils. Jonquils became an absolute obsession.
Mother said, "Honey, there's no more room for jonquils." And
still I kept on bringing in more jonquils. Whenever, wherever I
saw them, I'd say, "Stop! Stop! I see jonquils!" I made the young
men help me gather the jonquils! It was a joke, Amanda and her
jonquils! Finally there were no more vases to hold them, every
available space was filled with jonquils! No vases to hold them?
All right, I'll hold them myself! And then I—[*She stops in front of
the picture*. MUSIC] met your father!

Malaria fever and jonquils and then—this—boy....

Tom's final speech is another "set-piece," with its rhythmic flow, its recurrent
imagery, its colloquial tone heightened by both the freight of the emotion
and the suggestion of a pattern.

It is not only in the somewhat extended speeches that the poetic
qualities are evident; many of the dialogues are made up of brief exchanges
with the repetitive rhythmic patterns, almost like refrains, of verse but
avoiding the rigidity of metre. Tom's teasing announcement of the visit of
the Gentleman Caller is an example:

TOM. We are going to have one.
AMANDA. *What?*
TOM. A gentleman caller!
AMANDA. You mean you have asked some nice young man to
    come over? ...
TOM. I've asked him to dinner.
AMANDA. You really did?
TOM. I did.
AMANDA. And did he—accept?
TOM. He did!
AMANDA. He did?
TOM. He did.
AMANDA. Well, isn't that lovely!
TOM. I thought you would be pleased.
AMANDA. It's definite, then?
TOM. Oh, very definite.
AMANDA. How soon?
TOM. Pretty soon.
AMANDA. How soon?
TOM. Very, very soon. (pp. 27–28)

Here is approximately the give-and-take of traditional stichomythia retaining the quality of colloquialism.

Basic to the poetic qualities of Williams' language is his Southern origin, as several critics have noted. Marion Migid speaks of his

> long line, which achieves its most striking effects through a Steinian repetitiveness, through the use of unexpected archaisms, and the insertion of unexpected "literary" words and ironically elegant turns of phrase. It is a stylized rendering of Southern diction, which is more self-conscious, more evasive, but also more imaginative than Northern speech.[15]

Miss Jackson repeats this idea, stressing the fact that the natural symbolism of Southern diction has produced "a highly developed iconography." "This Southern aesthetic," she says, "has provided for the drama of Williams a kind of basic linguistic structure comparable to that which appeared in elementary stages of Greek tragedy."[16]

Modern studies of poetry have frequently developed the concept of the poet as a user of myth and a creator of new myths. Certainly in other plays, notably *Orpheus Descending*, *Suddenly Last Summer*, and *Camino Real*, underlying the action and characters are classical myths and pagan rituals. In his later plays especially, as Miss Jackson points out, Williams "has put together a kind of modern myth, a symbolic representation of the life of man in our time." She sees this myth as "synthetic," "composed, after the manner of cinematic montage, from the fragments of many ethical, philosophical, social, poetic, intellectual, and religious perspectives ... the image of modern man caught between opposing logics—man in search of a means of reconciliation."[17] In *The Glass Menagerie* Williams reaches out tentatively for the materials of this myth. Basic to it is the idea of man's alienation from the world around him, man still clinging to old values in an environment where they are no longer relevant. Certain archetypal Williams figures begin to take shape in the play: the poet-wanderer, later to acquire sexual elements from D. H. Lawrence; the fragile girl threatened with destruction and either escaping into a dream world of the past or being corrupted by the jungle world of the present; the same girl in maturity, strong and defensive in her struggle against the present but finding sustenance through cherishing the ideal of lost grace and beauty. It is the myth of the alienated, the lost, seeking some sort of tenable posture in the present chaos. It is the source of the poet's vision. Williams himself says, "Personal lyricism is the outcry of prisoner to prisoner from the cell in solitary where each is confined for the duration of his life."[18]

One of the constants of lyric poetry, and of much other poetry as well, is its immediacy, its capturing of the moment, the intense moment of experience and insight. Man is in constant battle with Time the Destroyer, and poetry is one of his oldest means of achieving victory. In his use of time and in his attitude toward it, Williams is typically the poet. He says, "Snatching the eternal out of the desperately fleeting is the great magic of human existence."[19] In most of his plays his characters fight against time, its attrition and its ravages, and time becomes a major symbol of the adversary, malignant and malevolent. Amanda and Laura seek to turn time back, to recapture a past which they have perhaps idealized out of all semblance to reality but the very search for which gives meaning to their lives. On the other hand, Tom looks forward, toward a future time as an escape, but when that future becomes his present, he finds himself a prisoner of the past.

In *The Glass Menagerie* time is used another way, an equally poetic one. Tom stands with us in the immediate present. At the start he wears a merchant seaman's outfit indicative of escape from the physical past, of his having left his mother and sister behind. But through his consciousness we are carried back in time to his life in the drab apartment before his escape, and we retrace with him events leading to his decision to leave. Within this train of memory there are two types of time, the generalized and the specific, and through the use of these two we are given a deeper insight into the lives and relationships of the Wingfields. The first scene in the apartment, the dinner scene, is an example of generalized time. It is not any one particular dinner but a kind of abstraction of all the dinners shared by the trio in their life of entrapment. Amanda's admonitory speeches are ones often repeated, her stories of the seventeen gentlemen callers are oft-told tales—and Tom's irritated responses are those he makes each and every time the stories are retold. Amanda's telephone call to Ida Scott, with its pathetic attempts at salesmanship, is not one specific call, but, as the isolating spotlight tells us, it is an action out of time and place, the essence of a repeated action rather than a unique event. There are also unique moments in the parade of Tom's memory, highlights with a significance of their own—the imaginative reconstruction of the visit of Jim (for Tom was not present during some of the dialogue with Laura), for example. Through this multiple use of time Williams embodies both the concrete, the particular, and the general, the typical, his images often achieving the force of what Eliot has called the objective correlative of abstract truth.

From one point of view, as in *Death of a Salesman*, *The Glass Menagerie* actually transfixes and holds up for insight a single, brief moment of Tom's consciousness, a moment in the present in which, like Proust, he recapitulates the past, a past inextricably intertwined with the present and the future, freezes this moment—the intense moment of poetic insight, of lyric intuition. And this is often what a poem does. Williams is himself well aware of what he is doing. He says:

> It is this continual rush of time, so violent that it appears to be screaming, that deprives our actual lives of so much dignity and meaning, and it is, perhaps more than anything else, the *arrest of time* which has taken place in a completed work of art that gives certain plays their feeling of depth and significance.... If the world of the play did not offer us this occasion to view its characters under that special condition of a *world without time*, then, indeed, the characters and occurrences of drama would become equally pointless, equally trivial, as corresponding meetings and happenings in life.

In such a timeless world, like that of Greek tragedy, man becomes aware of his potential nobility:

> The audience can sit back in a comforting dusk to watch a world which is flooded with light and in which emotion and action have a dimension and dignity that they would likewise have in real existence, if only the shattering intrusion of time could be locked out.[20]

By arresting time, by embodying in a single moment the past, the present, and the future, by making this frozen moment one of tremendous intensity permitting an insight otherwise impossible, Williams has made *The Glass Menagerie* a lyric drama.

In conclusion, by utilizing many of the elements of poetry and the non-verbal facilities of the theatre—controlling metaphors and symbols, "transformation," lighting, music, movement, patterned colloquial speech, mythic elements, and the arresting of time to permit insight into the particular and the general—and by organically shaping these through a poet's vision—Williams in *The Glass Menagerie* exemplifies twentieth-century American poetic drama, free of the anachronism of verse, a poetic drama peculiarly adapted to the complexities of the present. Linking Williams with Arthur Miller, Kenneth Tynan says that both men, "committed to prose drama ... have uncovered riches which snake the English 'poetic revival' [of Eliot and Fry, for example] seem hollow, retrogressive, and—to use Cyril Connolly's coinage—praeterist."[21]

NOTES

1. See his "A Prelude to Poetry in the Theatre," A Preface to *Winterset, Winterset* (New York: Anderson House, 1935). Also his "Poetry in the Theater," *Off Broadway: Essays about the Theater* (New York: William Sloane Associates, Inc., 1947).

2. "Poetry and Drama," *On Poetry and Poets* (London: Faber and Faber, 1957), pp. 74–75.

3. Eliot, *op. cit.*, p. 73, and Archibald MacLeish, "The Poet as Playwright," *Atlantic*, CXCV (Feb., 1955), 50.

4. Eliot, *op. cit.*, pp. 86–87.

5. *Fifty Years of American Drama, 1900–1950.* A Gateway Edition (Chicago: Henry Regnery, 1966), p. 110.

6. *Ibid.*, p. 105.

7. *The Glass Menagerie*, A Play in Two Acts. Acting Edition. (New York: Dramatists Play Service, 1948), p. vi. Hereafter quotations from this edition are followed in the text by page references in parentheses. With one exception, I have used this edition, which is supposed to be Williams' favorite, instead of the "bastardized script" published by New Directions in 1949 and widely anthologized. See L. A. Beaurline, "The Director, the Script, and Author's Revisions: A Critical Problem," in *Papers in Dramatic Theory and Criticism*, ed. David. M. Knauf (Iowa City: University of Iowa Press, 1969), pp. 88–89.

8. *The Broken World of Tennessee Williams* (Madison and Milwaukee: University of Wisconsin Press, 1965), pp. x–xii, 28.

9. Robert Frost, "Education by Poetry," *Robert Frost: An Introduction*, ed. Robert A. Greenberg and James G. Hepburn (New York: Holt, Rinehart and Winston, Inc., 1961), p. 80. Reprinted from *Amherst Alumni Council News*, IV (March, 1931), 6–13.

10. "The Constant Symbol," *Robert Frost: An Introduction*, p. 87. Reprinted from *Atlantic Monthly*, CLXXVIII (October, 1946), 50–52.

11. "Production Notes," *The Glass Menagerie*. The New Classics. (New York: New Directions, 1949), p. x. This is the "bastardized script."

12. Signi Lenea Falk, *Tennessee Williams*. Twayne's United States Authors Series No. 10. (New York: Twayne Publishers, Inc., 1961), p. 17.

13. "Foreword," *Camino Real*, in *Six American Plays for Today*, selected by Bennett Cerf. Modern Library No. 38 (New York: Modern Library, 1961), p. 5. Originally in the New York *Times*, March 15, 1953.

14. Eliot, "Poetry and Drama," p. 82.

15. "The Innocence of Tennessee Williams," *Essays in the Modern Drama*, ed. Morris Freedman. (Boston: D. C. Heath & Co., 1964), pp. 282–283. Reprinted from *Commentary*, January, 1963.

16. *The Broken World of Tennessee Williams*, p. 46.

17. *Ibid.*, p. 54.

18. "Person-To-Person," *Cat on a Hot Tin Roof*. Signet Book No. T 3547. (New York: The New American Library, n. d.), p. vii.

19. "The Timeless World of a Play," *Perspectives on Drama*, ed. James L. Calderwood and Harold E. Toliver (New York: Oxford University Press, 1968), pp. 247–250. Reprinted from *The Rose Tattoo*, New Directions, 1950.

20. *Ibid.*, pp. 248–249.

21. "American Blues: The Plays of Arthur Miller and Tennessee Williams," *The Modern American Theater*, ed. Alvin B. Kernan (Englewood Cliffs, N.J.: Prentice-Hall, 1967), p. 36. Reprinted from *Curtains*, 1961.

The author gratefully acknowledges the contributions to this essay by two of his graduate students, Jennifer Krugman and Mary Arnold Garvin.

THOMAS E. SCHEYE

The Glass Menagerie: *"It's no tragedy, Freckles."*

At the opening of *The Glass Menagerie*, Tom comes out of the shadows of the Wingfield apartment, the stage magician promising to explain the tricks in his pocket. But Tom is a creature of the shadows who never really admits what he has up his sleeve. He says "the play is memory"; it is also forgetting. In another version of *The Glass Menagerie*, the story called "Portrait of a Girl in Glass," the narrator is more honest about what he remembers: "In five years' time I had nearly forgotten home. I had to forget, I couldn't carry it with me" (*One Arm*, p. 112). That is what Tom would say too, except that he has been unable to shake his memories of home because his sister will not be forgotten: "Oh Laura, Laura, I tried to leave you behind me, but I am more faithful than I intended to be!" (I, 237).

In this "memory play" Tom remembers in order to forget. The contradiction in terms can be explained by the double game Tom is playing in the theater as "the narrator of the play, and also a character in it." He is inside the illusion that he calls "truth in the pleasant disguise of illusion," and he is on the outside, "an emissary from the world of reality" (pp. 144–45). In his first appearance, already dressed as a merchant sailor, Tom seems safely outside. But he is still haunted by the memory of his sister, still searching for anything that can relieve his feelings of guilt, "anything that can blow your candles out!" (p. 237). The intention of *The Glass Menagerie* is to leave Laura

From *Tennessee Williams: A Tribute*: pp. 207–213. © 1977 by the University Press of Mississippi.

in the past, in the shadows on the other side of the scrim, to plunge her "into everlasting darkness." The shadows fall across the stage after Tom uses the money for the light bill to pay his dues to the merchant marine; and at the end when he directs Laura to blow out the candles, the darkness is complete. Tom has to re-enter the past a final time, to make a play out of his memory, in order to leave memory behind. Once Laura, as a character in the play, can be brought to forgive and forget Tom's running away, he can make good his escape.

From the first moment he enters the play, Tom is trying to escape. He no sooner comes to the table than he pushes away because Amanda is carping at his table manners, and he plays most of the scene while standing at the portieres. Like the transparent scrim, the portieres curtain off an inner stage; they are another dividing line between illusion and reality or one kind of truth and another. According to Williams' stage directions, Amanda addresses Tom as if he were still at the table, and Tom answers her. Otherwise, "he plays this scene as though reading from a script" (p. 148), motioning once for music and then for a spotlight on Amanda. Tom is divided between two roles: the actor inside the illusion and the narrator or playwright on the outside. From the start he is trying to keep his distance. And his direction is clear: he is on the way out.

Scene three, which opens with Tom's soliloquy on the fire escape, closes with his making his move to escape. This time it is not Tom's table manners that provoke the quarrel with his mother, but his writing, Amanda's "interruption of Tom's creative labor" (p. 162). There is a contradiction between what Tom is doing and what he dreams of doing, between the day job which ties him to the apartment and the nightly creative labor which demands his freedom. "I'm leading a double-life," he tells his mother, "a simple, honest warehouse worker by day, by night a dynamic *czar* of the *underworld*" (p. 164). The foolishness here hardly disguises the terms of the conflict; it is the same conflict as between his two roles in the play. Either Tom stays inside, working for the Continental Shoemakers to pay the rent on the apartment, or he runs away to the merchant marines, gets free to write his play. And that course is threatening to the Wingfields.

After threatening to explode all their illusions Tom charges for the door. When he is caught up in his coat and throws it off, striking the shelf where the glass collection is, "there is a tinkle of shattering glass. Laura cries out as if wounded" (p. 164). Tom is drawn back into the room, into the world of the glass menagerie, in an attempt to comfort her. The symbolism, which is obvious without being a nuisance, states the predicament: Tom cannot escape until he finds the way to leave without shattering Laura's fragile self.

That is a trick he learns from the stage. At the movies' stage show the headliner was Malvolio the Magician—Tom came out of the audience to help him—and the magician proves to be his savior. Malvolio can turn water into wine, and triples the miracle of the wedding feast by turning the wine into beer and the beer to whiskey. "But the wonderfullest trick of all was the coffin trick. We nailed him into a coffin and he got out of the coffin without removing one nail.... There is a trick that would come in handy for me—get me out of this two-by-four situation!" (p. 167). In *The Glass Menagerie* the sorcerer's apprentice becomes the stage magician. He brings home a conjuring scarf which he gives Laura as a "souvenir," something to remember him by. And it is a conjuring trick—turning Jim O'Connor into a gentleman caller—that will solve Tom's predicament.

Tom conjures up Jim O'Connor as his surrogate after Amanda agrees that once "there's somebody to take your place" (p. 175), he is free to go. Turning Jim O'Connor into the gentleman caller turns the trick because he can do what Tom could never do by himself: get out of the two-by-four situation without removing one nail. Jim deserts Laura and she is not shattered by it; in fact she is able to say, "It's no tragedy" (p. 226).

Tom offers no reason why the incident with the gentleman caller should be his cue to leave, but Jim's identification with Tom provides a clue. Like Tom, Jim leads a double life, by day and night. Or, as he puts it more prosaically, "I have a couple of time-clocks to punch.... One at morning, another one at night" (p. 233). In the world of the play, he is as much a contradiction as Tom, both inside and outside the illusion. Tom captures the contradiction when he describes the gentleman caller in the opening monologue as "the most realistic character in the play" and also as a symbol. He is Tom's friend at the warehouse and the playwright's personal symbol. Tom calls him "an emissary from a world of reality that we were somehow set apart from" (p. 145). But it is precisely from that world that Tom returns in scene six, to usher on the gentleman caller. The acting edition of *The Glass Menagerie* specifies that Tom is dressed as a merchant sailor for the monologue in scene six as he is at the opening and close of the play.

The gentleman caller is "the long delayed but always expected something that we live for" (p. 145). All the Wingfields are living for the day he comes to call. "Haven't you ever liked some boy?" (p. 156) Amanda asks; Laura has never stopped loving Jim. Williams describes Laura's scene with the gentleman caller as "the climax of her secret life" (p. 210). He is what Amanda has wished for on the "little silver slipper of a moon" (p. 180) rising over Garfinkel's delicatessen and what Tom has wished for too.

Jim O'Connor is "A nice, ordinary young man" (p. 129) who is transformed, as if by magic, into the romantic figure of a gentleman caller.

Tom refers to this image as an "archetype of the universal unconscious," "this spectre, this hope"; he is drawn not from life but from the "serialized sublimations of ladies of letters" (p. 159) in the magazines Amanda sells over the phone. The sort of gentleman caller Amanda herself had known once has died out or disappeared; in the violence and confusion of the thirties, the world "lit by lightning" instead of candles, he no longer exists except in books—or plays.

Jim O'Connor seems the unlikeliest choice to fill the role. He is a great believer in the importance of the "right connections," the power of positive thinking, and the virtues of a night school course in public speaking. He is confident that "social poise" allows anyone to hold his own on any social level; he even tries to sell Laura on his own naive faith in "the cycle democracy is built on" (p. 222). All men are created equal, everyone is just like everyone else, only better: "Why, man alive, Laura! Just look about you a little. What do you see? A world full of common people! All of 'em born and all of 'em going to die! Which of them has one-tenth of your good points! Or mine! Or anyone else's as far as that goes—gosh!" (p. 221). But as he becomes aware Laura is truly different, he turns into something surprisingly different too. Under the spell of Amanda and her jonquils and romantic candlelight and the strains of "La Golondrina" he emerges as an emissary not from the world of reality but from Blue Mountain. When he observes that Laura's principal trouble is "a lack of confidence in yourself as a person" and tries to convince her to "think of yourself as superior in some way" (p. 221), he is using the words he has learned will make friends and influence people. When he asks Laura to dance, he is fumbling for the accents of the spectral gentleman caller: "Or is your program filled up? Let me have a look at it.... Why, every dance is taken! I'll just have to scratch some out.... Ahhh, a waltz!" (p. 224). And to the music from the Paradise Dance Hall he waltzes her uneasily around the room.

It is during their dance that the unicorn is knocked to the floor, the second time in the play that something from the glass menagerie is broken. The first time, Laura cried out as if she herself were wounded; now she can say, "It doesn't matter" (p. 226). All the figurines are part of Laura's own little world, but the unicorn is different, as Laura is different. It is, she says, her favorite of the glass menagerie; given the playwright's "weakness for symbols," the unicorn can be identified with Laura. And yet she can say, "It's no tragedy, Freckles" (p. 226), calling Jim by a special name.

In "Portrait of a Girl in Glass," Freckles is a character in a book that Laura reads over and over, "actually lived with." When Jim comes to dinner Laura mentions his freckles, and Jim says Freckles is his nickname. "She looked toward me," the narrator says, "as if for the confirmation of some too wonderful hope.... Yes, he had undoubtedly assumed the identity—for all practical purposes—of the one-armed orphan youth who lived in the Limberlost, that tall and misty region to which she retreated whenever the walls of Apartment F became too close to endure" (p. 109). But Jim's identification with the gentleman caller, and Laura's with the unicorn, are broken after the horn is broken.

Losing the horn, Laura thinks, is a "blessing in disguise" because it makes the unicorn less freakish, more like the other horses. "I'll just imagine he had an operation" (p. 226), she says. The line takes on nightmare proportions if the breaking of the horn is taken to symbolize Williams' own sister Rose's prefrontal lobotomy. But Rose's fate is not Laura's. By his stumblejohn gallantry Jim teaches Laura to have some confidence in herself, shows her that she is different from other people and should stay that way—even if it means never moving from the shelf, being left alone. It is the *gentleman* caller who speaks: "The different people are not like other people, but being different is nothing to be ashamed of. Because other people are not such wonderful people. They're one hundred times one thousand. You're one times one! They walk all over the earth. You just stay here. They're common as—weeds, but—you—well, you're—*Blue Roses!*" (p. 227).

Jim makes the final romantic gesture when he sweeps her up in his arms to kiss her. And having kissed her he takes leave—but not before she presses the broken unicorn on him as "A—souvenir" (p. 231). Since it is "just like all the other horses" now, it belongs in the world of reality where Jim lives; Laura does not. The unicorn is a painful reminder of what might have been but had better not, something for him to remember and for her to forget: the dream of ever liking some boy or ever having a gentleman caller.

Jim O'Connor has played the role in which he was cast, and played it well by playing it badly. His impersonation of a gentleman caller is so clumsy that Laura can see the apparition for what it is. And perhaps she sees that if her dream did come true, come to life, he might look like Jim O'Connor, he would not be made of glass and he could crush her fragile existence as he had broken the unicorn. And so she can say, "It's no tragedy, Freckles."

Tom's leaving her is no tragedy either; at least Tom can convince himself of that now. In his last speech, he describes his life from the day the gentleman called to this moment as a failed attempt to put some distance between past and present, Laura and himself. He has always been pursued by guilt, the memory of his sister; it is what he tries to forget: "I reach for a cigarette, I cross the street, I run into the movies or a bar, I buy a drink, I speak to the nearest stranger—anything that can blow your candles out!" (p. 237). During the monologue, with the scrim being lowered, the play comes back on itself; Tom is left safely outside. On stage he has cast his memory in the form of a play, and the play succeeds where everything else has failed. In the final scene, Laura stops her pursuit and takes her place in the past. A conjuring trick, the gentleman caller, has shown Laura what Tom could never tell her: that her life is on the other side of the scrim which divides illusion and reality, in the dark. Though Tom has tried every other trick to blow the candles out, it is only Laura who can do that for him and only as a character in the play that she will. The final line of *The Glass Menagerie* is a stage direction.

BRIAN PARKER

The Composition of The Glass Menagerie: *An Argument for Complexity*

I

Though Mrs. Edwina Williams has pointed out the many differences between the Williams family and the Wingfields,[1] *The Glass Menagerie* is nonetheless Tennessee Williams's most autobiographical play, accurate to the imaginative reality of his experience even when it departs from fact in detail. The essentials of that experience—the mismatched parents; the shock of the family's move from early years in his grandfather's Mississippi rectory to a series of shabby flats in downtown St. Louis; Williams's breakdown after working as a clerk in a warehouse, trying to write at night; his close companionship with his sister, Rose, disrupted by her withdrawal into schizophrenia; and the disastrous mistake of submitting her to a frontal lobotomy—are too well known to bear expansion. The recent publication of Williams's *Memoirs*,[2] however, with their startling frankness about his sex life, helps fill in some further details. In particular, Williams is explicit about his feeling of personal guilt because new companions and interests, the excitements of university life, and perhaps especially his gradual discovery of his own homosexual preferences led him to neglect and even be unkind to his sister at her period of greatest need. "It's not very pleasant to look back on that year [1937]," he writes, "and to know that Rose knew she was going mad and to know, also, that I was not too kind to my sister" (p. 121). He

From *Modern Drama*, vol. XXV, no. 3 (September 1982): pp. 409–422. © 1982 by the University of Toronto.

tells of her tattling on a wild party he gave at the house during their parents' absence, in resentment of which he hissed at her on the stairs, "I hate the sight of your ugly old face!", leaving her stricken and wordless, crouched against the wall. "This is the cruelest thing I have done in my life, I suspect", he comments, "and one for which I can never properly atone" (p. 122). Later that year Rose was put in an institution; and the following summer, while Williams was in Illinois with some of his new friends, his parents gave their permission for the operation that rendered Rose harmless but childish for the rest of her life.

This tragedy was one of the most traumatic experiences of Williams's life, from which he has never freed himself. It lies at the root of his feeling that love leads inevitably to loss and betrayal, as reflected in such poems as "Cortege" and "The Comforter and the Betrayer."[3] The pattern is extraordinarily clear in *Suddenly Last Summer*, written in the late fifties after psychoanalysis, in which the heroine is threatened with lobotomy for revealing the sadomasochistic homosexuality of her cousin, Sebastian, and an ambiguous brother–sister relationship recurs throughout Williams's work[4]; fittingly, the last pages of *Memoirs* express his concern to release his sister from her mental institution to live in a house he has bought for her near his own in Florida.

Not surprisingly, these events and tortured relationships are reflected in much more of Williams's early writing than just *The Glass Menagerie*: in short stories such as "Portrait of a Girl in Glass" and "The Resemblance between a Violin Case and a Coffin"; poems like "Cortege" and part 3 of "Recuerdo"; and one-act plays such as *The Long Goodbye, Auto-da fé, The Last of My Solid Gold Watches*, and perhaps *The Purification*[5]; and the produced but unpublished full-length play, *Stairs to the Roof*. But exactly how obsessive and intractable, how emotionally complex and contradictory the memories were, can be grasped only when one looks at the mound of rewriting which lay before *The Glass Menagerie* itself. To set the final play against these earlier efforts reveals nuances that are easily overlooked.

Before examining this material, however, a word should be said about Williams's habit of constantly revising and reworking his creations. Typically, a Williams play starts life as a poem or short story, is revised to a one-act, then a full-length play; the play itself is changed during performance and again between performance and publication; if the production has not been as successful as was hoped, the play is likely to be completely redrafted, or it may be drastically reworked as a script for a film or television or even a novel. Nor is it always the case that the revision moves from shorter versions to longer ones: the published version of the short story "Portrait of a Girl in Glass," for example, is much briefer than the draft versions at Texas which already contain many of the details, such as Laura's lameness and unicorn or Amanda's reminiscences of Blue Mountain, that later appear in *The Glass Menagerie*, where they must therefore be considered reversions, not new insights or additions. Such instability is apt to offend literary critics, but it is wholly typical of Williams's attitude to life and work, in which no position or creation is to be considered complete till the author decides to finish with it. It is well to bear this in mind not only when one comes to evaluate the radical alterations Williams has always been ready to accommodate for purposes of immediate production or filming, but also when one considers the differences among the short story "Portrait," the various drafts of *The Gentleman Caller* from which both "Portrait" and *Menagerie* emerge, the manuscript version of *The Glass Menagerie*, its acting version (as published by the Dramatists Play Service), the reading version authorized by Williams for publication by Random House and New Directions, and the alterations he agreed to, however reluctantly, for the movie and, more recently, for television. Though Williams's idol D.H. Lawrence may advise us to trust the tale and not the teller, in Tennessee Williams's case one is always faced with creation in process, and this turns one back inevitably towards the man.

II

Lester Beaurline's lucid appraisal of the Williams manuscripts in the Barrett Library of the University of Virginia pioneered the analysis of *Menagerie*'s development[6]; but since his article appeared, a great deal of extra material has been deposited at the Humanities Research Center of the University of Texas which shows that the genesis of the play was even more complex than he supposed. This new material is largely undated, however, and thus far has been sorted out only by text; so until an accurate time sequence can be worked out among the many drafts (and the Texas material collated with the archive in Virginia), nothing like a definitive analysis will be possible. Nevertheless, certain details are already clear which can affect interpretation of the finished play.

For example, it is usually assumed that *Menagerie* developed directly from the screen-play called *The Gentleman Caller*, but a glance at the screen-play itself shows that this assumption can only have been true in part. Texas has two copies of Williams's general "Description" of the screen-play, dated 13 May 1943 (plus six extra pages of draft, dated 28 June 1943), and a more elaborate but undated "Provisional Story Treatment" which recently turned up there during sorting of the David Selznick papers. The "Description" has no narrator but opens with a lengthy account of Amanda's life at Blue Mountain, her gentlemen callers, Wingfield's wooing, and his misadventure with an illicit still which forced the family to leave town. The "play" proper then begins on Christmas Eve with Laura, who is "morbidly shy" but not in this version lame, decorating a tree while her brother "Larry" reads poetry aloud; they attempt to attract passing carolers with a candle at the window; and Amanda gives them unsuitable Christmas presents, a six-month business course for Laura and books on salesmanship and "executive personality" for Larry. Laura fails at business college largely because she is bullied by a "hawklike spinster" instructor. Larry's restlessness is explained by the fact that "The Wingfields ... were pioneers, Indian fighters, trailblazers in the American wilderness," and there is "an amusing incidental scene" in which one of his wanderlust poems wins a $10.00 prize from the Ladies' Wednesday Club. Laura likes the gentleman caller Jim because his freckles remind her of the hero of her favourite Gene Stratton Porter novel (as in "Portrait"), not because she knew him in high school. The lights do not go off, there is no Paradise Dance Hall, little is made of the glass collection, and there is no unicorn to be broken. As in *Stairs to the Roof*, Larry loses his job for smoking on the roof, not for writing poems on cartons; and on the morning after his departure, Laura tries to comfort her mother by volunteering to telephone for magazine subscriptions, but does so too early—at 6:30 a.m.—which makes them both laugh and restores Amanda's morale.

The "Provisional Story Treatment" is even further from *Menagerie*. It is divided into three parts linked by an unidentified narrator. Part I dramatizes events at Blue Mountain, with scenes of gentlemen callers visiting Amanda, her first meeting with Wingfield, his proposal at a picnic and fight with another of her admirers, and her snubbing of his next visit but sudden decision to elope with him. The narrator then bridges to a hotel in Memphis where Amanda watches boats go down the river and tells Wingfield of her first pregnancy. Wingfield enlists for World War I and Amanda, pregnant with his second child, returns to Blue Mountain. Wingfield comes home a shell-shocked hero but begins bootlegging, and an elaborate sequence follows in which his still blows up, killing a Negro, and bloodhounds track him to his father-in-law's church. The dogs attack Laura on the church steps, and Wingfield, rescuing her, is arrested and taken to prison. Part II tells of the family's life in St. Louis, with the embittered father working in a shirt factory. Laura has been so traumatized by the bloodhounds that she cannot talk until her father delights her into speech by bringing home a Victrola on which he plays *Dardanella*. Amanda objects to the expense of this, and Wingfield leaves for good. The narrator then tells of the children growing up over shots of Tom (in this version) reading magazines instead of selling them and brooding despairingly in a warehouse, Amanda selling subscriptions over the telephone, and Laura having nightmares about dogs, failing to recite at school, playing *Dardanella*, polishing her glass collection, and endlessly rereading *Freckles*.

Part III covers the same sequence as the "Description," beginning with the Christmas Eve scene. Once more Laura is bullied by her typing instructor, but now the machine clatter is described as sounding like "hounds baying." There is no poetry prize scene, but again Laura likes Jim solely because of his freckles and again there is no unicorn. Tom's speech on leaving home is now made to echo his father's earlier recriminations; and after the scene in which Laura makes her comically early telephone call, three alternative endings are suggested: either Amanda and Laura return to Blue Mountain, where Laura insists her mother is "just as beautiful as she was—in the beginning"; or Laura is shown welcoming hosts of gentlemen callers at Blue Mountain, like her mother earlier; or one or other of the Tom Wingfields returns: "At any rate—Amanda has finally found security and rest. What she searched for in the faces of Gentlemen Callers." This "Story Treatment" is carelessly typed, and since it is in a Liebling-Wood folder and Part III announces that it "covers the part of the story contained in the stage play 'The Gentleman Caller' ('The Glass Menagerie')," possibly it was cobbled up either before or just after the New York opening of *Menagerie* when Selznick was alerted to take an interest in the play. Its differences from *Menagerie* suggest, though, that it drew on earlier material.

The discrepancies relate back, in fact, to the stage play of *The Gentleman Caller*, which survives in many partial versions but no complete one. The Texas archive contains multiple overlapping drafts, including a twenty-two-page fragment with the title "The Gentleman Caller, or Portrait of a girl in glass (A lyric play)," twenty-nine disorderly pages called "The Gentleman Caller (original and only copy of a rather tiresome play)" and subtitled "(the ruins of a play)," another twenty-page fragment entitled "The Gentleman Caller (A Gentle Comedy)," and a composite typescript of 156 pages, plus forty pages of pencil draft in a notebook and some 254 further draft pages in typescript. Names and details change bewilderingly throughout these drafts: Laura is sometimes called Rose or Rosemary (and once Miriam) and varies between eighteen, twenty, and twenty-three in age; Tom is often called Larry; Jim has several Irish surnames and hails variously from Oregon, Nebraska, or Wyoming; and the St. Louis apartment is located on Maple Street, Enright, or, most often, Côte Brilliante Avenue.

The confusion reflects the trouble Williams had controlling his material. "It's the hardest thing I have ever tried to say!", Tom assures the audience in the "ruins of a play":

I've written this over ten times and torn it up, I've sweated over it, raged over it, wept over it! I think I have it and then it gets all misty and fades away.... I must confine myself to a smaller ambition, not all but a little of it.[7]

Similarly, in the notebook pencil draft Tom says:

The original play filled several hundred pages. The top-heavy structure collapsed. And I lay under the ruins like a caterpillar. After a while I picked myself up again. I looked about me. Here and there I picked up a sound particle, a piece that survived. I put these fragments together. Out of the ruins of a monument salvaged this tablet, these remnants of a play, *The Gentleman Caller*.

This shortened version of *The Gentleman Caller* corresponds closely, but again not exactly, to the "Description" of the film-script,[8] and the sequence is complicated further by Williams's trying-out sections of the material also as one-acters. *The Pretty Trap* (*A Comedy in One Act*), for instance, has the title-page note: "This play is derived from a longer work in progress, *The Gentleman Caller*. It corresponds to the last act of that play, roughly, but has a lighter treatment and a different end." Jim's visit here takes place on Sadie Hawkins day (when girls may propose to men), and Laura is shy but not lame; the lights, however, do go out, much more is made of the glass animals than in the film-script, and the unicorn appears but is not broken. After Jim's kiss he mentions no fiancée but asks if he may take Laura for a walk; and when they have left, Amanda ends the play exulting to Tom: "Girls are a pretty trap! That's what they've always been, and always *will be*, even when *dreams* plus *action*—take over the world: Now—now, dreamy type—Let's finish the dishes!" A similar ending occurs in the full-length *The Gentleman Caller* (*A Gentle Comedy*), with the addition that Amanda tells Tom to take out the suitcase he has hidden under his bed and leave now with her blessing: "Then come home and I'll be waiting for you—no matter how long!"

Other one-acters which seem to have preceded either version of *The Gentleman Caller* are *Carolers, our Candle*[9] (dated April 1943), which covers the Christmas Eve sequence, and the fragmentary "A Daughter of the Revolution (A Comedy)," dated March 1943 and inscribed to "Miss Lilian and Miss Dorothy Gish for either of whom the part of Amanda Wingfield was hopefully intended by the author," which presents Amanda's comic telephone subscriptions. Another early one-acter, *If You Breathe, It Breaks! or Portrait of a Girl in Glass*, takes place at Blue Mountain, where Mrs. Wingfield is represented as the widow of an episcopal clergyman, supporting her family by running a boarding-house; Rosemary, her shy, plain daughter, is teased by malicious boarders and treated badly by a younger brother Ronald, but is taken off to the White Star Pharmacy for a soda by a middle-aged widower, Mr. Wallard, to whom she gives her prized glass unicorn. Another, more farcical Blue Mountain one-acter, *With Grace and Dignity or The Memorial Service*, included among *The Gentleman Caller* drafts, depicts Rosemary's inability to carry a white taper during Mrs. Wingfield's celebration of her election as regent of the local chapter of the D.A.R. and the substitution for her of the Negro cook with a candle stub from the kitchen.

What one needs to understand from this welter of alternatives therefore is the difficulty Williams had in coming to terms with his material and the complexity of his responses to it, because clearly there was no steady progression in one direction—details come and go bewilderingly—and though in *Menagerie* he found a form which brilliantly controls the material, some of the rejected alternatives are still faintly there like an imaginative penumbra.

For instance, in drafts of the longer version of the stage *Gentleman Caller*, one can trace Williams's efforts to "place" the story. One recurring experiment is to try to set it within a "pioneer" framework, recounting the Williams family history in Sandburg-like verse at the beginning (against a large map of America) and returning to it at the end to explain the necessity of Tom's choice and to reassure the audience of the women's ability to survive "because we're daughters of the Revolution." The same element comes up more obliquely in a version where Williams introduces a young vagrant, Tom Lee, whom Amanda invites to breakfast when she finds him stealing milk bottles, then dismisses to the fire-escape again for "bolshevik" opinions, only to find that Tom prefers to join him there; and in another draft one of Williams's "fugitive kind," a street-musician named Tony, who calls Amanda disrespectfully "Mother Wing" and is dismissed by her as an "artistic bum," persuades Tom to join the merchant marine and leave the stolid Jim to take his room and place in the family.[10] A related experiment has the play remembered by Tom himself sleeping in a doss-house and deciding to return home when he hears carolers outside. Shades of this left-wing comment and romantic bohemianism remain in the Tom of *Menagerie*, but in a more qualified, ironic tone that is linked to another of Williams's experiments in *The Gentleman Caller*—the theatricalism of a framework in which Tom criticizes the lighting man and at several points argues directly with the audience in justification of the play. The combative, slightly aggressive relation to the audience in these last experiments is worth remembering.

A different kind of framework tries to set the children within a context of their parents, showing Amanda's relationship with Wingfield at the beginning and, in at least two versions, having the husband return to resolve the situation at the end; and this reflects a different kind of light that the drafts can shed on *Glass Menagerie*. Critics react so sympathetically to the Wingfields that they are apt to miss shades of characterization, but familiarity with the earlier attempts alerts us to Williams's own ambivalences, particularly his unexpected siding with his father. Amanda can be very sympathetic, as Williams surely meant her to be, but she is also grotesquely comic, and the drafts often emphasize this—by the story of the exploding still, for instance, which in some versions Tom uses to deflate her reminiscences of Blue Mountain, or the description of her waiting up for him in a dingy flannel wrapper, "smelling of Vicks' Vap-o-rub—a portrait of Motherhood that would make Whistler turn in his grave." There is also a certain flexibility in the presentation of Laura. Besides varying her age and only occasionally making her lame, Williams presents her with very different degrees of neurasthenia, ranging from completely fey fantasies that she and Tom will escape to Freckles's "Limberlost" in a blue coupé and live together in an old, abandoned house, to a moral strength that enables her both to assure Tom that she will not be harmed by the disappointment of Jim or by Tom's departure and to take over when her mother finally breaks down. And in the curious version with the street-musician Tony, she is transformed to a high-strung member of the local Little Theatre who wants to be "Duse! Bernhardt! Duncan! Pavlova! Garbo! Joan of Arc!", with a sharp, sarcastic tongue that is more than a match for her mother's, whereas Tom is the withdrawn and quiet one. This interesting transfer of identities was anticipated in the one-act *The Long Goodbye*, where the promiscuous sister is forced from home and the poetic brother finds it difficult to leave, and it also prefigures characterization in the revised version of *The Two-Character Play* more recently.

Most important of all, however, is the draft versions' evidence that Williams was uncertain how to end the story and constantly tempted to use optimistic conclusions, ranging from loud assertions of American independence, through happy returns of Wingfield Senior, Tom, or Jim, to attempts to show the women prospering in some way on their own. With hindsight, we can see that Williams was right to discard these experiments, but it is important to bear them in mind when, for instance, we consider the sentimental conclusion of the 1950 film, in which Laura, cured by her encounter with Jim, has her pick of gentlemen callers, "And the one she chose was named Richard."[11] It is usual to blame this travesty on Hollywood, noting that the script is credited to Williams and a rewrite man named Peter Berneis. But we have seen Williams experimenting with such conclusions in his drafts,[12] and Texas has a film-script of *The Glass Menagerie* by Williams alone in which Laura, cutting business school, makes friends with a little girl sketching in the botanical gardens and eventually falls happily in love with the child's sympathetic art teacher. To do Williams justice, he has scrawled across the cover of this script, "A Horrible Thing! Certified by Tennessee Williams."

A similar caution must be exercised with changes introduced into the original production and subsequently enshrined in the Dramatists Play Service acting edition. The director, Eddie Dowling (who also played Tom), influenced by George Jean Nathan, thought the play was not funny enough and introduced Tom's drunken return in scene 4. According to Williams (*Memoirs*, p. 82), Dowling wanted Tom to sing "My Melancholy Baby" and swig from a red, white, and blue flask,[13] but though Williams agreed to include the scene, he wrote it in his own way, weaving it into the pattern of the play by its motifs of rainbow scarf, magician, coffin, and escape. Actually the play is full of humour, but it is of Williams's own oblique and mordant kind. He credits Laurette Taylor with a special gift for this sort of wild, black comedy, and it was because she could balance it so carefully against Amanda's sympathetic qualities that he allowed her many small revisions of lines that, without the counterbalance she provided, can combine to make Amanda overly sympathetic.[14] Much the same reason may have influenced him in permitting the projection of titles to be cut. To my knowledge, the play has only once been produced as originally intended, and that quite recently and in German[15]; nonetheless, Williams insisted that the Random House-New Directions reading edition largely return to his original script. He has been criticized for doing this,[16] but when we remember his laborious experiments through draft after draft of *The Gentleman Caller*, searching for the proper framework, it seems probable that he was as right to do so as he was later in printing the original end to *Cat on a Hot Tin Roof* that Elia Kazan had sentimentalized in production. To insist, as most critics still do,[17] that the projection device is jejune or pretentious is to do Williams and his play a grave injustice.

III

The reasons for the original neglect of the projection device are not far to seek. In the early 1940's American audiences were familiar with realism and theatricalism separately but not with the simultaneity and tension between them on which Williams depends in *Menagerie*; the first production was so phenomenally successful that it is hardly surprising that critics should assume the projections must have been unnecessary; and Williams's own justifications for the device in his Production Notes to the play were rather misleading.

Reflecting the influence of Erwin Piscator, with whom he had studied during the period of his Rockefeller fellowship in New York, the first two reasons Williams gives are that, in an "episodic" drama, captions serve to clarify the central values of each scene and to emphasize the structural relationships between them—arguments that the critics had no difficulty refuting by pointing out that scenic focus and structural sequence were perfectly clear without such aids. Williams goes on to suggest a third function, however, which was largely ignored, perhaps because its phrasing was so vague: "... I think the screen will have a definite emotional appeal, less definable but just as important."[18] It is here that the importance of the projections lies. *The Glass Menagerie* is explicitly "sentimental," a play whose "first condition" is "nostalgia," and its besetting danger, therefore, is the sentimentality of which it has often been accused (ironically, sometimes by the same critics who dismiss the projections). It was by the complexity of its presentational effect that the original version guarded against this.

Just as the wording of Tom's framework speeches in the New Directions reading edition is much more ironically qualified than in the acting edition,[19] so too theatrical devices—Tom using an imaginary knife and fork (p. 24), or playing the first scene "*as though reading from a script*" (p. 26), with projections such as the "sailing vessel with the Jolly Roger" (p. 51) which accompanies his dreams of adventure (and links them to Jim's high-school performance in *The Pirates of Penzance*)—all serve to maintain an ironic distance between the early Tom-within-the-play and the later Tom-remembering, through whose presentation the audience must, willy-nilly, experience the play.

Moreover, this device not only slakes sentimentality, but also reflects aspects of Tom's character. Its slightly jaunty, occasionally jarring irony is typical of Williams's black comedy, the not-quite-funny humour (that in *Out Cry* he calls the "jokes of the condemned")[20] by which his characters try to protect themselves against painful feeling. The exaggeration of projections such as "Annunciation" (p. 56) or "The Sky Falls" (p. 111), for example, like the obtrusive playing of the Ave Maria off-stage, both mocks Amanda's self-dramatizing and reflects Tom's attempt to control his pain at recognizing the hope and despair beneath his mother's absurdity.

The theatricalism has a further effect besides. It creates a gap between Tom-remembering and the audience (which is really why the projections are resented); there is a slight, Albee-like abrasiveness involved that recalls the element of antagonism in those early drafts where Tom was made to argue with the spectators directly. This appears most disturbingly in relation to Laura, who is a wholly sympathetic character without the absurdity that is clear in Amanda, Jim, and the early Tom himself. She is given such a dimension of absurdity, however, by projections like "Not Jim!" (p. 72),

"Terror," "Ah!" (p. 83, followed soon by "Ha!" [p. 86]), or "Gentleman caller waving goodbye—gaily" (p. 109), which seem to run directly counter to the audience's response.

The significance of this effect is subtle, and can perhaps best be arrived at by noticing Williams's surprising lack of personal enthusiasm for this, his most popular play. In an early interview with *Time* he warned that in *The Glass Menagerie* "... I said all the nice things I have to say about people. The future things will be harsher,"[21] and in letters to Donald Windham during the summer of 1943 he complained, "'The Gentleman Caller' remains my chief work, but it goes slowly, I feel no overwhelming interest in it. It lacks the violence that excites me, so I piddle around with it," and "It is the *last* play I will try to write for the now existing theatre."[22] What *The Glass Menagerie* seems to lack, in fact, are Williams's characteristic ingredients of sex and violence. Yet it is clear from the drafts and alternative treatments that there were elements of both in his full response to the situation; and adumbrations of them can still be traced in the complexity of tone produced by the original theatricalism and by a certain exaggeration in the style of Tom's framework speeches, especially towards the end.

The play is usually talked of as Tom's exorcism of memory, but it can just as accurately be seen as repetition. After all, he does not really escape the family trap. The memory which forces him constantly to relive events that give so much pain and regret can be compared to Yeats's *Purgatory* or, even more closely, to Sartre's *Huis clos*—for which Williams has expressed great admiration (*Memoirs*, p. 149). And when the play is seen in this way, one must recognize that, besides its gentle sadness and remorse, there is also ruthlessness in Tom's final command, "Blow out your candles, Laura—and so goodbye ..." (p. 115). Like Othello's "Put out the light," this is a kind of loving murder, a repetition of the original violation. For Williams, in fact, love and betrayal are always two sides of the same emotion, as in his poem "The Comforter and the Betrayer"; his "brutal and gentle characters do more than co-exist, they interexist, one creates the other in a vicious circle of disaster."[23]

More interesting still, Laura is bidden to put out her own light. The image is of enforced self-killing, of ruthlessness turned in upon itself, because in rejecting Laura, Tom is also denying part of himself. This is more complex than the idea that "To leave home and Amanda is to insure self-preservation, but at the same time to kill something vital within the self."[24] It goes beyond the emotions of remorse and escape to touch the sadomasochism that is central to Williams's sensibility, according to which idealized love must be violated precisely because it is ideal, and in hurting others one also punishes oneself.

The element of bravado in Tom's attitude, the uneasiness in his insistence on the need to break away in spite of the damage that will be caused (seen most flagrantly in the rodomontade of the pioneer America drafts), is reflected in *The Glass Menagerie* by a slightly false, posturing, overelaborate quality in his poetic self-justifications, a forcing of tone which has often been remarked but is usually condemned. And Williams's comment in the *Memoirs* (p. 84) that he too has never felt Tom's narrations were up to the rest of the play interestingly beats out an observation by Peggy Prenshaw on Williams's use of art as therapy:

> viewing art as an extension of the artist, either for what he is or what he needs, leads solipsistically back to the mortal and flawed being that the artist seeks to transcend.... Tom Wingfield casts a magical web over experience, transforming the ordinary and ugly, and even painful, into a thing of beauty. But undermining ... [his] transformations of life into art is [his] ... (and [his] ... creator's) lurking doubt that the vision is wholly truthful....[25]

Williams may not have intended this uneasiness consciously, of course, but it adds immensely to the richness of the play (besides avoiding the trap of sentimentality) and also relates *The Glass Menagerie* more closely to the rest of Williams's canon. In various displaced, oblique ways the mixture of guilt and identification which Williams feels for Rose has been a recurrent theme throughout his work.[26] In *Memoirs* he says: "My sister and I had a close relationship, quite unsullied by any carnal knowledge.... And yet our love was, and is, the deepest in our lives and was, perhaps, very pertinent to our withdrawal from extrafamilial attachments" (pp. 119–120). He sees in Rose's retreat from life to imagination and in her final dreadful fate an equivalent of his own inescapable self-consciousness as an artist and of the confinement he talks of as his greatest fear (*Memoirs*, p. 223); and in no work is this to be seen more clearly than in the play called variously *Out Cry* (1973) and *The Two-Character Play* (1967, 1975), which has been described as "in some respects like a sequel to *Glass Menagerie*...."[27]

Though there are considerable revisions between the versions (particularly to make the relationship of the framework characters more antagonistic), the basic Pirandellian situation of *The Two-Character Play* remains unchanged. Two actors, a brother and sister androgynously named Felice and Clare Devoto, on tour in the capital of an unnamed northern country, find themselves abandoned by their company as "insane." They are alone on a stage dominated by a gigantic statue—representing, we are told, "things anguished and perverse" (p. 7); but since "if we're not artists, we're nothing" (p. 22), they put on a play that the brother is still in process of writing, ad-libbing as seems necessary. In this play within the play they represent a brother and sister, also called Felice and Clare, who are incapable of leaving the family house, where their father killed their mother, then himself. It is hinted that their love for each other has a sexual element (with sadistic overtones in the final revision), and as it becomes evident that Felice is shaping his play towards a repetition of the parents' killing-suicide, the actress Clare abruptly brings the performance to a halt—only to discover that their audience has left and they are now alone, locked in the darkening, icy theatre. To escape the cold, their one expedient is to go back into the southern past of the brother's play, where the killing-suicide can provide a solution to both levels of imprisonment. When it comes to the point, however, neither can kill the other, and the play ends with their embrace in what Williams has described as a *"Liebestod,"* as the stage blackens out to represent death theatrically.[28] As epigraph Williams quotes the *Song of Solomon*: "A garden enclosed is my sister."

Such a summary does no justice to the subtlety of this play, of course, which Williams calls "the big one," "close to the marrow of my being" (*Memoirs*, pp. 129, 228), but it is sufficient perhaps to show its relevance to the reciprocal fantasies in *Menagerie*—Laura's retreat to a private world of glass reflected in Tom's theatrical obsession with the past, and his conscious cruelty of abandonment mirrored in the guilt she returns to him—as two aspects of the "Comforter-Betrayer" syndrome. Like Felice and Clare, though less schematically, Tom and Laura can be seen as related aspects of the "fugitive" sensibility,[29] and only if this complementarity is accepted, can the full complexity of Williams's brilliant final balancing of tones between love, pity, regret, guilt, self-lacerating ruthlessness, posing, and bravado be imaginatively realized, and the superiority of his original theatricalized version of the play become quite clear. Perhaps like Felice's *Two-Character Play* itself, this may be "a little too personal, too special for most audiences" (p. 62), in which case the acting edition will continue to be preferable for performance, as Beaurline reports Williams's agent as indicating.[30] But until the theatricalism has been shown to fail, there is certainly no *a priori* case for this; and Williams has ensured that in reading we pay attention to his original version, which reflects more truthfully the complexity of response that can be traced throughout his many drafts and rewritings of the play.[31]

NOTES

1. See Edwina Williams and Lucy Freeman, *Remember Me to Tom* (New York, 1963).

2. Tennessee Williams, *Memoirs* (Garden City, N.Y., 1975). Subsequent references will appear in the text.

3. Tennessee Williams, *In the Winter of Cities* (Norfolk, Conn., 1964), pp. 53, 44.

4. See John Strother Clayton, "The Sister Figure in the Works of Tennessee Williams," *Carolina Quarterly*, 12 (Summer 1960), 47–60. A more extreme position is argued by Daniel A. Dervin, "The Spook in the Rain Forest: The Incestuous Structure of Tennessee Williams' Plays," *Psychocultural Review*, 3 (1979), 153–183.

5. All are in *27 Wagons Full of Cotton and Other One-Act Plays* (Norfolk, Conn., 1945)

6. Lester A. Beaurline, "*The Glass Menagerie*: From Story to Play," *Modern Drama*, 8 (1965), 143–149.

7. My ellipsis; the speech is a very long one.

8. Cf. Williams's "scenic out-line of the play-script" in an undated letter to Audrey Wood, reproduced in Richard F. Leavitt, ed., *The World of Tennessee Williams* (New York, 1978), pp. 52–53.

9. This may be the earliest element in *The Gentleman Caller*. The Texas archive has a note scribbled on two loose sheets in what looks like a very early, juvenile hand, recording a brother's musing about what his sister can be thinking as she decorates a Christmas tree.

10. Jim is characterized in much the same way in *Stairs to the Roof*.

11. *Screen Hits Annual*, No. 5 (1950), p. 50.

12. As he also did with happy endings for *Streetcar*; cf. Vivienne Dickson, "*A Streetcar Named Desire*: Its Development through the Manuscripts," in *Tennessee Williams: A Tribute*, ed. Jac Tharpe (Jackson, Miss., 1977), p. 157.

13. Mrs. Williams remembers the song as the bawdiest verse of the "St. Louis Blues" (E. Williams, p. 145).

14. See James L. Rowland, "Tennessee's Two Amandas," *Research Studies* (Washington State University), 35 (1967), 331–340, though Professor Rowland prefers the revised, sympathetic version.

15. Cf. pictures and discussion of a 1966 production at Ulm in Christian Jauslin, *Tennessee Williams* (Munich, 1976), pp. 129, 123–125. I am indebted to Professor Gilbert Debusscher for this reference.

16. See, for instance, Lester A. Beaurline, "The Director, the Script, and the Author's Revisions: A Critical Problem," in *Papers in Dramatic Theory and Criticism*, ed. David M. Knauf (Iowa City, 1969), p. 89.

17. E.g., Beaurline, "The Director"; S. Alan Chesler, "Tennessee Williams: Reassessment and Assessment," in Tharpe, p. 853; Mary Ann Corrigan, "Beyond Verisimilitude: Echoes of Expressionism in Williams' Plays," ibid., p. 392. A notable early argument against this attitude can be found in George Brandt, "Cinematic Structure in the Work of Tennessee Williams," in *American Theatre*, ed. John Russell Brown and Bernard Harris (London, 1967), pp. 184–185.

18. Tennessee Williams, Production Notes, *The Glass Menagerie* (New York, 1966), p. 8. Subsequent references to *The Glass Menagerie* are to this edition and will appear in the text.

The Texas archive has the typescript draft of what appears to have been intended as an open letter, entitled "A Reply to Mr. Nathan" and dated 9 April 1945, which throws further light on Williams's concept of the projections:

> It is true that in the original script I suggested—not insisted upon—the use of magic lantern slides to serve at intervals, carefully chosen, as a sometimes satirical and sometimes poetic counterpoint to the dialogue, and to sustain the narrative point of view even when he was not present on stage, *for these slides were the narrator's own commentary on what was taking place* (my italics).

Williams goes on to say that he did not object to the removal of the device in the first production and does not regret its loss because "the extraordinary power of Miss Taylor's performance, which I and nobody else had quite anticipated, made this play a play where that performance should be set as a pure jewel in the simplest of all possible settings." The letter seems never to have been published.

19. Cf. Thomas L. King, "Irony and Distance in *The Glass Menagerie*," *Educational Theatre Journal*, 25 (1973), 207–214.

20. Cf. Williams's unpublished Author's Notes for director and actors as quoted in Thomas P. Adler, "The Dialogue of Incompletion: Language in Tennessee Williams's Later Plays," *Quarterly Journal of Speech*, 61 (1975), 56. Subsequent references to *Out Cry* in my article refer to the New Directions edition (New York, 1973) and will appear in the text.

21. "The Theater: The Winner," *Time*, 23 April 1945, p. 88.

22. Tennessee Williams, Letters of 28 June 1943 and [18 or 25] August 1944, Letters 48 and 74, *Tennessee Williams' Letters to Donald Windham, 1940–1965*, ed. Donald Windham (New York, 1977), pp. 94, 148. Cf. Williams's statement, "I had never been able to avoid the undeniable fascination with violence until I wrote *The Glass Menagerie*," quoted in E. Williams, p. 253, and Williams's admission that this violence is the obverse of constant fear (ibid.).

23. John Buell, "The Evil Imagery of Tennessee Williams," *Thought*, 38 (1963), 185.

24. Nancy M. Tischler, "The Distorted Mirror: Tennessee Williams' Self-Portraits," *Mississippi Quarterly*, 25 (Fall 1972), 389–403; rpt. in *Tennessee Williams: A Collection of Critical Essays*, ed. Stephen Stanton (Englewood Cliffs, N.J., 1977), p. 160.

25. Peggy W. Prenshaw, "The Paradoxical Southern World of Tennessee Williams," in Tharpe, p. 24.

26. Cf. Clayton; Victor A. Kramer remarks on the same obsession: "to write of his sister is to write of a complexity which can be observed but not understood; but it is also to find 'release' ..." "Memoirs of Self-Indictment: The Solitude of Tennessee Williams," in Tharpe, p. 673.

27. Prenshaw, p. 17.

28. Cf. Williams, Author's Notes, in Adler, 57, n. 27.

29. Esther M. Jackson goes further and suggests that Amanda and the father are also "masks" of Tom: *The Broken World of Tennessee Williams* (Madison, Wis., 1966), p. 86.

30. Beaurline, "The Director," p. 89.

31. Quotations from the Texas archive are by permission of Tennessee Williams and the Humanities Research Center, The University of Texas at Austin.

ROGER BOXILL

'The Glass Menagerie' (1944)

TOM WINGFIELD. I didn't go to the moon, I went much further—for
time is the longest distance between two places.

T he first production of *The Glass Menagerie* opened in 1944 at the Civic
Theatre in Chicago and in the following year at the Playhouse Theatre in
New York. It was directed by Eddie Dowling and Margo Jones with Laurette
Taylor as Amanda, Julie Haydon as Laura, Eddie Dowling as Tom and
Anthony Ross as Jim. The music was by Paul Bowles and the set and lighting
by Jo Mielziner. The 1948 London production was directed by John Gielgud
with Helen Hayes as Amanda. The 1950 screen version was co-written by
Williams and Peter Berneis, and directed by Irving Rapper with Gertrude
Lawrence as Amanda, Jane Wyman as Laura, Arthur Kennedy as Tom and
Kirk Douglas as Jim. In major revivals of *Menagerie*, Amanda has been
played by Helen Hayes, Maureen Stapleton and Jessica Tandy. A television
adaptation was produced in 1966 with Shirley Booth, and another in 1973
with Katharine Hepburn.

In the play, a young merchant seaman (Tom Wingfield) looks back on
his life before the outbreak of the Second World War. He had shared a small
apartment in a poor section of St Louis with his sister (Laura), a painfully
shy girl who spent most of the time polishing her glass collection, and his
mother (Amanda), a minister's daughter from Mississippi whose husband, a

From *Tennessee Williams*: pp. 61–75. © 1987 by Roger Boxill.

telephone-company employee, had deserted her. Tom, who serves both as the narrator and as a participant in the enactment of his memories, was in those days a would-be poet working as a clerk in a warehouse to support the family. All that occurs in *Menagerie* is that the friend Tom brings home to meet Laura (Jim O'Connor), although he happens to be the boy she secretly admired in high school, turns out, unfortunately, to be already engaged.

The play is cradled in the playwright's recall of the Depression years when he worked in the warehouse of the International Shoe Company by day and wrote by night. The faded belle as doting mother derives from Miss Edwina. The absent father who fell in love with long distance alludes to C. C. during his happy days as a Delta drummer. Rose Williams's short-lived business studies, disappointing relationships and withdrawal from life inform the character of Laura as the predestined spinster with a lost love. Even the title refers to the collection of little glass animals that Rose and Tom kept in her room in St Louis, tiny figurines that came to represent for him all the softest emotions that belong to the remembrance of things past.

The theme of this gentle confessional work is aspiration and disappointment. The action is contained in the dashing of Laura's hope for romance, anticipated in the break-up of Amanda's marriage, and echoed in the failure of Tom's effort to become a writer. The plot centres on Laura's non-Cinderella story. A shy, crippled girl encounters in the flesh the very man she loves, who leads her on and quickly lets her down. The exposition of Amanda's ideal girlhood in Blue Mountain and unfortunate middle age in St Louis is like an organ point that sounds the play's nostalgic note. She was once the belle of the ball, surrounded by suitors, and is now a deserted housewife, struggling for survival. As the disillusioned narrator, Tom looks back to a time when adventure and success seemed possible. Even Jim, although not discouraged, finds life after adolescence disappointing.

The historical setting provides an enveloping action that ironically reflects the play's theme. The economic recovery following the Great Depression came with the Second World War. The optimistic phrases in which Jim forecasts his future—'*Knowledge—*Zzzzp! *Money—*Zzzzp!—Power!'—hint at the sounds of battle. The customers of the Paradise Dance Hall across the alley from the Wingfield apartment house find an end to boredom in a hell on earth. Tom gets his wish to live the life of a hero in an adventure movie through his role as a merchant seaman in a world lit by lightning.

The full historical background extends from the Second World War, in which Tom serves, to the First World War, in which his father served before him, and even to the American Civil War, which ended in the fall of the Old South, to whose vestiges of gracious living his mother still so desperately clings. Amanda Wingfield is an anachronism in the St Louis of the 1930s and may even have been one in the Blue Mountain of her girlhood. Besides the story of her failed marriage, she brings to the play the sense of a world that, like herself, has long since faded. Her expectation that she would marry a wealthy planter and settle down to raise her family on a large plantation with many servants is a *belle rêve* of Southern aristocratic life in antebellum times. Her reminiscences are a confusion of wish and reality consistent with the play's premise that memory is primarily seated in the heart.

The Glass Menagerie is a dramatic elegy that plays within three concentric spheres of time: the time of the Second World War, in which Tom speaks to the audience as a merchant seaman; the time of the Depression, in which Tom lived with his mother and his sister in St Louis; and the time that Amanda thinks of as a vanished golden age—her girlhood in the rural South before the Great War. Like Tom's, the memory of her cherished past is partly enacted when she appears for the evening of the dinner party with a bunch of jonquils on her arm and skips coquettishly around the living-room, dressed in the girlish frock of yellowed voile with blue silk sash in which she led the cotillion long ago, won the cakewalk twice at Sunset Hill, and went to the Governor's Ball in Jackson.

The primary conditions of Amanda's poignant resurrection of her youth—spring and courtship—conform to the conventions of pastoral romance. Invitations poured in from all over the Delta that enchanted season when she had her craze for jonquils. In the evenings there were dances, and in the afternoons picnics and long carriage rides through the countryside, lacy with dogwood in May, and flooded with the jonquils that she made her young men help gather for her. On a single Sunday afternoon in Blue Mountain, she had seventeen gentleman callers, and extra chairs had to be brought in from the parish house to accommodate them. She could have become the wife of the brilliant Duncan J. Fitzhugh or of the dashing Bates Cutrere, who married another after Amanda refused him but carried her picture on him until he died. Amanda's arias on the lost dreams of her youth echo spring rites and tall tales of princesses wooed by many suitors.[1] Tom's memory of his mother's memory modulates easily into legend because it is twice removed from reality, recessed within the play's innermost sphere of time.

The Christian symbolism with which *Menagerie* is filled suggests that the time of Amanda's youth, the time of the Depression and the time of the Second World War are analogues, respectively, of Paradise, Purgatory and Hell. From the midst of global conflagration Tom looks back to the years of trial in St Louis that followed the disappearance of the Edenic South his mother remembers. The idea of the gentleman caller as saviour is clear from the 'Annunciation' to Amanda by her son that Jim is coming to dinner. One night at the movies Tom sees a stage magician turn water into wine and escape from a coffin. Amanda exhorts her children to 'rise and shine' and calls her ailing magazine-subscribers 'Christian martyrs'. In an atmosphere that is relatively dusky, the light on Laura has a pristine clarity reminiscent of that on saints in medieval paintings. The qualities of intimacy and reverence combine in her scene with Jim, the only light for which is provided by a candelabrum that once stood on the altar of a church.

As the gentleman caller does not fulfil his role as redeemer, the altar candles in Laura's heart are soon extinguished. The play's central image—light playing on a broken surface—suggests the ephemeral nature of life, beauty and human feeling. Joyful moments flicker only for an instant within the surrounding darkness of eternity, as when Jim and Laura look at the little glass unicorn together by candlelight, Amanda wishes on the moon, or couples find brief comfort in fleeting intimacy at the nearby dance hall, whose glass sphere, revolving slowly at the ceiling, filters the surrounding shadows with delicate rainbow colours. In the dim poetic interior of the Wingfield living-room, the picture of the absent father with smiling doughboy face is intermittently illuminated, while outside, beyond the dark alleyways and murky canyons of tangled clotheslines, garbage cans, and neighbouring fire escapes, the running lights of movie marquees blink and beckon in the distance. The movies themselves are no more than images of light that pass quickly into oblivion like cut jonquils or spring showers. For even art in *The Glass Menagerie* is presented as a feeble consolation for the sorry transience of life—fragile glass, scratchy phonograph records, scraps of poetry scribbled on shoe boxes.

Like the spotty, shadowy lighting, other extra-literary effects, drawn principally from film, emphasise the first condition of the play, which is nostalgia, and help to project the sense of an insubstantial world, wispy as memory itself. Transparent gauze scrims, one representing the outside wall of the tenement, another the portieres in the archway or second proscenium between the living-room and dining-room up stage, not only make scene transitions cinematic in their fluidity but also create a stage within a stage within a stage—a use of space which relates to the idea of containing time within time within time. After Tom's introductory speech, the grim wall of the building before which he has stood fades out as the Wingfield living-room fades in behind it. In turn, the portieres upstage dissolve and separate like a second curtain or inner veil of memory as soft lighting slowly reveals the family seated at the dining-table. The first scene is played without food or utensils. The last is played without words. During Tom's closing speech, Amanda appears to comfort Laura as if behind sound proof glass, her studied gestures reminiscent of the silent screen.

Music from three sources weaves through the scenes, bridging the spheres of time. On the on-stage Victrola Laura plays the music of her parents' youth, records her father left behind. The dance hall mixes the hot swing of the thirties with the slow tangos of the twenties and the tender waltzes of Amanda's girlhood. The music to which Jim and Laura dance, 'La Golondrina', is the same Mexican waltz that Alma Winemiller sings on Independence Day 1916 in *Summer and Smoke*. Most prominent is the recurring theme that comes out of nowhere and fades away again in accordance with film convention, like the images in a reverie. It is primarily Laura's *Leitmotiv* and suggests her fragile beauty as does the spun glass with which she is also identified. Williams's idea of barely audible circus music is consistent with his central image of light glimmering sporadically in the void. The immutable sorrow of life persists under the superficial gaiety of the passing moment. The distant calliope, with its associations of sad clowns, trapeze acts and performing animals, is an invitation occasionally to escape into a garish, itinerant world of make-believe. Human creativity is once more presented in the most pathetic terms. Indeed the circus animals are continuous with the figurines of Laura's menagerie, whose tiny size on stage corresponds to the remoteness of the fairground.

In the course of this memory play, some forty projections of images, speeches or titles associate the graphic with the verbal in the sometimes whimsical manner of the mind when in the relatively free condition of sleep or reverie. Williams's explanation notwithstanding, the projections do not make structural points but instead spoof the sentiment of the scenes in which they appear. A pirate ship, a magazine cover, or the gentleman caller waving goodbye are pictures that undermine the pathos of the play like the farcical moments in Chekhov. Since the first production, directors have almost without exception cut the device as an expressionist intrusion upon an essentially naturalistic work. Perhaps they are right. Yet the projections are indebted less to the German theatre than to the silent screen. Such lines as 'Ah!' or 'Not Jim!' and such titles as 'The Annunciation', 'The Accent of a Coming Foot' or 'The Sky Falls' appear to derive, like so much else in *Menagerie*, from the playwright's frequent movie-going in childhood.

The call in Williams's production notes for 'a new, plastic theatre' to replace the outworn theatre of conventional realism is essentially a manifesto of the cinematic stage. The writer is to become more visual. He is to use lighting to suggest mood and assert relationships—such as the clear pool of light in which the fragile and unearthly Laura sits while Jim, Tom and Amanda are having supper upstage. He is to bring in music from out of the blue or flash images on a screen in order to give a plastic, mobile quality to plays that are relatively actionless. The lyric naturalism of the twentieth-century play of sensibility depends for its theatrical expression upon the writer's imaginative use of the methods and resources with which motion pictures have enriched theatrical art.

This explains why the American theatre became more of a director's medium, like film, in the time of Williams. When Elia Kazan founded the Actors Studio in 1947, three years after *Menagerie*, it was for the purpose of training actors to give film-size performances. His successor, Lee Strasberg, would later train them in the requisite docility. Actors were to become more compliant, more 'plastic', like the scenery and the lighting through which the all-powerful director would express his predetermined 'concept'. The neo-Stanislavskyan American Method repudiates 'projection consciousness' as leading to oversized mannerisms put out of date by the microphone and camera.

It is partly the convention of film, although chiefly that of the short story, from which the episodic structure of *Menagerie* derives. The play is an adaptation of a film script (*The Gentleman Caller*) based on a short story ('Portrait of a Girl in Glass'). The seven scenes mingle with allusive narrative speeches to convey a casual sense of order that accords with the nature of memory. In neither the story nor the play is the tiny plot the point. It is the revelation of characters locked in time. This explains why nothing much happens in *Menagerie*. Its lyrical, non-linear form is rooted in the gently exfoliative 'Portrait of a Girl in Glass'. It is also rooted in a particular character's point of view, a technique common enough in fiction but atypical of drama. Since that character happens to be an aspiring poet in both the story and the play, an inclination to lyricism is obligatory.

'Portrait' is essentially a character sketch of Laura, as its title from the static art of sculpture implies. Her brother, Tom, remembers her from the time they lived in St Louis with their mother and he worked in a warehouse. Their father had long ago deserted them. Laura was a frightened, reclusive girl who appeared to exist in a world of make-believe. While decorating the tree one Christmas, she picked up the star that went on top and asked Tom if stars really had five points. She spent most of the time listening to her father's old records, polishing her collection of glass figurines, and rereading Gene Stratton Porter's *Freckles*, with whose hero, a young one-armed lumberjack, she carried on an imaginary relationship. He would drop by her room for an occasional visit just as her brother habitually did. When she was twenty, she was unable to face the demands of secretarial school. When she turned twenty-three, her mother asked Tom to bring a friend home to dinner in order to meet her. He turned out to be a hearty and befreckled fellow employee (Jim Delaney), with whom Laura, much to her family's amazement, got along famously because she confused him in her mind with the hero of the much-read book. Unfortunately, he was already engaged. Not long after Jim's visit, Tom lost his job at the warehouse, left St Louis and took to wandering. He became independent and succeeded in forgetting his home, although from time to time he thinks of his sister.

The revelation that Jim is already engaged becomes more pathetic in the play because Williams makes the gentleman caller into Laura's real rather than her imaginary love. Her abnormality is less mental but more physical. Instead of the obsession to reread the same book, she has the more playable handicap of a slight limp. It is particularly effective when she and Jim dance together by candlelight (they are never alone in 'Portrait') and accidentally break the glass unicorn's horn—a piece of business, missing from the story, that uses the play's titular symbol and suggests, among other things, the sudden collapse of male ardour upon the removal of maidenly defence.

'Portrait' is a wistful memory, *Menagerie* a moving elegy. The play gains power from an intensification of theme and a strengthening of logic in the progression of events. The three years that pass in the story between the mother's discovery of her daughter's truancy and the appearance of the gentleman caller are reduced to three months in the play, long enough considering Amanda's determination to find Laura a husband if she is not to be a secretary. In the story, Tom's departure is peremptory because it is not preceded by a climactic quarrel with his mother. Jim Delaney makes no thematic contribution of his own because he is not a former high-school hero like Jim O'Connor. The mother is a minor character with neither reminiscences nor a name. Nor are the Wingfields specifically from the South.

The Glass Menagerie combines Williams's two archetypal actions. The climax of the outer play is the spoiled occasion, the climax of the inner play the eviction or loss of home. Laura does not sit at table with Jim. The gentleman caller, having declined his hostess's offer of lemonade, leaves early to meet his fiancee. After all the preparation, Amanda's party is ruined. Tom's curtain speech reminds us that everything has happened within his memory, and we may be sure that it will do so again and again. Whether the two belles, one faded, one never having bloomed, manage to keep their home after his departure we can only guess; but it is clear that the wanderer has none apart from them.

In the play's last moments, Tom's two roles, narrator and participant, coalesce. Dressed as a merchant seaman, the one who broke free to seek adventure stands before the audience and admits that he is a haunted fugitive. He calls out to Laura that he has tried but not been able to forget her. The many cities to which he has sailed seem to sweep about him like dead leaves torn loose from their branches. A strain of familiar music, a display of perfumes in a store window, or simply a fragment of transparent glass is enough to remind him of what he has lost. Upstage, behind the gauze scrim which marks the outside wall of the St Louis tenement that was once his home, the mother and sister he left behind enact a scene without words, like silent ghosts, visible only to the eye of memory. Still facing the audience, he tells Laura to blow out the candles which light the dim interior. She does so, he says goodbye, but on his exit the elusive, nostalgic music that has dipped in and out of the scenes from the beginning breaks off without resolution. Tom's climactic realisation that he will play out his 'memory play' for the rest of his days is like the 'epiphany' in a short story by Joyce. His confession throws all of the events that have preceded it into a different light; or, more precisely, it casts them into a greater elegiac darkness.

The problem of playing *The Glass Menagerie* arises from the fact that, whereas from a dramatic critic's point of view it is Tom's play, from an actor's it is Amanda's. The same distinction applies to Shakespeare's *Henry IV, Part One*, which is Hal's play although Falstaff appropriates it in performance. While students are invited to see the work as the education of the Prince, actors ask to read for the fat knight or the fiery rebel. Similarly, although *Menagerie* is really the chronicle of the Son, its production record shows that it has nearly always been construed as a starring-vehicle for the Mother.

Laurette Taylor's legendary performance established the tradition. The first Amanda was a plump little woman of sixty with a bright, eager face, her grey hair cut into girlish bangs. From all accounts, her characterisation was a composite of vague, fluttery gestures, sudden pauses, and unexpected shifts in pace or stress. Her delivery was quiet. A good deal of the time she gave the impression of mumbling. Bit by bit, her subtle revelations of hope, sorrow, despair, decision, longing, annoyance, snobbery, playfulness, coquetry, fatigue and resignation merged into a stage portrait of such fidelity to truth that reviewers were at a loss to define its method. Garland of the *New York Journal-American* called it 'Duse-like in the poignancy of its serio-comic detail', Gibbs of the *New Yorker* said one hardly knew what to write, and Young of the *New Republic* confessed that its depth and spontaneity defied analysis.[2]

On the other hand, Eddie Dowling as the first Tom did not altogether succeed. The actor-director was a short man of nearly fifty with a still boyish face. His characterisation was evidently congenial and subdued. He read his narrative speeches straightforwardly, putting the house at ease with his off-hand manner and personal charm. Most reviewers praised his performance much as they did Julie Haydon's ethereal Laura and Anthony Ross's workmanlike Jim. But his double role made others uncomfortable. It seemed too derivative of the narrator-participant in John Van Druten's *I*

Remember Mama, then running on Broadway, or of the narrator in Thornton Wilder's *Our Town* before it. Krutch of the *Nation*, who disliked the cinematic effects created by Jo Mielziner's set and lighting, took even greater exception to what he called the 'pseudo-poetic verbiage' of the narrative speeches. Young, however, blamed Dowling rather than Williams. The narrations, he believed, only appeared to be a mistake on the playwright's part because the actor did not read them from character. If they had been delivered with the 'variety, impulse, and intensity' they needed, then the whole story would have been different.

It was thirty years before Young's thesis was put to the test. In 1956 the younger and more matter-of-fact Tom of James Daly appeared opposite the spirited Amanda of Helen Hayes (she played the role three times). In 1965 the gentle and disarmingly simple Tom of George Grizzard appeared opposite the earnest Amanda of Maureen Stapleton (she played it twice). But, according to Kerr of the *New York Herald-Tribune*, Daly's Tom made the narrations seem 'a trace heavy', and according to Watts of the *New York Post* Grizzard was less effective as the commentator than as the participant.[3] The narrations were largely cut from the 1950 screen adaptation, in which the caustic Tom of Arthur Kennedy appeared opposite the musical-comedy Amanda of Gertrude Lawrence. A flashback showed Amanda as a young girl dancing with her many admirers. A close-up showed her as a giddy mother peeping through the curtain to see how Jim and Laura were getting on. The obligatory Happy Ending came when the lame daughter, accompanied by the gentlemen caller, went out to the Paradise Dance Hall and met a man of her own.

In 1973 Thomas L. King published a valuable article arguing that *Menagerie* belongs to Tom, who tricks the audience into shouldering the pain he exorcises by creating his memory play.[4] In 1975 Rip Torn, cast opposite Maureen Stapleton's second Amanda, made the only all-out effort to read the narrations from character. The curtain speech was the key to his portrait. The result was a wild, brooding, quirky, homosexual Tom who flung his words at the house like accusations. Torn's performance did not receive a unanimous welcome; but neither was it damned with faint praise. Those who attacked it were inclined to do so without reserve; others were as absolute in their esteem. Barnes of the *New York Times* was reminded of a Greek tragic hero, Kalem of *Time* thought it 'just right', and Watt of the *New York Daily News* made the telling observation that Torn was at his best in 'the beautifully written narrative sections'.[5]

At the end of 1983 Jessica Tandy, the original Blanche DuBois, played Amanda in a New York revival directed by John Dexter. She was seventy-four. It was a reserved, grandmotherly Amanda who, together with Amanda

Plummer's far-gone Laura and John Heard's fidgety Jim, was at odds with the postcard prettiness of the production. No filmy gauze or dusky light made unclear for long the big, elegant set of Ming Cho Lee. The Wingfield apartment was a store window at Christmas exploiting our nostalgia for the 1930s. The menagerie itself was set on matching tables down right and left. Attractive bookshelves marked the exit, upstage of the telephone table. Lamps hung from the suspended ceiling, beyond which, in the distance, the abstract forms of buildings were visible. Paul Bowles's original music was used selectively. One soft roll of thunder announced the rain. Bruce Davison's blond, clean-cut Tom, although he occasionally imitated Williams's drawl, read most of his lines with swift precision. The decorative look of the whole extended from his handsome sweaters to the pink and yellow light in which the stage was swathed, and above it to the proscenium arch, where, for the first time in a major production, some of Williams's legends (and others not his) were periodically illuminated in a graceful script. Like one of Laura's statues, *The Glass Menagerie* had been handled like a little treasure and remounted for commemorative display following the death of the author at the beginning of the year.

NOTES

1. For an excellent demonstration of this point, see Judith Thompson, 'Symbol, Myth, and Ritual in *The Glass Menagerie*, *The Rose Tattoo*, and *Orpheus Descending*', in *Tennessee Williams: A Tribute*, ed. Jac Tharpe (Jackson: University Press of Mississippi, 1977) pp. 697–711.

2. The cited reviews of the 1945 premiere production of *The Glass Menagerie* are: Robert Garland, in *New York Journal-American*, 2 Apr 1945, repr. in *New York Theatre Critics' Reviews, 1945*, p. 235; Wolcott Gibbs, in *New Yorker*, 21 (7 Apr 1945) 40; Stark Young, in *New Republic*, 112 (16 Apr 1945) 505–6; Joseph Wood Krutch, in *Nation*, 160 (14 Apr 1945) 424–5.

3. For the 1956 production, see Walter Kerr, in *New York Herald-Tribune*, 22 Nov 1956, repr. in *New York Theatre Critics' Reviews, 1956*, p. 190. For the 1965 production, see Richard Watts, Jr, in *New York Post*, 5 May 1965, repr. in *New York Theatre Critics' Reviews, 1965*, p. 332.

4. Thomas L. King, 'Irony and Distance in *The Glass Menagerie*', *Educational Theatre Journal*, xxv, no. 2 (May 1973) 207–14.

5. The cited reviews of the 1975 New York production of *The Glass Menagerie* are: Clive Barnes, in *New York Times*, 19 Dec 1975, and Douglas Watt, in *New York Daily News*, 19 Dec 1975, repr. in *New York Theatre Critics' Reviews, 1975*, pp. 125 and 128; T. E. Kalem, in *Time*, 107 (12 Jan 1976) 61.

DREWEY WAYNE GUNN

"More than Just a Little Chekhovian": The Sea Gull *as a Source for the Characters in* The Glass Menagerie

For nearly fifty years one of Tennessee Williams's abiding passions was his love for Chekhov. In 1979 he claimed, "I have not been subjected to any influence but that of Chekhov in my profession." Above all, he consistently praised *The Sea Gull*. In a letter to a friend in 1950 he called it "the greatest of all modern plays." And in his 1972 *Memoirs* he was willing to admit only a play of Brecht's into the same august company.[1] Williams's infatuation began in the summer of 1935 when he first read *The Sea Gull*, as well as *The Cherry Orchard* and some of Chekhov's short stories and letters.[2] For the plays he probably read the translations of Constance Garnett available in Modern Library. Although he did not see it, the spring 1938 Theatre Guild production of *The Sea Gull*, using a translation by fellow Mississippian Stark Young and starring Alfred Lunt and Lynn Fontanne, undoubtedly drew his attention.[3] At the time, Williams was finishing his studies at the University of Iowa and was immersed in all aspects of theatre.

Towards the end of his life Williams tried to absorb *The Sea Gull* completely into his own corpus by adapting it according to his own vision. The result, the unpublished *Notebook of Trigorin*, was presented in Vancouver in 1981 and in Los Angeles the following year. One reviewer of the American production, wrote, "Williams has pared down the play and quickened the sluggish ebb and flow of life on a *fin de siècle* Russian country estate. He has

From *Modern Drama*, vol. XXXIII, no. 3 (September 1990): pp. 313–321. © 1990 by the University of Toronto.

abbreviated Chekhov's cadences and augmented the poetry with his own choices." Most significantly, the reviewer felt that the portrait of Trigorin "reflects much of Williams's own person," particularly since Williams depicted the writer as homosexual or at least bisexual.[4]

But Williams in a sense had already injected his life into *The Sea Gull*, for he used the Russian play as early as 1944, I am convinced, in order to create and shape his first and perhaps still greatest success, *The Glass Menagerie*. The reviewer Louis Kronenberger, two days after its New York opening, wrote that "in its mingled pathos and comedy, its mingled naturalistic detail and gauzy atmosphere, its preoccupation with 'memory,' its tissue of forlorn hopes and backward looks and languishing self-pities, *The Glass Menagerie* is more than just a little Chekhovian." Twenty years later Francis Donahue, in a brief discussion of Chekhov's influence on Williams, quoted the reviewer's observations with approval. But neither Kronenberger nor Donahue—nor for that matter Young in his review of Williams's play—noted the specific, close similarities between the four characters in *The Glass Menagerie* and the four principals in *The Sea Gull*.[5] The fact that Williams's play is so undeniably autobiographical has obscured how much these characters resemble one another.

To describe the four in one play is to describe those in the other. There is a frustrated son who wants to be a writer but who feels trapped by circumstances. There is a silly and vain mother who, living in her own world of artificial dreams, largely ignores her son's needs. There is a frail young girl who also is trapped by her weaknesses and by her own unrealistic dreams. Finally, there is a seemingly practical but somewhat crass outsider who wreaks havoc on the dreams of the others. In neither play is there a father. Other similarities besides character relationships exist. They seem altogether too close to be entirely coincidental. Just as *The Cherry Orchard* probably provided Williams clues for developing *A Streetcar Named Desire*[6] almost surely—though the evidence must remain circumstantial—*The Sea Gull* was indispensable for his realization of *The Glass Menagerie*.

It was not, of course, a source in the same sense that *Look Homeward, Angel* was the source for Ketti Frings's play or even that *Finnegans Wake* was a source for *The Skin of Our Teeth*. But it would seem that Williams, probably subconsciously, saw that significant configurations in his life could become a play because Chekhov had already provided him a model by which to order his experience. In 1943 Williams finished "Portrait of a Girl in Glass," a short story which anticipated the play.[7] Though the four characters are all present (and the father is absent), a number of key personality traits and symbolic motifs had not yet appeared. Brian Parker, in his synopsis of the many differing versions of *The Glass Menagerie* in manuscript at the University of Texas, shows how Williams tried out many variations on his family plot. It was not until late in the drafts that the present pattern emerged.[8] It was as if Williams had finally locked onto the model thus provided for him in *The Sea Gull*.

Konstantin Treplev provides the prototype for Tom Wingfield. Both are struggling writers who are frustrated in their efforts. A comment the doctor makes about Konstantin applies almost as well to Tom: "There is something in him! He thinks in images; his stories are vivid, full of colour and they affect [one] strongly. The only pity is that he has not got definite aims. He produces an impression and that's all, but you can't get far with nothing but an impression" (*SG*, p. 52).[9] Both aspiring writers feel trapped by their background and their environment, and both are faintly rebellious. Neither has finished his formal education: Konstantin has had to leave the university in his third year, "owing to circumstances 'for which we accept no responsibility'" (*SG*, p. 7); Tom has graduated from high school and begun working in a shoe warehouse. Though with different handicaps, they struggle to overcome their adversities. Konstantin does manage to publish short stories, but ultimately he is a failure. Rather than master his circumstances, he kills himself after one previously unsuccessful attempt. In joining the merchant marine, Tom runs away from family responsibilities, abandoning all but the memory of his mother and his sister. Yet he is more successful at least in defining his life.

Tom and Konstantin may even share literary theories. Apparently Tom is to be considered as the author of the play that we are witnessing: he says, "I give you truth in the pleasant disguise of illusion" (*GM*, p. 22),[10] and in other comments he indicates that he has created the theatrical world we have entered. If we look at *The Glass Menagerie* thus, we can see that there are striking similarities between the literary forms with which he and Konstantin experiment. The latter wants to bring a new form of drama to the stage. In his desire to shed the worn-out trappings of realism, of "tradition and conventionality," he asserts, "We need new forms of expression" (*SG*, p. 6). To this end Konstantin writes a highly symbolic drama that dispenses with scenery altogether. His actress complains, "There is very little action in your play—nothing but speeches"; but he insists, "One must depict life not as it is, and not as it ought to be, but as we see it in our dreams" (*SG*, p. 9). *The Glass Menagerie* as a play is quite different from the snippet of Konstantin's play we see (in fact, Konstantin's drama seems to be Chekhov's satire on the misty symbolism of the Maeterlinck school). Still, *The Glass Menagerie* satisfies many of Konstantin's theories and intentions. As Tom tells us at the beginning, "The play is memory" (*GM*, p. 23)—a haunted dream. It has many speeches, its most startling action being a kiss. Instead of the three walls denounced by Konstantin, we have transparencies with the suggestions of rooms; instead of the show, loathed by Konstantin, of the way "people eat, drink, love, move about, and wear their jackets" (*SG*, p. 153), we have a scene in which "*Eating is indicated by gestures without food or utensils*" (*GM*, p. 6). Tom also acknowledges that he has "a poet's weakness for symbols," stating explicitly that he is conscious of his use of the Gentleman Caller as a symbol (*GM*, p. 23).

Neither son has a father. It is impossible to gather what has happened to Konstantin's—although one assumes he has died—while much is made of the older Wingfield's disappearance. Still, their personalities were apparently similar. Wingfield had great charm, just as the older Treplev, an actor, was presumably attractive. Yet both were common enough men: Wingfield was an ordinary worker with a telephone company, while the older Treplev was "an artisan of Kiev" (*SG*, p. 7). The sons apparently resemble their fathers, at least in their mothers' eyes. Konstantin's mother seems to be accusing him of being like his father when she labels her son "a Kiev shopman" (*SG*, p. 37), and Tom's mother criticizes him as becoming, "More and more" like his father (*GM*, p. 53). The motif is all the more striking since Williams's own father was very much present during the period he was depicting and since in some drafts of the play Williams actually had the father figure on stage.[11]

The similarities between Irina, Madame Arkadin, and Amanda are even closer than those between the sons. The women's personalities are very close. As a consequence, the relationship between mother and son is likewise similar. First, in their efforts to become writers, both sons must struggle against the incomprehension of dominant mothers. Irina makes fun of the play her son presents, goading him into angrily calling off the performance, and there are later quarrels between the two. Amanda irritates Tom several times until he bursts out in fits of anger. Irina repeatedly accuses Konstantin of being decadent (*SG*, pp. 12–13, 37). Amanda removes all of Tom's books which she considers "the output of diseased minds" and which she fears are endangering him morally (*GM*, p. 39). Second, both sons feel hampered by their mothers' over-solicitousness about money. Irina insists that she has none to give her son, that she needs to keep all she has for her costumes and life as an actress.[12] Amanda, stung by the Depression, less selfishly wants the means to provide for her daughter, but she harps on any waste she perceives Tom making. As a result, both sons question their mothers' love. Certainly Irina does not care enough to read his stories once he becomes a published author. Tom tells Amanda, "It seems unimportant to you, what I'm *doing*—what I *want* to do" (*GM*, pp. 40–41), and at times Amanda seems to consider Tom's most important functions to be to pay the rent and to launch his sister into a marriage. Both mothers declare their love for their sons, but their statements sound faintly insincere.

For both women are chiefly engrossed with themselves, vain to the point of being comical about their appearance and their position in society. Irina is an actress by profession. Almost certainly one reason Konstantin has begun writing plays is to win her approval. But his role as playwright, as well as his dislike of the kinds of plays in which she acts, detracts from her own importance. Konstantin himself calls her "a psychological freak" who wants to hear praise only for herself (*SG*, pp. 5–6). She is proud of the fact that she can look like "a girl of fifteen" (*SG*, p. 20). Amanda is an actress by nature; throughout she plays roles: loving mother, deceived provider, Southern belle. When the gentleman caller arrives, she literally dresses her adolescent past and plays it for all she can: *"the legend of her youth is nearly revived"* (*GM*, p. 71). Amanda's jonquils monologue is one of the great moments of *The Glass Menagerie*, analogous to her earlier recital about her beaux, but it is the speech of a self-absorbed actress, not that of a mother. This aspect of Amanda's personality is missing from "Portrait of a Girl in Glass." For example, with the gentleman caller she merely has "the conversational honors, such as they were" (*CS*, p. 116) and she is dressed in no special way. It is another bit of circumstantial evidence that Irina colored Williams's development of Amanda's character.

Williams also followed Chekhov in depicting a woman who has been unlucky with men. Amanda's reminiscence about Blue Mountain and Moon Lake (*GM*, p. 27), though longer, is similar to Irina's memory of life on the lake "Ten or fifteen years ago" when there were "laughter, noise, shooting, and love affairs without end" (*SG*, p. 14). Both women want love. Irina talks about the way a woman may "captivate" a man (*SG*, p. 20). We learn nothing about her relationship with her husband, but we see a probable pattern in her relationship with Trigorin. When he openly admits to her that he is attracted to a younger, more appealing woman, Irina all but gives her consent to the fling. Then, when the episode ends, she accepts him back. Amanda tells Laura, "All pretty girls are a trap" (*GM*, p. 70). But she likewise has chosen the wrong man out of all the beaux who she claims presented themselves for her hand. Even though her husband has deserted her, she still clings to a larger-than-life-size photograph of him, which dominates her living room. Like Nina, she cannot give up a man who has wronged her. Again Williams has expanded considerably on Amanda's relationship with her husband as depicted in the short story. There he simply made a "sudden and unexplained disappearance" and his name is "spoken rarely" (*CS*, p. 112).

Williams throughout his career depicted the ravages of time as vividly as had Chekhov. Here both comically and sympathetically he portrays the way Amanda is affected. On this point, there are more differences than similarities between the two mothers. Nevertheless, both talk about time's passage and both suffer the loss of their sons. Irina says, "it is my rule never to look into the future. I never think about old age or death. What is to be, will be" (*SG*, p. 19). One cannot know whether she accepts her son's death with such equanimity since it provides the play's curtain. Perhaps she does, since she is so absorbed in herself. In contrast, Amanda worries about the effects of time. She tells Tom, "You are the only young man that I know of who ignores the fact that the future becomes the present, the present the past, and the past turns into everlasting regret if you don't plan for it!" (*GM*, p. 63). She worries particularly about what will happen to Laura and warns her about unmarried women, who become "barely tolerated spinsters living upon the grudging patronage of sister's husband or brother's wife" (*GM*, p. 34).[13] Since Tom's departure also provides the curtain, likewise we cannot know how Amanda accepts his being gone.

Mothers, sons, and even absent fathers in the two plays then have much in common. What Williams gained from Nina for his depiction of Laura seems more tenuous. While Nina is a potential wife for Konstantin, Laura is Tom's sister, and even the subconscious incestuous desire Tom probably feels for her is a very distant echo of the passion Konstantin feels for Nina. Yet again there are a number of very important similarities. First, both men are equally helplessly enslaved by the magnetism of the two women. One of Konstantin's last speeches to Nina is highly similar to Tom's curtain speech (and even closer to the ending of "Portrait of a Girl in Glass"): "wherever I look I see your face, that tender smile that lighted up the best days of my life" (*SG*, p. 56). Second, Laura and Nina are alike in being weak women, psychologically crippled and unable to cope with life. Both are infatuated with a romanticized vision of a male: Laura worships Jim, the high school star of Gilbert and Sullivan operettas, just as Nina idolizes Trigorin, whom she has long read. When Jim leaves, Laura gives him the unicorn, now turned into a horse, as a souvenir, much as Nina, who thinks she will not see Trigorin again, gives him a medallion to remember her by. And finally, while Nina actually tries to break out of her seclusion when she thinks Trigorin returns her feelings, Laura at least seems momentarily on the verge of finding new strength. Both women, however, subsequently retreat into their own little worlds created in their own minds.

None of these similarities appears in Williams's portrayal of Laura in the short story. She has never previously admired Jim, the unicorn (and thus the souvenir incident) is missing altogether, and Laura seems unchanged when Jim leaves. In fact, in "Portrait of a Girl in Glass" Laura actually seems simple-minded. There is yet another piece of circumstantial evidence that Nina influenced Williams's changing conceptions of Laura. When Nina runs away, she tries to become an actress. In one early version of *The Glass*

Menagerie at the University of Texas, Laura becomes "a high-strung member of the local Little Theatre," while Tom is "the withdrawn and quiet one."[14] (In the published version, Nina's decision to run away from her unhappy homelife more closely adumbrates Tom's decision, of course.) As for Laura's being physically crippled, an affliction equally absent from the short story, *The Sea Gull* too may have provided the idea. At one point Chekhov shows another woman (Masha, whose foot has fallen asleep) as walking with "a lazy, lagging step" (*SG*, p. 22).[15] Williams was always keenly sensitive to such stage images.

Jim seems to have even less relationship to Trigorin than the two women do to each other. But again there is a pattern. First, both men are outsiders who stir the emotions of the young women they encounter. An idea that Trigorin has for a story can serve to sum up both men's powers: "a man comes by chance, sees [a young woman], and having nothing better to do, destroys her" (*SG*, p. 30). Nina follows Trigorin into a life of misery and failure. Jim, on his own this evening while his girlfriend is away, impulsively kisses Laura, an act that he recognizes is wrong, even potentially dangerous, and he is indirectly the cause for the unicorn's horn being broken. At the same time, both men affect the older women. Trigorin is Irina's lover. Amanda plays the coquette when she encounters Jim; he clearly becomes a surrogate for the lost beaux of her past. All these similarities are again missing from the short story version. Finally, even though Trigorin, the published author with some fame, seems more successful than does Jim, the high school singer now filled with dreams of a future in television, both men are essentially second-raters, egotistical and only apparently practical in their approaches to life. Nevertheless, these men are not objects of the authors' scorn. Thus Trigorin and Jim are, in much the same ways, ambivalent figures. It is probably significant that the older Williams, when he came to write *The Notebook of Trigorin*, focused on the older rather than the younger man.

In addition to characters, there are a few other ideas that Williams could have obtained from *The Sea Gull* for *The Glass Menagerie*. Both plays, for example, call for striking lighting effects. Particularly interesting is the use of candlelight at the end of both works. Just before Konstantin and Nina's last interview, the servant blows out the candles on the table. Every viewer remembers the expressive extinction of the candles at the end of Williams's play. *The Sea Gull* is filled with references to the moon, so much so that it becomes another one of the play's dominant symbols. Williams has Amanda become excited at the appearance of the moon and beg Tom to join her in making a wish on it; her last words to Tom are, "Go to the moon—you selfish dreamer!" (*GM*, p. 114). However, the fact that characters in *The Sea*

Gull quote lines from *Hamlet* and Jim nicknames Tom "Shakespeare" does not seem particularly significant. The music that runs throughout Williams's play is found in other Chekhov plays as much as in *The Sea Gull*. And the "ominous cracking sound in the sky" (*GM*, p. III) most definitely comes from *The Cherry Orchard*.

Other than the all-important relationships of the characters, possibly a few images, and the general atmosphere, there seem to be no indications then of borrowing, consciously or unconsciously, from *The Sea Gull*. Could it be that, instead of a direct influence of the one play on the other, the characters in the two works appear so similar because both dramatists were exploring the same basic narrative patterns? The very real differences between Nina and Laura would seem to preclude that possibility. With the one we are examining the attractions of a neighbour, disdained by her family and aspiring to make her own life; with the other, the role of a crippled sister unable to leave the security of her family and home. Therefore, their similarities seem all the more significant. Although not evidence *per se*, to see how *The Glass Menagerie* is not merely "Chekhovian" but is so very close to *The Sea Gull* in its pattern of character relationships, one can think about Chekhov's other plays. None of them resembles *The Glass Menagerie* so much.

There are, to be sure, as many differences between the two plays as there are similarities. Their structures are in no way alike, and despite all the attention given to the Chekhovian dramaturgy in Williams's plays, it is often more a matter of atmosphere than of imitation. The scope of Chekhov's play allows thirteen characters, subplots of various sorts, four sets, a time period of several years, and different themes from those found in Williams's. Williams's four characters are seen in only one set during a relatively short period of time. Other playwrights as diverse as Strindberg, O'Neill, Wilder, and perhaps Brecht have influenced *The Glass Menagerie*. Nevertheless, in shaping this fragment of Williams's autobiography into dramatic form, Chekhov's model would seem to have played a decisive, probably the crucial role.

NOTES

1. Tennessee Williams, "Author's Note" to *All Gaul is Divided*, in *Stopped Rocking and Other Screenplays* (New York, 1984), p. 3; letter quoted by Benjamin Nelson, *Tennessee Williams: The Man and His Work* (New York, 1961), p. 76; *Memoirs* (New York, 1975), p. 41. See also Richard F. Leavitt, *The World of Tennessee Williams* (New York, 1978), p. 50.

2. Donald Spoto, *The Kindness of Strangers: The Life of Tennessee Williams* (Boston, 1985), pp. 45–46.

3. See John Gassner, ed., *Twenty Best European Plays on the American Stage* (New York, 1957), p. 348. The cast also included Sydney Greenstreet, to whom Williams would dedicate "The Last of My Solid Gold Watches," as well as Margaret Webster, the director-to-be of *Battle of Angels*, and Uta Hagen, a future Blanche.

4. Charles Faber, "Theater Ticket," *Advocate* (Los Angeles), 14 October 1982, p. 51.

5. Louis Kronenberger, "A Triumph for Miss Taylor," *New York Theatre Critics' Reviews*, 6 (1945), 135–36; Francis Donahue, *The Dramatic World of Tennessee Williams* (New York, 1964), p. 215; Stark Young, *Immortal Shadows* (New York, 1948), pp. 183–88.

6. See John Allen Quintus, "The Loss of Dear Things: Chekhov and Williams in Perspective," *English Language Notes*, 18 (1981), 201–06.

7. The story was fast published in a limited edition of *One Arm and Other Stories* (New York) in 1948. The text used here is Williams, *Collected Stories* (New York, 1985), pp. 110–19, cited as *CS*.

8. Brian Parker, "The Composition of *The Glass Menagerie*: An Argument for Complexity," *Modern Drama*, 25 (1982), 409–22.

9. All references are to *The Plays of Anton Tchekov*, trans. Constance Garnett (New York, 1930), cited as *SG*. Although this translation of *The Sea Gull* is the one Williams most likely knew, the Library of Congress printed catalog lists three others available: by Marian Fell, 1912; George Calderon, 1912; and Fred Eisemann, 1913. Two later translations appeared before *The Glass Menagerie* was finished: by S.S. Koteliansky, 1937, and Stark Young, 1939

10. All references are to the 1970 New Directions text of *The Glass Menagerie* (New York), cited as *GM*.

11. Parker, 415–16.

12. The first note struck in *The Sea Gull*—by the schoolmaster—is a sense of deprivation and poverty as intense as anything felt in *The Glass Menagerie*.

13. On this point Amanda echoes Irina's brother. He admits that he has "nowhere else to go" than his sister's house, adding, "I've got to live here whether I like it or not" (*SG*, p. 5).

14. Parker, 415.

15. In Young's translation she walks "slow and hobbling" (Gassner, p. 357).

C. W. E. BIGSBY

Entering The Glass Menagerie

In *The Seagull* Chekhov's Trepliov insists that "We need new art forms ... and if they aren't available, we might just as well have nothing at all."[1] The statement is not without its irony given Trepliov's own incapacity, but it carried the force of a playwright who was himself dedicated to such innovation. Fifty-five years later, and in a world as much in transition as Chekhov's, Tennessee Williams was conscious of trying to create just such a new form, a "plastic" theatre which owed something, indeed, to the Russian writer for whom a detailed realism was never really a primary objective. As Stanislavsky had remarked of Chekhov's work, "At times he is an impressionist, at times a symbolist; he is a 'realist' where it is necessary."[2] A tracery of the real was an essential scaffold for his exploration of character and subtle recreation of mood, but his characters inhabit more than a tangible world and reach for something more than the merely material. Much the same was true of Williams, so that what Stanislavsky said of Chekhov could equally well be said of him:

> A purblind eye would see only that Chekhov lightly traces the outward lines of the plot, that he is engaged in representing everyday life, the minute details of ordinary living. He certainly does these things, but he needs all this only as a contrast to set

From *The Cambridge Companion to Tennessee Williams*, edited by Matthew C. Roudané: pp. 29–44. © 1997 by Cambridge University Press.

off the high ideal which is ever present in his mind and for which
he longs and hopes all the time. In his dramatic works Chekhov
has achieved an equal mastery over the internal as well as external
truth ... he knows how to destroy both the inner and outer falsity
of the stage presentation by giving us beautiful, artistic, genuine
truth.[3]

Williams was concerned with exploring precisely this internal truth,
a world of private need beneath the routines of social performance. For
Stanislavsky "These subtle moods and emotions which Chekhov conveys
through his art are suffused with the undying poetry of Russian life."[4]
Williams's work is also suffused with poetry. His, though, derives from a
region of America which has self-consciously invested itself with a romantic
mythology, as it does from characters whose struggle with the real leaves a
residue of poetry in their broken lives. His dramatic strategy, however, is
close to that pioneered by his Russian master whose plays, as Stanislavsky
explained, "are full of action, not in their external but in their inner
development. In the very inactivity of his characters," he insisted, "a complex
inner activity is concealed."[5]

This was precisely the quality singled out by Arthur Miller in his
memorial tribute to Williams, following his death in 1983. For Arthur
Miller, though, what was most striking was his celebration of a lyrical quality
in characters whose lives were, indeed, in one sense inactive but which
constituted the action of plays which set out to stage the drama of the self's
encounter with the ineluctable fact of mortality. As he remarked, Tennessee
Williams

> broke new ground by opening up the stage to sheer sensibility,
> and not by abandoning dramatic structure but transforming it.
> What was new in Tennessee Williams was his rhapsodic insis-
> tence on making form serve his utterance. He did not turn his
> back on dramatic rules but created new ones.... With *The Glass
> Menagerie*, the long-lost lyrical line was found again, and sup-
> porting it, driving it on, an emotional heroism, that outflanked
> even values themselves; what he was celebrating was not approval
> or disapproval but humanity, the pure germ of enduring life.[6]

You could say of Williams's work what Jean Cocteau said of his own,
that "the action of my play is in images, while the text is not: I attempt to
substitute a 'poetry of the theater' for 'poetry in the theater.'"[7] Nowhere,

perhaps, were the above observations more relevant to Williams's work than in his first Broadway success, *The Glass Menagerie* (1945).

When New Directions published *The Glass Menagerie* as part of the first volume of the collected plays of Tennessee Williams, they included an essay entitled "The Catastrophe of Success."[8] Indeed the reader entering the play text passes through a series of other texts, including this essay, character notes, production notes, and elaborate stage directions. Each one modifies our response to the play and in some sense throws light on Williams's own reading of it.

In the essay, which he published in the *New York Times* to mark the third anniversary of the Chicago opening of *The Glass Menagerie*, Williams described the life which he had led prior to the success of that play as "one that required endurance, a life of clawing and scratching along a sheer surface and holding on tight with raw fingers to every inch of rock higher than the one caught hold of before" (136). It was a description which could have applied to virtually any of his principal characters, from Blanche, in *A Streetcar Named Desire*, and Val, in *Orpheus Descending*, through to Maggie, in *Cat on a Hot Tin Roof*, and Shannon, in *The Night of the Iguana*. It could certainly apply to the characters in *The Glass Menagerie*.

In the essay he speaks of his paranoid response to finding himself suddenly in the limelight, in a world in which the ordinary seems imbued with threat, and explains the pressures which had led him to write. He had turned to writing, he explained, because it is "only in his work that an artist can find reality and satisfaction, for the actual world is less intense than the world of his invention and consequently his life ... does not seem very substantial" (138). Again the observations which he makes about himself could apply with equal force to his characters for whom the imagination is a principal resource, while "the actual world" is the origin of threat and a destructive banality.

It is ironic, therefore, that in that same essay Williams speaks disparagingly of the Cinderella story, with its account of moving from rags to riches, as a primary and destructive American myth, for it is the fate of his characters, and particularly those in his first Broadway success, to miss life's party, to be left with no more than the ashes of a once-burning fire. However, where Cinderella succeeds and inherits a suspect world of tainted wealth, his characters transform their lives with nothing more than a fantasy born out of need. The irony is, however, that the imagination which sustains them also isolates them, insulates them from those others pressed to the margins of a society whose priorities have little to do with the artist, the dispossessed, or the abandoned.

The essay is a curious document. Much of it is taken up with Williams's confession of guilt at moving so easily into the role of successful playwright, living in expensive hotels and treating the staff as social inferiors. In particular he denounces a service economy which requires social inequity. He announces that American ideals can no longer even be stated, let alone enacted, and insists on the importance of struggle. "Security," he announces, "is a kind of death." The essence of that struggle, however, does not so much lie with challenging the class system as resisting the deprivations of time because, as he reminds us, "time is short and it doesn't return again. It is slipping away while I write this and while you read it, and the monosyllable of the clock is Loss, loss, loss, unless you devote your heart to its opposition" (140–41). The need for social justice thus becomes entwined with a more fundamental struggle to discover meaning and identity in the face of absurdity.

On the face of it his insistence that security can be equated with death would seem a curious observation when applied to *The Glass Menagerie*, a play set during the Depression. What Amanda needs more than anything else, both for herself and her daughter, is, arguably, precisely security. It was what the Depression had destroyed. His own sense of self-disgust, however, leads him to celebrate the insecurity which had characterized his own earlier life. Yet in a sense if Tom, his alter ego in the play, had settled for what he had got, if he had offered his mother and sister the security they needed, he would have destroyed himself as a poet. *The Glass Menagerie*, then, is concerned with the insecurity which on the one hand drives some to a lonely desperation, redeemed only by hermetic fantasies and myths, and on the other creates poets scarred by guilt but elevated by their avocation.

As Williams himself insisted, in the production notes which precede the printed text, this is a "memory play" which, "because of its considerably delicate or tenuous material," justifies "atmospheric touches and subtleties of direction." He chooses the occasion to reject the "straight realistic play with its genuine Frigidaire and authentic ice-cubes, its characters who speak exactly as its audience speaks." Everyone, he insists, "should know nowadays the unimportance of the photographic in art" because "truth, life, or reality is an organic thing which the poetic imagination can represent or suggest, in essence, only through transformation, through changing into other forms than those which merely present in appearance" (131). This is something more than a manifesto, though, at the beginning of his career, it is certainly that. For the fact is that this is not only a description of the play's dramatic tactics, it is an accurate account of the strategy of characters who themselves distrust the real until it is transformed by the imagination.

All the key words of Williams's work are to be found in these introductory notes: paranoia, tenderness, illusions, illness, fragile, delicate, poetic, transformation, emotion, nostalgia, desperation, trap. These defining elements are to be projected not merely through character and dialogue. He envisages a production in which all elements will serve his central concern with those who are the victims of social circumstance, of imperious national myths, of fate and of time as the agent of that fate. He envisages the projection of magic-lantern slides which will amplify elements of a scene. He calls for music to give "emotional emphasis," music which is to be "the lightest, most delicate music in the world" emphasizing "emotion, nostalgia, which is the first condition of the play." He identifies the need for non-realistic lighting, "in keeping with the atmosphere of memory," a lighting which, when it falls upon the figure of Laura should have "a pristine clarity such as light used in early religious portraits of female saints or madonnas." Indeed, he suggests that "a free, imaginative use of light can be of enormous value in giving a mobile, plastic quality to plays of a more or less static nature" (133–34). As Jo Mielziner, the play's designer and lighting director, remarked of Williams: "If he had written plays in the days before the technical development of translucent and transparent scenery, I believe he would have invented it." Explaining his own use of translucent interior walls, he insisted that, "it was a true reflection of the contemporary playwright's interest in—and at times obsession with—the exploration of the inner man." As he remarked, "Williams was writing not only a memory play but a play of influences that were not confined within the walls of a room."[9] Those influences were in part artistic and in part social for the pressure which threatens to break not only Laura but all the characters in this St. Louis apartment derive, at least in part, from the brutal urgencies of 1930s America, from the imperatives of a society dedicated, in the words of Jim, the "gentleman caller," to "*Knowledge—Zzzzzp! Money—Zzzzzp!—Power!* ... the cycle democracy is built on!" (222).

The opening stage direction seems somewhat curious, a hangover from the radical plays he had written in the 1930s. The Wingfield apartment, we are told, is

> one of those vast hive-like conglomerates of cellular living-units that flower as warty growths in overcrowded urban centers of lower middle-class population and are symptomatic of the impulse of this largest and fundamentally enslaved section of American society to avoid fluidity and differentiation and to exist and function as one interfused mass of automatism. (143)

It is true that the apartment is both literally and metaphorically a trap which Tom and his mother, at least, wish to escape, but the determinism is not primarily presented as politically or socially rooted. The alienation and despair go deeper than this. His characters are, beyond anything, the victims of fate (Laura), of time (Amanda), and of a prosaic and destructive reality. However, the social and political backdrop is not as irrelevant as it may appear.

The Wingfields live on credit. The electricity is cut off following Tom's failure to pay the bill. Amanda scrapes together money by demonstrating brassieres at a local store, itself a humiliation for a woman of her sensibility. Otherwise she has to suffer the embarrassment of selling subscriptions to women's magazines over the telephone, enduring the abrupt response of those she calls. The daughter's failure to complete a typewriting course is more than a blow to her self-esteem. Amanda has invested what little money she has to free both herself and Laura.

In this context her son's decision to leave has financial as well as personal implications. He earns a wretched sixty-five dollars a month but in Depression America any job is valuable and, though Tom feels suffocated by work which leaves him little time or space for his poetic ambitions, it has at least served to sustain the family. By leaving he condemns mother and sister to something more than spiritual isolation. The gentleman caller, Jim, meanwhile, recalls visiting the Century of Progress Exposition in Chicago, an exhibition not without its irony in Depression America (an irony frequently invoked by David Mamet thirty years later). To Jim it reveals that the future of America will be "even more wonderful than the present time is!" (222). But we have seen the present, a present in which the Wingfields have been reduced to something approaching a subsistence existence. Indeed Jim's confidence is paper thin for within a few moments he confesses that "I hoped when I was going to high school that I would be further along at this time, six years later, than I am now" (216), his high-school yearbook having predicted inevitable success. If knowledge, money, and power do, indeed, constitute democracy then democracy is itself under threat. And, indeed, Tom is seen, at one stage, reading a newspaper which announces Franco's triumph, a curious stage direction but one which goes to the heart of Williams's sense of the imperious and implacable power which threatens all his characters.

Tom's first speech reiterates that sense of social oppression which Williams had sought to imply through the stage set. "In Spain," he tells us, "there was revolution. Here there was only shouting and confusion. In Spain there was Guernica. Here there were disturbances of labor, sometimes pretty violent, in otherwise peaceful cities such as Chicago, Cleveland, Saint Louis." This, he asserts, "is the social background of the play." The middle class of America, he tells us, had "their fingers pressed forcibly down on the fiery Braille alphabet of a dissolving economy" (145). And there is a powerful sense not merely that the animating myths of America have failed those who look for some structure to their lives, but that those myths are themselves the root of a destructive materialism or deceptive illusion.

The play is set at a moment of change, change in the private world of the characters but also in the public world, as though it resonated this private pain. As Tom tells us, "Adventure and change were imminent in this year. They were waiting around the corner for all these kids. Suspended in the mist over Berchtesgarden, caught in the folds of Chamberlain's umbrella. In Spain there was Guernica! ... All the world was waiting for bombardments!" (179). It is a speech which does more than situate the play, provide a context for what, by contrast, must seem a minor drama. It is an invitation to read the events ironically, and to see in the desire to live with comforting fictions, rather than confront brutal truths, a doomed and ultimately deadly strategy. For, as Tom indicates in the same speech, whatever consolations or distractions existed—hot swing music, liquor, movies, sex, glass menageries (the last hinted at by his reference to a chandelier)—flooded the world with rainbows which he characterizes as "brief" and "deceptive."

The Glass Menagerie is more than a lament for a tortured sister (Laura is based on Williams's mentally damaged sister, Rose); it is an elegy for a lost innocence. The Depression had already destroyed one American dream; the war destroyed another, and Tom looks back on the events which he stages in his memory and imagination from the perspective of an immediately postwar world. Neville Chamberlain's piece of paper promising "peace in our time" was no less a product of desperation, no less a symbol of the triumph of hope over despair, than Laura's glass menagerie. Chamberlain's piece of theatre, as he emerged from an aircraft and waved the flag of surrender, believing it to be evidence of his triumph, was no less ironic than Amanda's stage-managed drama of the gentleman caller. In the end brute reality trampled on both.

The Glass Menagerie is no more a play of purely private emotions and concerns than Chekhov's *The Cherry Orchard*. In both cases society, no less than the characters who are its expression and in some senses its victims, is caught at a moment of change. Something has broken. We even hear its sound. In Chekhov "A distant sound is heard, coming as if out of the sky, like the sound of a string snapping, slowly and sadly dying away."[10] In *The Glass Menagerie* "There is an ominous cracking sound in the sky ... The sky falls" (233). The snapping of the horn from a glass unicorn thus stands for something more than the end of a private romantic myth. It marks the end of a phase of history, of a particular view of human possibility.

The origins of *The Glass Menagerie* lie in a short story which Williams wrote around 1941. "Portrait of a Girl in Glass" differs in certain respects from the final play version, not least in the absence of that detailed social and political context which broadened the metaphoric significance of *The Glass Menagerie*. The character of Laura is much closer to being a portrait of his sister, Rose. In the play she suffers from a deformed foot; in the story the flaw is more cruel. She is mentally rather than physically fragile. At the age of twenty she believes that stars are five-pointed because they are represented as such on the Star of Bethlehem which she fixes to the top of her Christmas tree. She treats the characters in her favorite book as real and responds to her gentleman caller not because they had shared the same high school but because, in her mind, he resembles a character from that book, though there is an echo of that in the play when Laura suddenly addresses Jim as Freckles, the protagonist of the novel which is no longer alluded to.

The setting is similar, though with certain crucial differences. There is no dance hall across the street, with its overtones of a smoldering sexuality. Instead the alleyway is a scene of death as a dog regularly attacks and kills stray cats in a cul-de-sac which mirrors that confronting the characters in the story. That sense of entrapment, social and metaphysical, survives into the play version, though without this reminder of mortality.

Other elements fed into *The Glass Menagerie*. A projected series of plays, to be called "Mississippi Sketches," included a comedy entitled "The Front Porch Girl," in which a shy girl ultimately finds companionship with one of the lodgers in her mother's boarding house. Expanded into a play called *If You Breathe, it Breaks! or Portrait of a Girl in Glass*, it featured a girl who sat on the front porch of her house awaiting gentlemen callers while finding consolation in a menagerie of glass animals, which becomes an expression of the fragility she believes characterizes those so easily broken by the world. Finally, under contract to Metro-Goldwyn-Mayer in Hollywood, Williams worked on a script, then titled *The Gentleman Caller*, about a woman awaiting a gentleman caller. This, revised, became *The Glass Menagerie*.

Story and play are rooted firmly in Williams's own life. As he explained, speaking in the year of the play's first production, his family had lived in an apartment not essentially different from that featured in his drama. He recalled his sister's room which was "painted white" with shelves which he had helped her fill "with the little glass animals" which constituted her menagerie. "She was the member of the family with whom I was most in sympathy and, looking back, her glass menagerie had a meaning for me ... and as I thought about it the glass animals came to represent the fragile, delicate ties that must be broken, that you inevitably break, when you try to fulfill yourself."[11]

This, indeed, is a clue to why Tom, the narrator who shares Tennessee Williams's first name, chooses to "write" the play, in the sense of recalling what seem to him to have been key moments in his past life. For the fact is that the play does have a narrator and his values and perceptions shape the way we see the action, indeed determine what we see. The story is told for a purpose and serves a need outside that story. Tom Wingfield recalls the past for much the same reason that Willy Loman does in *Death of a Salesman*: guilt. He revisits the past because he knows that his own freedom, such as it is, has been purchased at the price of abandoning others, as Williams had abandoned his mother and, more poignantly, his sister. He "writes" the play, more significantly, perhaps, because he has not effected that escape from the past which had been his primary motive for leaving. The past continues to exert a pull on him, as it does on his mother and sister, as it does on the South which they inhabit.

For his mother, Amanda, the past represents her youth, before time worked its dark alchemy. Memory has become myth, a story to be endlessly repeated as a protection against present decline. She wants nothing more than to freeze time; and in this she mirrors a region whose myths of past grace and romantic fiction mask a sense of present decay. In Williams's words, she clings "frantically to another time and place" (129). The South does no less and Williams (here and in *A Streetcar Named Desire*), like William Faulkner, acknowledges the seductive yet destructive power of a past reconstituted as myth. At the same time she knows that compromise is necessary. Survival has its price and Amanda is one of Williams's survivors. She survives, ironically, by selling romantic myths, in the form of romance magazines, to other women.

For her daughter, the glass animals of her menagerie transport her into a mythical world, timeless, immune from the onward rush of the twentieth century. It is an immunity, however, which she buys at too high a price for, in stepping into the fictive world of her glass animals, she steps out of any meaningful relationship with others in the present. She becomes one more beautiful but fragile piece in the collection, no longer vulnerable to the depredations of social process or time but no longer redeemed by love.

Tom, meanwhile, prefers the movies, or, more importantly, his poetry. A poet in an unpoetic world, he retreats into his writing because there he can abstract himself from the harsh truths of his existence in a down-at-heel St. Louis apartment. It is not, however, a strategy which has brought him success or peace of mind. He narrates the play in the uniform of the Merchant Marine. He has traded a job in the warehouse for one at sea. There is no suggestion that his desertion of mother and sister has been sanctified by the liberation, or public acknowledgment, of his talent. Like his father before him he has fallen in love with long distance, mistaking movement for progress. Williams himself may have seen Laura's glass animals as representing the fragile, delicate ties that must be broken "when you try to fulfill yourself,"[12] but it is clear that in *The Glass Menagerie* Tom has not fulfilled himself. Tennessee Williams may have felt guilty that his success with the play was built on the exploitation of others; Tom lacks even the consolation of success. Fired from his job in the shoe warehouse, he wanders from city to city, looking for the companionship he had failed to offer his sister. In the story version he tells us that he has grown "firm and sufficient." In the play there is no such assurance as, in that Merchant Marine uniform which is the very symbol of his homelessness, he returns, in his memory, to the home he deserted for the fulfillment he failed to find. When his mother asks him to "look out for your sister ... because she's young and dependent" (175), she identifies an obligation which Tom refuses. In his own life Williams never quite absolved himself of a feeling of guilt with respect to his sister.

For Tom, memories of the past are a distraction from present failure for though situated in time they exist outside of time. In summoning those memories into existence, he transposes experience into a series of images, transforms life into art, and in so doing mimics the process which his namesake Tom Williams adopts in creating plays, for, as Williams has remarked, the virtue of a play lies in the fact that it occurs "*outside of time*," indeed that it is "*a world without time.*"[13] It is, to his mind, time which renders experience and, indeed, people, inconsequential. Art ascribes meaning to the moment, neutralizes a fear of "*not meaning.*" It is a world in which "emotion and action have a dimension and a dignity that they would ... have in real existence, if only the shattering intrusion of time could be locked out" (52). The theatrical metaphor, indeed, is central, with Tom as author of a metadrama in which he self-consciously stages his memories as a play in which he performs as narrator. But if he is the primary author, he acknowledges the centrality of Amanda as director, designer, and lighting technician of the drama which has been his life and the life of his tortured sister.

Early in the play Amanda is presented as an actress, self-dramatizing, self-conscious. Her first part is that of martyred mother. When she removes her hat and gloves she does so with a theatrical gesture ("a bit of acting" [151]). She dabs at her lips and nostrils to indicate her distress before melodramatically tearing the diagram of a typewriter keyboard to pieces. When the gentleman caller arrives for her daughter she changes roles, dressing herself in the clothes of a young woman and becoming a Southern belle, rendered grotesque by the distance between performer and role. But at the end of the play all such pretenses are abandoned. As we see but do not hear her words of comfort to her daughter, so her various roles—shrewish mother, coquettish belle, ingratiating saleswoman—are set aside. The tableau which we see as Tom delivers his final speech is one in which mother and daughter are reunited in their abandonment. "Her silliness is gone," Williams tells us. Amanda "withdraws through the portieres," retreating from the stage which Tom has summoned into being but also from the arena in which she has chosen to play out her own drama. Just as Stanislavsky had rejected those who try to "act" or "pretend" in a Chekhov play, praising only those who "live them ... and follow the deeply buried arteries through which their emotions flow,"[14] so Williams presents Amanda as most completely human when she lays aside her performance and allows simple humanity to determine her actions.

Laura, too, is an actress, though of a different kind. If she has learned "to live vitally in her illusions" (129), she is forced to deceive when her enrollment in a typewriting course ends in fiasco. Each day she leaves home supposedly to go to the business college but in fact to watch movies, visit museums, the zoo, or the botanical gardens. At home she pretends to study a keyboard chart. When this performance proves futile she is cast in a part of her mother's making for the visit of Tom's friend, Jim, the gentleman caller. Laura is costumed by Amanda ("The dress is colored and designed by memory," her breasts enhanced by powder puffs). She is made up ("The arrangement of Laura's hair is changed; it is softer and more becoming") and placed center stage ("Laura stands in the middle of the room"). The stage has been set and the lighting adjusted by Amanda as stage manager ("The new floor lamp with its rose silk shade is in place, a colored paper lantern conceals the broken light fixture in the ceiling, new billowing white curtains are at the windows, chintz covers are on the chairs and sofa ..." [191]). She even directs the action ("Laura Wingfield, you march right to that door!" [197]). The failure of this performance, however, leaves Laura with only one theatre in which to live out her life, that of her glass menagerie.

Even Jim, the gentleman caller, is an actor. Once the baritone lead in *The Pirates of Penzance*, he is studying public speaking, the better to enter the public stage. He, too, has his fantasies. In his own mind he is something of a psychoanalyst. He is interested in "electro-dynamics" and taking a course in radio engineering at night school. Each new enthusiasm implies a scenario which will transform him, including his engagement: "The power of love is really pretty tremendous! Love is something that—changes the whole world" (230). Once again, however, this is a performance which fails quite to convince as his prosaic description falls some way short of the life-transforming experience which he claims: "She's a home girl ... and in a great many ways we—get along fine" (229). The dash indicates a momentary hesitation as he reaches for a language adequate to the self-confident role he wishes to project. Recognizing the inadequacy of "get along fine" he moves quickly to a confession of love, born on a moonlit boat trip and leading to the construction of "a new man" (280). It carries no real conviction. Jim is a huckster for success, no longer confident of the substantiality or inevitability of his dream, an actor increasingly uncertain of his lines or his role.

One of the ironies of the play lies in the fact that performance, the imagination's abstraction of the self from its social environment itself, leads into a cul-de-sac not dissimilar to that which lies just beyond the windows of the St. Louis apartment. Tom is fated to restage his drama of the glass menagerie as surely as Ishmael is to recount the story of a white whale, as surely as is his sister to dramatize the lives of animals who are touching at least in part because they, like Amanda and Laura in Tom's memory, are unchanging. No matter how many times Tom steps forward to introduce the memories which haunt him, Laura will never escape on the arms of her gentleman caller, nor Amanda redeem her own failed life by finding romance for the daughter she loves but who must always stand as a reproach. The theatre offers a certain grace, as does all art, but beyond the obvious irony always implicit in an unyielding beauty, uncorrupted by time and hence uncontaminated by an imperfect humanity, is the hermetic atmosphere conjured by a world constructed by the imagination out of memory and desire.

The theatrical metaphor was to remain central to his work. *A Streetcar Named Desire* ends with Blanche DuBois, always a performer but now a pure actress, walking out of a New Orleans apartment towards the sad theatre of the madhouse, no longer able to distinguish fantasy from the real, no longer able, therefore, to reach out to those who might have been able to rescue her from despair. *Camino Real*, whose title is doubly ironic, stages the lives of the dispossessed and the marginal wholly through fictional characters who are never allowed access to the tangible world of tortured humanity, acting out their romantic scenarios entirely in the fictive world which is their protection against time but which also defines the limits of their possibility. Fiction as consolation: fiction as imprisonment. Decades later he was to write a play, *Out Cry*, in which the theatre is presented as the central metaphor, as two characters perform their lives in an empty theatre in a country whose coldness is itself an image of their lives, drained of human warmth because abstracted from time, from mortality, and hence from humanity.

Why this theatrical metaphor? In part, perhaps, because his plays are set in a South which is self-dramatizing, which performs its history as myth refusing the dynamic of time because this contains an account of failure and defeat. In part because the self he wishes to present is one sustained essentially by the imagination. The real proves so relentless and unforgiving that it has to be transformed, restaged, so that it becomes tolerable to those who lack the qualities required for survival. The national drama of progress, albeit denied by a national reality of Depression, is one which has no place for the fragile, the poet, the betrayed, the deserted. For progress, beyond its insistence on the material, invokes time and time, as we have seen, for Williams and his characters, was always the enemy. In his personal life he, like Tom, like Blanche, and like so many of his characters, sought some ultimate meaning in an art which granted him the only real refuge from the deprivations of natural process while at the same time leaving him to rely on the comfort offered by "the nearest stranger."

When Amanda says that "in these trying times we live in, all that we have to cling to is—each other" (171), she voices a conviction which was equally Williams's own, as she does when she observes that "Life's not easy, it calls for—Spartan endurance!" Indeed, though in interviews he often derided his mother, on whom Amanda was modeled, it is clear that it is Amanda who bears the greatest burden, twice abandoned and left to watch over her daughter. Though querulous and puritanical, she is allowed moments of touching vulnerability when she exposes the nature of her own pain ("I've never told you but I—loved your father..." [172]). And though she sustains herself with memories and fantasies of a reassuring future, she is forced to an acknowledgment of her situation, as Tom is not. Indeed, Williams himself confessed as much, remarking that, "the mother's valor is the core of *The Glass Menagerie* ... She's confused, pathetic, even stupid, but everything has got to be all right. She fights to make it that way in the only way she knows how."[15] By necessity she has a practicality which none of the other characters show. At the beginning of the play she proscribes the word "cripple"; at the end she uses the word herself. It is her first step towards accepting the truth of her daughter's situation and hence of the need which she must acknowledge and address.

Williams comments on her cruelty and tenderness, on her derisory yet admirable character, her confused vitality, confused because it appears to lack real purpose. As he remarks in the character notes which precede the play, "she is not paranoiac, but her life is paranoia" (129). The conspiracy of which she is a victim is a fact of existence: youth gives way to age, beauty decays, optimism is subverted by experience, fantasies ground on the rock of the real. She has, he insists, "endurance," but as William Faulkner was to say in his Nobel Prize acceptance speech, endurance is not enough. It is simply the ability to live with irony. He looked, at least in the rhetoric of his speech if not in the action of his novels, for a degree of triumph. There is no real triumph in Williams's plays and precious little in Faulkner's novels.

What there is is "a kind of heroism," and that is precisely the quality which he has ascribed to Amanda. Deserted and betrayed, she stays and continues her losing battle with time in the company of her doomed daughter and, in what is virtually the play's final stage direction, Williams finds a "dignity and tragic beauty" in that sad alliance. It is no longer the absurdity of this abandoned woman he chooses to stress. At the beginning of the play he had described her expression as "grim and hopeless" (151). She shakes her head in despair, having just learned of her daughter's deception in abandoning her typing course. At the end we are told that her "gestures are slow and graceful, almost dancelike" (236), as she comforts that same daughter.

Early in the play we are told that her face has "aged but childish features," that it is "cruelly sharp, satirical as a Daumier print" (169). At the end, with her words inaudible to us, she is once more presented to us in visual terms in a kind of *tableau vivant*. This time, though, it is an image drained of irony. What communicates is less cruelty than charity, less sharpness than a soft maternal attentiveness. At least in memory Tom embraces the woman he has otherwise blamed for his own problems, for the suffocating years in the shoe warehouse and for the guilt which has made him return, in memory, to St. Louis where he had abandoned her and failed to redeem his sister from her isolation.

In a world "lit by lightning," Laura's candles cast a softer glow. In the end the lightning will prevail, at least in the short term. Art can never really be a protection against the real. Chamberlain's betrayals, Franco's victories, Hitler's barbarity were not defeated by wishing they might be so, and, as Auden lamented, poetry did not save a single Jew. Williams was acutely aware of this. Why else have Tom open the play with a reminder of what lay in wait for those caught in the Depression and consoling themselves with movies, glamour magazines and dance music entitled, "The World is Waiting for the Sunrise"? At the same time he was wedded to art, whose power does indeed lie in its ability to outlive even the traumas of history. He was wedded to theatre whose form and whose substance exposed the nature of the paradox, as it offers truth through lies and reveals a tensile strength in the most fragile of creations.

NOTES

1. Anton Chekhov, *Plays*, translated Elisaveta Fen (Harmondsworth: Penguin, 1959), 123.

2. *Ibid.*, 7.

3. *Ibid.*, pp. 7–8.

4. *Ibid.*, p. 8.

5. *Ibid.*, p. 7.

6. Arthur Miller, "A Memorial Tribute to Tennessee Williams," a speech to the American Academy, 1984. Unpublished typescript.

7. Manuel Duran, *Lorca* (Englewood Cliffs, 1962), 171.

8. Tennessee Williams, *The Theatre of Tennessee Williams*, vol. 1 (New York 1971). Further references to this essay, and *The Glass Menagerie*, which also appears in this volume, appear in parentheses in the text.

9. Jo Mielziner, *Designing for the Theater* (New York, 1965), 124.

10. Chekhov, *Plays*, 398.

11. Tennessee Williams, *Conversations with Tennessee Williams*, ed. Albert Devlin (Jackson: University Press of Mississippi, 1986), p. 10.

12. *Ibid.*, 10.

13. Tennessee Williams, *Where I Live* (New York: New Directions, 1978), 50.

14. Anton Chekhov, *Plays*, 8.

15. Williams, *Conversations*, 14.

GILBERT DEBUSSCHER

"Where Memory Begins":
New Texas Light on The Glass Menagerie

T he early drafts or discarded versions of a masterpiece have always interested scholars because they seem, more than the finished product, to reveal the secrets of an artist at work. In the case of Tennessee Williams they are all the more fascinating since the playwright has always been comparatively reluctant to provide information about his works in progress. In his article on the Texas drafts of *The Glass Menagerie*, R. B. Parker could therefore confidently predict that "the genesis of the text remains a promising area for further research and criticism." Indeed, the texts finally acted and published—and there are minor but not insignificant variations between these two—were the result of a protracted sequence of trial and error testifying to "the difficulty Williams had in coming to terms with his material and the complexity of his responses to it."[1] In the course of selecting material for his final version, Williams discarded much that he originally intended to include in a story that would have sustained comparison in length with *Gone with the Wind*. The rejected drafts, some of which Williams himself designated as "the ruins of a play," are contained in four boxes of miscellaneous texts, partial versions, overlapping fragments, composite typescripts, a handwritten notebook, and numerous single draft pages that constitute a manuscript librarian's nightmare to sort out, date, and classify chronologically. Parker's examination of them has already thrown new light

From *The Tennessee Williams Annual Review* (1998): pp. 53–62. © 1998 by *The Tennessee Williams Annual Review*.

on the origins of the play and on some of its final aspects. However, not contained in the humanities Research Center boxes specifically connected with *The Glass Menagerie* (sometimes catalogued as an "unidentified" play or story or, in other instances, bearing a title that suggests its relationship with the play) are a number of items that reveal, upon examination, their close connection with the final text. Some of these announce, more clearly than the *Gentleman Caller–Menagerie* manuscripts, many of the techniques finally used in the play; they prefigure some of its best passages or provide a glimpse at its most memorable images or phrases. In these early contexts, the materials of *Menagerie* possess shades of meaning which can only be guessed at in their final dramatic settings but which contribute to the textual richness of the play, its "imaginative penumbra" in Parker's apt formulation.

The most important of the *Menagerie* related items is a six-page typewritten manuscript, on brownish-beige paper of poor quality, which comprises a first page simply inscribed "For my Grandmother Rosina Maria Francesca von Albertzart-Otte Dakin (or Rose)" and five pages of actual text, unnumbered. It starts with a stage direction describing *The Boy Who Tells the Story* as he steps out of the wings and addresses the audience. He is a twenty-five year old hitchhiker on an invisible highway, "indistuinguishable [sic] from the rest of his kind, the youths in nondescript dusty clothes with battered valises who stand about the country's highways in summer wanting a ride to California from New York or from New York to California—or wanting a ride anywhere...." His first speech, on the theme of memory, establishes the background of the action—the house, the sky, the birds—, the properties—the swing on the hill, the stairs, the chandelier, the piano, the dining room table—, the characters, their way of speaking, their actions. He claims that everything is memory and therefore different from actuality but nevertheless essentially true in fact. He, only, is not memory: "I am the one who remembers." On his imaginary way back to where the memories started, he tentatively invites the spectator to accompany him: "I want you to go back with me! (Light fading) Will you?—Will you?—Will you...?" Music is heard as a spot of light reveals the boy and girl as children in white clothes on the steps by a single white column representing the porch of a Southern house. With them is a "black negro mammy" who sings to them of heavenly grass.

As she stops singing and prompts them to scatter "everywhere—all over," the children run out from the steps and the Boy resumes his narrator's comments to introduce the singer as "Ozzie, our negro nurse." And as he makes the gesture of the hitchhiker and a great rumble suggests the approach of a truck, he adds "I think that memory begins with her...." Light returns to the black nurse who is now joined on the steps by the mother "very lovely, unbelievably lovely in a long and indefinite dress the color of morning skies, very early" who inquires if her children are happy and instructs Ozzie to "keep them happy—Keep them blind for while." But the servant claims that the sun does that for them and that only when their eyes get used to the light will they begin to see around.

As she starts singing her ballad again, the mother leans on the pillar and muses on the ephemeral character of all things before turning back to the house. The children are heard laughing in the distance as Ozzie's singing fades. The last four lines of the text, arranged as poetry and not specifically attributed but presumably spoken by the youth, return to his previous comments: "Memory begins with her—Ozzie—the black singer. Life. Death. The earth—All wisdom and all understanding—Who knew the secrets of the sun before time even started. Ozzie—the black singer—the nurse—Where memory begins...."

The points of resemblance with *The Glass Menagerie*—as well as some significant differences—are immediately apparent from the initial stage direction. The fragment has, like the full-length play, a narrator who is also a character in the action. He is not a merchant marine sailor but a road traveler, which brings him closer to a self-portrait of the playwright than Tom in the final play, and is reminiscent of Val Xavier in *Battle of Angels*, the play in which Williams by his own avowal had put his whole heart in 1938. Also more clearly perceptible here than in the final play is the generic character of the narrator/hero. After identifying him with "the rest of his kind," the initial description introduces him as one of those

> youths who seem to breathe the salt air of the Atlantic in Kansas and walk the earth of Texas in Manhattan. Who say hello with the tongue of Mississippi in Chicago. Who remember the Great Lakes in Arizona. Who can tell a chance acquaintance in San Francisco where to get a good meal for twenty cents in New Orleans. Their landscape is America: and the bigness of it seems to have widened their eyes and lengthened their bodies.

A number of the early drafts of *Menagerie* examined by Parker indicate that Williams originally conceived of the story of the Wingfields as representative of American experience in general: some of them start with the Narrator in front of a map of the United States pointing at cities as he mentions them; another, dated April 1943, Clayton Mo., is subtitled "An American Family Portrait" but none establishes so clearly as this fragment that in one of his original incarnations Tom was meant to be, physically almost, as Kilroy in *Camino Real*, "the Son of America." This opening stage direction ends with "They own very little and they are owned by nothing: and they aren't afraid," a comment in which can be glimpsed Tom's later preoccupations with "freedom" but, in this case, conceived not in terms of individual experience but in a perspective closer to Williams's socioeconomic commitments of the late 30s and early 40s.

Of these political preoccupations traces can be found in other Texas drafts, most evidently on the front page of *Ruins of a Play* which has inscribed in pencil, recognizably in Williams's hand, a quotation from "Clark Mills ... in a conversation" which reads "capitalistic society is a pyramid of boxes." This image may have inspired the very first stage direction of the final play in which the Wingfield apartment is described as part of one of those "vast hive-like conglomerations of cellular living-units that flower as warty growths in overcrowded urban centers of lower middle-class population."

Absent from this early version, perhaps because of its attempt at generalization, is the contrast, also of political import, briefly established in Tom's introductory speech, between the relative peace that prevailed in the United States—now represented by a much abbreviated list of three cities—and the Spanish Civil War, the forerunner of a major international conflagration abroad. Judging then from a comparison between this and other early drafts and *The Glass Menagerie*, a first conclusion imposes itself without completely obliterating them, the movement in the final version is away form the general, the emblematic and the political towards a more intimate, more immediate, less ponderous—indeed less pretentious statement. The notebook draft corroborates this as the Narrator there, obviously trying too explain why the play is finally reduced to "commonplace incidents," says:

> This is the preface to a larger play than I am able to give you. I know how incongruous it is going to seem attached to the commonplace episodes that follow—you see I'm admitting this play to be a failure. I make this admission not just to disarm criticism but more to engage your participation in probing back of what is displayed for that which is hidden or lost or not remembered.

That which is hidden, fortunately not lost and now slowly remembered, is precisely what is preserved at the Humanities Research Center.

Before turning to the dialogue and action of the fragment, it is interesting to note Williams's preoccupation, in even such early stages of the work, with the lighting—fade-out to separate scenes, spots of light on specific characters for emphasis—and with the music, two devices that would acquire prominence in his conception of a new plastic theatre "destined to take the place of the exhausted theatre of realistic conventions," as outlined in the

Production Notes of the final play. They appear to have grown organically with the material rather than constituting a redundant illustration of it.

The first words of the Boy, "The play is memory," are of course preserved, although not as overture; in the final version of *Menagerie* where they are also developed—as they are, but to a lesser extent, in this fragment—to emphasize that memory operates through selection and transformation, which makes accessible the essential, emotional truths embedded in the action. However distorting its effects—the sky is "clearer and paler than any sky could be," the birds are "always in one place and always flying-away," the properties are "fused with the landscape for that's how memory is—it runs together," the speeches are "wilder and more impassioned than any speech could be," the costumes are "soft, indistinct—not any definite color"—this stylization is, as Williams will later state in the preface of *The Rose Tattoo*, the necessary legerdemain by which "events are made to remain *events*, rather than being reduced so quickly to mere *occurrences*"—thus bringing about "the great magic trick of human existence" viz. "snatching the eternal out of the desperately fleeting." It is surprising to find early sketches such as this one replete with so many indications of Williams's conception of a "new" theater destined to replace the "exhausted" modern realistic mode. It is as if, very early on, Williams had conceived this new form, a combination of dialogue, music, sound, and visual effects built into a series of dramatic episodes, of which the successive full-length plays represented tentative realizations.

Ozzie, the black nurse, constitutes the real originality of this dramatic fragment. She is well-known from Williams's biographical studies as the servant who took care of the Williams children and fascinated them with her stories. It is from her presumably that the playwright acquired his taste for fabulation, and it is natural, then, that he would make her here the source of information, the repository of the family's lore. The fragment is thus provided with a double perspective, the Narrator's and Ozzie's, made necessary by the playwright's original project to tell the story of his family from the beginning, i.e. long before he could become a plausible narrator of the events. This double viewpoint has left slightly problematic traces in the finished play: it raises questions as to Tom's access to information about such things as Amanda's return from the D.A.R. meeting and her subsequent conversation with Laura or the final tete-a-tete of Laura and Jim, but since the scope of the events is limited to the period of Tom's young adulthood, one may accept there the explanation, as one could not in the fragment, that whatever he could not have witnessed directly, he may have gathered from conversations with his sister or remarks by his mother. But if making Ozzie into the chronicler—where memory begins—solves the problem of the reliability of the information, one may wonder how Williams envisaged solving the problem of this double point of view. The fragment breaks off conveniently long before the narrated events would have forced him to confront it.

The presence of the black Ozzie as the original narrator pairs together with her description in the final lines as "the black singer Life—Death—the earth. All wisdom and all understanding. Who knew the secrets of the sun before time even started" and brings this short draft, in this respect, close again to *Battle of Angels*, in which the Conjure Man is also the mysterious source of knowledge, the character closely associated with nature and its elemental processes.

As she appears on the stage, Ozzie is singing to two children, a boy and a girl, presumably Tom and his sister Rose, dressed in white clothes, and her ballad is arranged in four stanzas as is the poem reproduced later in the volume *In the Winter of Cities* (1956) in the section "Blue Mountain Ballads" under the title "Heavenly Grass" where the text is presented as one poem of nine lines. That it was reproduced by Williams in this collection testifies to its lasting importance for him and to his belief that it had, with the formal rearrangement, reached its final expression. It was set to music by Paul Bowles, the playwright's friend who also composed the music for *The Glass Menagerie*; it was used again in *Orpheus Descending*, the remake sixteen years later of *Battle of Angels*, and there again, as in the draft, it expressed one of Williams's perennial themes, viz. that of the inevitable corruption of innocence and the concomitant nostalgia for lost purity. Here, as musical background accompaniment to the scene in which the children, in virginal white, are prompted literally to "inherit the world"—"the earth is yours—everywhere is yours" exclaims Ozzie at the end of her song—it ties in with the later image of the blinding sun, expressing the confidence that they can, at least for some time yet, remain blissfully unaware of the corruption attendant upon growing up.

Finally, in the short scene in which the mother appears, the rapturous description of her as "very lonely, unbelievably lovely" testifies to the author's wavering attitude towards the character and his original conception of her as totally sympathetic. Interestingly enough, her first inquiry "Are my children happy?" and the few words she exchanges with Ozzie reveal a deep-seated anxiety, an apprehension about the future which is concurrent with the nostalgic message of the song which Ozzie repeats in reply. It is surprising that in this very early incarnation of Amanda, an Amanda at an early age, one would find what is going to become a major character trait which, one usually assumes, is the result of a particular painful existence. Here it appears as a constituent trait of the character. The echo of this young version of Amanda in the later final woman is made clear when she says, in the draft, leaning against the pillar:

> This pillar is solid—but sometime it may fall.
> Nothing is safe and nothing is everlasting.
> I think that even—sometime—the sky will fall!

This constitutes the early version of the last of the legends to be projected on the screen in the play after the announcement that Jim has a girl with whom he goes steady: "Legend: 'The Sky Falls.'" In the early draft it introduces the mother's awareness that everything decays and that her world, however happy and secure it seems in the present, is doomed to collapse sooner or later. As such it reinforces the ominous tension, the premonitory note introduced by the "Heavenly Grass" ballad which Ozzie repeats contrapuntally as if to stress its congruence with the mother's words.

It is significant in this context, although perhaps not immediately conclusive, that one of the short stories preserved at the Humanities Research Center should be titled "In Spain there was revolution." One remembers the phrase from the introductory words of Tom in *The Glass Menagerie* where as narrator he seems to establish the contrast between Europe, where World War II is in rehearsal, and the United States, where "there was only shouting and confusion." The story is on a typed manuscript of eight pages by Thomas Lanier Williams with a penciled note on the title page that reads "Not a bad story and rather prophetic. T. W. (written about '36)." A small slip in the same file indicates that the text was originally "rejected by Story—sept. 21, 1936." This early offering concerns the brief summer idyll of Steve, a lifeguard on a lake resort in the Ozark Hills (also a favorite summer retreat of the Williams family) with a school girlfriend who is a counselor at a nearby camp. The bulk of the story is comprised of their sensual encounter in a rowing-boat, hidden amidst the rushes on the banks of the lake overhung with willows—an encounter not very different from that which Val recalls at the end of Act II Sc I in *Battle of Angels* and that curtains the lovers from sight. As Steve returns to his place at the dock to survey the bathers, a fat man engages him in conversation about "this trouble in Spain." When Steve reports that he is not aware of any and asks what it is all about the man retorts "Revolution. Next it will be the Whole world!" Disgusted at Steve's indifference, the fat man swims off the dock with an inner tube girdling his middle while the lifeguard "looked down at him and shook with noiseless laughter."

At first sight the short story illustrates Steve's indifference to anything except his intense concern with the girl and their love affair: "He avoided the fat man's searching squint, kept his eyes fixed stonily on the water. He wanted to think of the girl. Nothing else." And Thomas Lanier Williams seems to be distributing the roles: "Steve is a muscular lifeguard with coffee-brown shoulders, his girlfriend an expert oarsman who has tanned deeply and smoothly"; by contrast the fat man is described as a "stooge," a "white collar nonentity" who tries ineffectually on vacation to be a "vital and specific" personality by "exposing [his] moist white skin immoderately to the sun's indifferent burning," one of those men who "lived narrow, slavish lives in cooped-up places, ... caught in ruts, graves with both ends kicked out." Such a person largely justifies Steve's attitude towards him and forces the fat man and his news into unwelcome intrusions in an otherwise quiet and idyllic world. However, on the back of the final page, obviously in Williams's own hand in brown, fading ink, resembling an afterthought or constituting a note for a further bit of dialogue between Steve and the man, appear the words "Spain is a long way off but not the Revolution. Which Revolution? The one in which you will be killed. You and all the other young fools who think that Spain is such a long way off!" The passage cannot have been conceived as an addition, since it could have served as an alternative or, even less likely, an added ending to the short story. It must, therefore, be read in conjunction with Williams's (this time Tennessee's) later remark on the title page about the prophetic quality of the text. And indeed the short story informs *The Gentleman Caller* draft and *The Glass Menagerie* itself with a sense of things running irretrievably towards a major change, quickly approaching an end: the summer's plenitude is almost over and, although the young lovers will see each other again in school, things will never again be the same:

> "He looked up and smiled.
> "Sure it will be just the same.
> "What? She asked ...
> "At school—The way it is here.
> "I don't know," she repeated gloomily. School isn't like here."
> "I know it isn't, he admitted. "Here it's just perfect."

Tom's later words, then in the final play, about the difference between Spain and the United States may not be as clearly contrastive as I had thought previously: rather they may be hinting, as Williams's handwritten note makes clear, that although major trouble was limited so far to Spain, the United States would soon be drawn into the conflagration, of which the final blackout is the scenic realization.

It is obvious from our investigations at the Humanities Research Center that *The Glass Menagerie*, probably the best known play in the American repertoire, has not yet and might very well never reveal all the secrets of its long and painful conception. It is equally obvious that the published short story "Portrait of a Girl in Glass" or the film treatment *The Gentleman Caller* in its various guises cannot account, as Parker already demonstrated, for all the material. Williams seems throughout his career to have worked at various projects simultaneously, many of which ended up not in the dustbin but carefully preserved in the material that is today housed at the Humanities Research Center. That material is daunting: fragments of it, sometimes small like phrases, names of characters, or addresses, sometimes more important like an episode in a story or the sketch for a narrator frame, are used as raw materials, the building brick of a house, ultimately meant to stand on their own. Consistently, the blocks in their original setting appear clumsy, uncut, undeveloped, revealing sometimes aspects that were later occulted but, systematically almost, less rich than the final product. It seems to have been Williams's particular flair or poetic genius to have worked on the material and altered it until he had found for it a setting, be it a poem, a one-act play, but most often a full-length play, a short story or sometimes all three, in which the blocks of imaginative material had been sorted out and shaped neatly together to make the clearest sense of the emotional experience.

That long and compulsive process of transmutation to which the archives at Austin eloquently and abundantly testify is that of transforming experience into art or, as Williams himself put it, mere occurrences into lasting events. To observe the process is to appreciate the playwright's craft; to look at the final result is to marvel at his mastery.[2]

NOTES

1. Parker, R. B., "The Composition of *The Glass Menagerie*: An Argument for Complexity." *Modern Drama*, XXV, 3, (Sept., 1992), 409–22.

2. This essay was first presented at the Tennessee Williams Scholars' Conference, New Orleans, March 1997. It will appear in the volume "Union in Partition"; *Essays in Honour of Jeanne Delbaere*. Liege L3 Press, 1997.

BERT CARDULLO

The Blue Rose of St. Louis:
Laura, Romanticism, and The Glass Menagerie

Laura Wingfield of *The Glass Menagerie* hardly qualifies as a Romantic superwoman, a majestic ego eager to transcend the "mereness" of mundane human existence. In his narration of the drama at the same time as he plays a part in it, together with his final, self-centered leavetaking from the domestic misery-cum-ménage of his mother and sister, Tom owns that role. But Laura does represent the kind of person for whom the Romantics of the early nineteenth century felt increasing sympathy: the fragile, almost unearthly ego brutalized by life in the industrialized, overpopulated, depersonalized cities of the Western world.

This physically as well as emotionally fragile woman of almost twenty-four escapes from her mid-twentieth century urban predicament in St. Louis, as someone of Romantic temperament would, through art and music through the beauty of her glass menagerie and of the records she plays on her Victrola. Moreover, although she failed to graduate from high school, Laura fondly remembers a choral class she took with Gentleman Jim O'Connor and the three performances of *The Pirates of Penzance* in which he sang the baritone lead. And instead of attending Rubicam's Business College, as her mother had planned, this high-school dropout went daily to "the art museum and the bird houses at the Zoo.... Lately I've been spending most of my

From *The Tennessee Williams Annual Review* (1998): pp. 81–92. © 1998 by *The Tennessee Williams Annual Review*.

afternoons in the Jewel Box, that big glass house where they raise tropical flowers" (33).

Like a Romantic, then, Laura has a love for Nature in addition to Art—a nature that is artfully memorialized in her collection of little animals made of glass, and that is painfully absent from the area surrounding the Wingfield apartment, which Williams describes as "one of those vast hive-like conglomerations of cellular living units that flower as warty growths in overcrowded urban centers of lower middle-class population" (21). Indeed, even Laura's name signifies her affinity for the natural together with the transcendent: "Laura" is somewhat ironically derived from the laurel shrub or tree, a wreath of which was conferred as a mark of honor in ancient times upon dramatic poets, military heroes, and athletic victors; and "Wingfield" brings to mind the flight of birds across a meadow and on up into the sky.

Jim's nickname for Laura, "Blue Roses," itself signifies her affinity for the natural—flowers—together with the transcendent—*blue* flowers, which do not occur naturally and thus come to symbolize her yearning for both ideal or mystical beauty and spiritual or romantic love. That beauty is also symbolized by Laura's favorite among the animals in her glass menagerie, the fabled, otherworldly unicorn, as well as by the place where Laura has spent many of her afternoons, the Jewel Box, and what she saw there: tropical flowers, which could be said to come from another world, and which can survive in St. Louis only by being placed in the artificial environment of a hothouse. And that love comes to her, however fleetingly, in the person of her namer, Jim O'Connor, who beatifies Laura by emphasizing what is special, even divine, about her and downplaying her physical disability. He opines:

> A little physical defect is what you have. Hardly noticeable even! ... You know what my strong advice to you is? Think of yourself as superior in some way! ... Why, man alive, Laura! Just look about you a little. What do you see? A world full of common people! ... Which of them has one-tenth of your good points! Or mine! Or anyone else's, as far as that goes—gosh! Everybody excels in some one thing. Some in many! (99)

In this speech Jim adopts a Romantic-subjective view of human creation, as opposed to a naturalistic, deterministic, objective one—ironically so, because he himself appears to be one of the common people with his freckle face, flat or scant nose, and mundane job in the same shoe factory where Tom works, and also because, in his aspiration to become a television engineer, he identifies himself with the utilitarian world of mathematics and machines. Nonetheless, Jim echoes here the same sentiment expressed by Amanda when she misunderstands Tom's own rather Romantic notion of instinct and declares that Christian adults want "Superior things! Things of the mind and the spirit! Only animals have to satisfy instincts!" (52). Just as surely, Amanda wanted the same "superior things" when she was a debutante in the Mississippi Delta being courted by the sons of plantation owners, but this Daughter of the American Revolution settled instead for marriage to a "commoner" who worked for the telephone company.

Such a union between a woman of superior if by then effete heritage and a man of lower social status yet vital animalism, or let us say the psychosexual conquest of the former by the latter, is the subject of the book of Tom's that his mother returns against his will to the library, D. H. Lawrence's *Lady Chatterley's Lover*. Amanda dismisses its heady, equal mixture of Freud and Darwin as the filthy output of a diseased mind, but one can surmise that its obscenity is not the only aspect of this novel that troubles her. Her stated idea of a good read is naturally *Gone with the Wind*, Margaret Mitchell's mythic romance of the Old South, the Civil War, and Reconstruction, in which at one point the wellborn Scarlett O'Hara kills a vulgar Yankee intruder who would rape her.

The workaday Jim O'Connor, of course, has no intention of sexually subjugating or psychologically dominating Laura Wingfield. On the contrary, he idealizes rather than reifies her by placing her on a pedestal and equating this young woman with a blue rose. In so identifying Laura, Jim unwittingly recalls that widely recognized Romantic symbol of longing for the infinite, of unrequited yearning for absolute emotional and artistic fulfillment: the blue flower, drawn from the representative novel of early German Romanticism, Novalis' *Heinrich von Ofterdingen* (1802). This prose romance in two books is about the evolution of a young poet of great potential—in this case, a legendary medieval poet and master singer. It chronicles his apprenticeship to his art and search for the archetypal symbol, the blue flower, which had appeared to him in a dream.

For Heinrich, this flower comes to represent not only his artistic longing but also his loving fiancee, who has mysteriously died by the time the second book of the novel begins; this book, never finished by Novalis, was to have shown Heinrich von Ofterdingen's transfiguration into a poet, even as the first book depicted his preparation for the artistic vocation. Similarly, *The Glass Menagerie* is about the evolution (if not the artistic maturation) of the poet Tom—a man in his early twenties who is not by accident given by Jim the nickname of "Shakespeare," one of the heroes of the Romantic movement. *The Glass Menagerie* is also about Tom's effort, through the art of this play, both to find himself and to rediscover or memorialize his beloved sister, a blue flower in human form. The character of Tom, of course, is based in part on Tennessee Williams himself, whose given name was Thomas, even as Laura is modeled after Williams's only sister—Rose.

Laura herself happens to think that "blue is wrong for—roses" (106), but Jim insists that it is right for her because she's pretty "in a very different way from anyone else.... The different people are not like other people, but ... other people are not [so] wonderful. They're one hundred times one thousand. You're one times one! They walk all over the earth. You just stay here. They're common as—weeds, but—you—well, you're—*Blue Roses*!" (105). As her gentleman caller speaks, Laura is aptly bathed in the soft light coming from the new floor lamp her mother has especially purchased for the occasion—a lamp covered by a shade of rose-colored silk that helps to bring out her "fragile, unearthly prettiness" (85)—and she stands before the living-room sofa, suitably framed by its equally new pair of blue pillows. Moreover, Jim's words are reinforced by the image of blue roses projected onto a screen or section of wall between the living- and dining-room areas of the Wingfield apartment.

Laura is indeed different, as Jim maintains, but her difference stems from her physical frailty in addition to her fragile prettiness—both of which are symbolized not only by the figurines of her glass menagerie, but also by the "delicate ivory chair" (29) with which Williams identifies Laura in Scene 2. By physical frailty, I am referring not only to the "childhood illness [that] has left her crippled, one leg slightly shorter than the other, and held in a brace" (5), but also to her frequent faintness, nausea, and colds together with her bout with pleurosis as a teenager. Jim misheard "Blue Roses" when Laura told him, back in high school, that she had had pleurosis, an inflammation of the thin membrane covering the lungs that causes difficult, painful breathing.

His oxymoronic mishearing is similar to Williams's own "incorrect" hearing of "glass menagerie" for "grass menagerie," the enclosure where a collection of *live* wild animals is kept—a "mishearing" underlined by the dramatist's assertion in the "Production Notes" that a single recurring tune [of the play in production] "is ... like circus music ... [which paradoxically should be] the lightest, most delicate music in the world and perhaps the saddest" (9). Jim's mishearing for its part suggests the oxymoronic existence of Laura Wingfield, a young woman of this world who simultaneously, like the lovely but easily broken creatures of her glass menagerie, seems physically unfit for or unadapted to an earthly life. She is too good for this world, the Romantics might say, and for this reason she could be said to be sadly beautiful or bluely roseate, like the soft-violet color of her kimono (29) in Scene 2—the first scene where the screen-image of blue roses appears.

Indeed, Laura's physical as well as emotional frailty betokens an early demise, if not a death-wish on her part—a death that would bestow upon her the ultimate union with Nature so prized by the Romantics and so elusive or unattainable in life. Death imagery may not pervade the surface of *The Glass Menagerie*, but it is at the heart of two poems quoted or invoked by Williams on the screen device included in the authoritative version of the play. The first is "The Ballad of Dead Ladies," by the medieval French poet François Villon, from which the following, recurring line is projected onto the screen as Amanda and Laura appear onstage for the first time in Scene 1 (24), in addition to being projected later in the same scene when Amanda reminisces about the gentlemen callers she once entertained and would now like her daughter to receive (27). The line reads, "Où sont les neiges [d'antan]?", or "Where are the snows of yesteryear?" Villon uses snow here as a symbol of worldly life's evanescence as well as its natural provenance-cum-dissolution, its inevitably lost innocence or tarnished purity"; and Williams ironically connects the humble Laura and her humbled Southern belle of a mother with the great but departed women of Villon's part historical, part legendary ballad, among them Joan of Arc.

Like much of Villon's work, this poem elevates death to the status of a supreme law that ineluctably ends all earthly life yet ushers in the eternity of the Christian afterlife—an afterlife unironically intimated, embraced, or augured in so modern a drama as *The Glass Menagerie* by the title of Scene 5, "Annunciation" (56); by the mid winter-to-late spring time frame of the action; and by verbal references in the play to God the Father, the Virgin Mary, Christian martyrs, resurrection, baptism, paradise, grace, souls, and the erstwhile Catholic practice of eating fish every Friday. There are aural references to resurrection as well in the early-morning church bells at the start of Scene 4 (44), and we find a musical reference to Christ's rising from the dead in the song "The World is Waiting for the Sunrise!" from Scene 5 (57). There is no direct reference to Easter in the play, but certainly such allusions to resurrection as Amanda's calls to her son to "Rise and Shine!" in Scene 4 (46), together with Tom's own blasphemous tale to Laura in the same scene (45) of Malvolio the Magician's escape from a nailed up coffin, suggest that *The Glass Menagerie* takes place around the time of this annual Christian commemoration of Jesus' return to life and ultimate ascension into heaven.

The second poem quoted by Williams is less obviously associated with death, since the playwright uses two lines from it—which, again, appear on the screen between the living and dining rooms of the Wingfield apartment to anticipate, then announce, the arrival of the Gentleman Caller for dinner in Scene 6. The poem is Emily Dickinson's "The Accent of a Coming Foot," which I quote in full:

Elysium is as far as to
The very nearest Room
If in that Room a Friend await
Felicity or Doom—

What fortitude the Soul contains,
That it can so endure
The accent of a coming Foot—
The opening of a Door— (1180, Vol. 3, 1963)

Williams cites this poem's penultimate line first, then the final line as Tom brings Jim home to meet his sister (69, 74).

Now we know that all of Dickinson's transcendentalist-inspired work was composed within the characteristically American, late nineteenth-century range of relationships among God, man, and Nature. Furthermore, she was preoccupied in her poetry with the idea of death as the gateway to the next existence, as a special glory that has something in common with the conventional paradises offered in hymns and sermons of her day. Death for Dickinson means leisure, grandeur, recognition; it means being with the few, rare people whom it was not possible to know fully upon earth: she writes, for example, that "Death is potential to that Man / Who dies—and to his friend—" (420, Vol. 2, 1955). Much of life for her is anguish endured in an anteroom to death, which is but a prelude to immortality.

Although Dickinson speaks again and again of transitoriness and isolation in this world, she is not a mystic or a religious poet. Rather, from the whimsical, domestic, even rococo cast of her mind, she flirts with eternity, she is coquettish with God, forgiving Him for his "duplicity" and sometimes going so far as to be brash with Him. God is indeed a puzzling figure in her work, the Creator who perhaps does not know why He has created. He is burglar, banker, father; gentleman, duke, king: a being personified at times as Death, at other times as a sort of lover.

So too is Jim O'Connor of *The Glass Menagerie* a kind of gentleman, just as he was a champion high-school debater and baritone lead, if he will probably never be a captain of industry. For his part, Laura's absconding father (whose presence as a fifth character of sorts hovers over the play through his larger-than-life-size, beatifically smiling photograph above the mantel) can be called a burglar but not a banker, and a lover of other women if no longer of Amanda. Jim certainly never becomes *Laura's* lover, even though she secretly loves him, since he is engaged to be married to another woman; he does, however, adumbrate the death of Laura, her release from this life and return to nature, together with her rebirth in heaven.

In this sense, Jim is indeed, as Tom describes him in his narration, "the long-delayed but always expected something that we live for" (23). The anticipated arrival of someone or something that will provide a form of religious, political, or existential salvation and release to those who await him or it is a familiar subject of modern drama, from Maeterlinck's *The Intruder* to Odets's *Waiting for Lefty* to Beckett's *Waiting for Godot.* Although, ironically, the "expected something" usually does not arrive, the Gentleman Caller does make an appearance in *The Glass Menagerie*—one that is tellingly heralded by Tom's "annunciation" of his upcoming visit (59); by Jim's association with a traditional symbol of Christ, the fish (61); and by Laura's mentioning of his high-school yearbook picture right after she refers to the picture of Jesus' mother in the local art museum (33–34). Yet it is the Gentleman Caller's departure rather than his arrival that provides a final solution to Laura's problems, for in intensifying her desperation and isolation, Jim's permanent disappearance after Scene 7—in combination with the subsequent disappearance of Tom—could be said to hasten her physical and mental deterioration to the point of death.

"The accent of a coming foot" is, of course, Jim's, but it is also that of the Grim Reaper, who awaits Laura, his "friend," in "the very nearest room." Death will spell her *felicitous* doom, however, for it is identified in Dickinson's poem with Elysium, which in classical mythology represents the paradisiacal abode of the virtuous and blessed after they die. It is there that Laura may finally know fully Mr. James Delaney O'Connor, a man who on earth remained for the most part a figment of her imagination. It is on earth as well that Laura's soul may have had the fortitude to endure the accent of Jim's coming foot, his opening of her apartment door, because that accent and that opening would mean not only momentary escape from the prisonhouse of her imagination along with her shyness, but also ultimate, perpetual release from the cellblock of her physically crippled body, the wasteland of her emotionally crippled mind, and the enslavement of urbanized subsistence.

Certainly it is not by accident that Williams gives Laura a June birthday at the same time as he makes Jim's wedding day the second Sunday in June (111). Through her birth, Laura is thus associated with Juno, the ancient Roman queen of heaven; Juno, the goddess of marriage and childbirth; and Juno, the wife of Jupiter, the supreme deity of the ancient Romans, whose weapon was the thunderbolt that can be heard toward the end of Scene 6 (83). Laura may not marry and bear children on earth, but the implication is that in death she will become, or after death she will be resurrected as, the celestial bride of Jesus if not of James-Jupiter.

And surely her death will paradoxically be hastened by the celebration of her birth, for on that day or near that day the man of Laura's dreams,

Gentleman Jim O'Connor, will marry someone else, the unseen and prosaically named "Betty." Since Easter is celebrated at some time in the course of *The Glass Menagerie*'s episodic action, Laura's birthday occurs near Pentecost, or is closer to Pentecost than any other major Christian festival: the seventh Sunday after Easter, the religious holiday marking the descent of the Holy Spirit on the Apostles—and therefore the ideal day to signify or encapsulate the earthly yet transcendent life the chaste Laura Wingfield has led among the lowliest as well as the most noble creatures of God's menagerie.

As further evidence that Williams conceived of Laura as someone experiencing life-in-death or death-in-life, I offer a third poem from which he quotes—this time in the stage directions accompanying the screen title "The accent of a coming foot" in Scene 6. The dramatist writes that "It is about five on a Friday evening of late spring which comes 'scattering poems in the sky'" (69). His direct quotation is slightly inaccurate, but he clearly has in mind "Impressions, IX," by that romantic anarchist of American poetry, E. E. Cummings. I must refer the reader to this work in its entirety, for its dominant images—of life-in-death or death-in-life, ascent and descent, of dawn's early light and the candlelight of dusk, the dreams of sleep or the dreaminess of poetry, of harsh city life and the starry, songful life of the mind—recapitulate those of *The Glass Menagerie*. Here I can only offer the first two stanzas:

> the hours rise up putting off stars and it is
> dawn
> into the street of the sky light walks scattering poems
>
> on earth a candle is
> extinguished the city
> wakes
> with a song upon her
> mouth having death in her eyes (67)

As I intimated earlier, the lighting of Laura Wingfield—called for most prominently by Williams in the "Production Notes" to the play—is as poetic or expressive as its quotations and signifies just how different or special, if not heavenly, she is in comparison with the Betty O'Connors of this world. Williams writes that "the light upon Laura should be distinct from the others, having a peculiar pristine clarity such as light used in early religious portraits of female saints or madonnas" (9–10). Furthermore, the playwright sometimes makes Laura the visual focus of our attention "in contradistinction to what is the apparent center. For instance, in the ... supper scene ... her silent figure on the sofa should remain the visual center" (9). Beyond this, Williams suggests that the light surrounding Laura, as well as Tom, Amanda, and the Gentleman Caller, show "a certain correspondence to light in religious paintings, ... where the figures are radiant in atmosphere that is relatively dusky" (10). "Relatively dusky"—that is, "blue," as in the "deep blue dusk" from which there issues a "sorrowful murmur" in Scene 6 (83) as a summer-like storm abruptly approaches and Laura becomes too ill to sit down to dinner with Jim O'Connor, her mother, and her brother.

Williams calls for "dim" or "poetic" atmospheric lighting throughout *The Glass Menagerie*, however, not just during the three scenes that occur at twilight or dusk. He writes that such faint illumination is "in keeping with the atmosphere of memory" (9) in this memory play, but it must also be remembered that the time from twilight to dusk—the time of dim or poetic lighting—was the Romantics' favorite because, in its mixture of darkness and light, it is more infinite, more all-embracing, than any other part of the day. In addition, twilight-to-dusk suggested to them a mind that was half awake and half asleep and therefore in sentient retreat from the workaday world, alive to the dreamlike workings of memory. As is Laura's mind toward the end of Scene 5, in the "early dusk of a spring evening" (56), when—in response to her mother's demand that she "make a wish on the [little silver slipper of a] moon" that has just appeared—Laura "looks faintly puzzled as if called out of sleep" (67). Not by chance, the moon appears again in Scene 7, for, in its blending of blackness and brightness, moonlight creates the nighttime equivalent of twilight at sunset.

Twilight can thus be seen as the retiring Laura's favorite time of day, despite the fact that Jim calls it—or its artificial equivalent, candlelight—his favorite after a power outage plunges the Wingfield apartment into what Amanda terms an "everlasting darkness" (87). Jim appropriately comes to his "date" with Laura in Scene 7 "carrying [a] candelabrum, its candles lighted, in one hand and a glass of wine in the other" (88), together with a pack of Life-Saver mints (107). The virtually sacramental wine, in combination with his warmth and charm, gradually "lights her inwardly with altar candles" (97), which is Williams's way of saying that Jim's apparent love has touched Laura's soul by way of her eyes. This naturally is the manner in which romantic or spiritual love, as opposed to animalistic or carnal lust, works, and has been thought to do so since the early Renaissance when the sight of Dante's Beatrice created a hunger for empyreal rather than fleshly beauty: by touching the spirit in emulation of God's love for mankind as well as man's love of God.

When Laura realizes that she has misperceived Jim's intentions or that he has unintentionally misled her, "the holy candles on the altar of [her] face" are accordingly "snuffed out" (108). Indeed, at the end of the play Laura herself blows out the candles that Jim had brought to their encounter, and she does this in recognition not only of her brother Tom's departure from her life, together with that of her father before him, but also of the Gentleman Caller's leave-taking. The implication is that no gentleman caller will ever enter her life again; none will ever be gentle enough among an American people so crassly materialistic to perceive her inner beauty, to appreciate her love for beauty, to understand her unnatural, if not supernatural, place in a world ruled by science and technology instead of heart and soul. That Laura requires such a man—a man, period—to guarantee her happiness, if not her very survival in an unequal contest with the fittest, is a comment less on the man-made oppressiveness of the patriarchal order or the blind selectivity of the biological one, than on her need-cum-desire to anchor the eternal, unearthly feminine in the world of the temporally masculine. In this man's world, waiting for the second global war of the century after having recently weathered the economic war of the Great Depression, and therefore soon to be lit by lightning from mass bombardments, Laura is figuratively condemned to live out her earthly existence in an "everlasting darkness" that has already literally begun to descend on what will become millions of other human beings.

One of them may turn out to be Tom Wingfield himself, for he is a member of the Merchant Marine in the play's present or framing time of 1943–1944. This means, of course, that he was a sailor on the ships that carried weapons and supplies to our armed forces overseas—ships that were prime, and easy, targets for enemy submarines and cruisers. In *The Glass Menagerie*'s past action of 1936–1937, as remembered by Tom, he twice discusses his imminent joining of the Merchant Marine, and in each instance the image of a "sailing vessel with Jolly Roger" is projected onto the screen (51, 78). Now such a vessel is normally a pirate ship flying the traditional skull-and-crossbones flag, which obviously symbolizes death. Yet, as a merchant seaman, Tom will be furnishing food, clothing, and arms to other men and ships, not stealing such resources from them, as murderous pirates would do. So the image of a sailing craft with the skull-and-crossbones flag seems intended both to mock Tom's fantasy of high adventure on the oceans of the world and to augur his own demise, or descent into darkness at sea, at the hands of a *modern* pirate ship, the privateer.

Tom's death will leave the world in the hands of people like Jim O'Connor, the mock-pirate of the Gilbert and Sullivan comic operetta. Jim's real-life adventures, however, will be limited, as he himself says, to accumulating—or dreaming of accumulating—knowledge, money, and power in that order (100). This is the triad on which democracy is built as far as he's concerned, but it is the foundation of rampant capitalism for most of the rest of us. The Gentleman Caller's cravenly opportunistic dream of material success, or coldly rationalistic strategy for achieving monetary gain, may point the direction in which the American-led, postwar free world must go, but Laura and Tom Wingfield's heroically Romantic dream of spiritual or artistic fulfillment doubtless embodies what that world will lose by going there.

WORKS CITED

Cummings, E. E. *Complete Poems, 1904–1962*. New York: Liveright, 1991.

Dickinson, Emily. *The Poems of Emily Dickinson*. Ed. Thomas H. Johnson. 3 vols. Cambridge, Mass.: Harvard Univ. Press, 1955.

———. *The Poems of Emily Dickinson*. Ed. Thomas H. Johnson. 3 vols. Cambridge, Mass.: Harvard Univ. Press, 1963.

Novalis (Friedrich von Hardenberg). *Heinrich von Ofterdingen*. Trans. Palmer Hilty. New York: Frederick Ungar, 1964.

Villon, François. *Poésies complètes*. Ed. Claude Thiry. Paris: Librairie Générale Française, 1991.

Williams, Tennessee. *The Glass Menagerie*. New York: New Directions, 1966. First published, New York: Random House, 1945.

WILLIAM FORDYCE

Tennessee Williams's Tom Wingfield and Georg Kaiser's Cashier: A Contextual Comparison

T om Wingfield in Tennessee Williams's *The Glass Menagerie*, a defining work of "plastic theatre," written and first produced in 1944, has a distant relative, namely, the Cashier in Georg Kaiser's *Von morgens bis mitternachts*, a defining work of German Expressionism, written in 1912, first produced in 1917, and first translated into English in 1920 by Ashley Dukes as *From Morn to Midnight*. Each character—Tom and the Cashier—is the mainstay of his family in money matters: Tom is the son who earns a living for his mother, his sister, and himself because his father deserted the family; the Cashier is the conventional head of the household who does, in a mindless way, what society expects him to do. In particular, each character is a wage-slave who thinks he can become a complete human being only by escaping from an imprisoning environment. Although both characters are in analogous situations, determining whether Williams was aware of a similarity between Tom and the Cashier is not the issue in this article. Instead, the emphasis is on the fact that a comparison of these two characters clarifies how Williams's world-view differs from Kaiser's. Moreover, the precise implications of each world-view are more apparent when they are scrutinized in the context of the other world-view.

In its selective use of Expressionistic techniques, *From Morn to Midnight* anticipates the "plastic theatre" that Williams elucidates in his

From *Papers on Language & Literature*, vol. 34, no. 3 (Summer 1998): pp. 250–272. © 1998 by the Board of Trustees Southern Illinois University.

Production Notes to *The Glass Menagerie*. Williams, like Kaiser, is seeking a stagecraft that allows him to transcend "the exhausted theatre of realistic conventions." He asserts that Expressionism and all other unconventional techniques in drama have only one valid aim, and that is a closer approach to truth.... truth, life, or reality is an organic thing which the poetic imagination can represent or suggest ... only through transformation, through changing into other forms than those which were merely present in appearance" (7). As it developed in Germany just before World War I, Expressionism used all the resources of the theatre, such as lighting, sound effects, extended monologues, stylized dialogue and gestures, etc., to find ways of representing on the stage the protagonist's highly subjective, even dream-like, point of view. The ways and means of this movement continue to be a fertilizing influence on stagecraft.[1]

Mary Ann Corrigan suggests how Williams might have become aware of and responsive to various aspects of Expressionism (377). She goes on to show how the impact of Expressionism on Williams's sensibility can be documented in a work begun in 1940: "That Williams was familiar very early in his career with not only the theory of Expressionism but also its earlier dramatic manifestations seems evident from his unpublished play, *Stairs to the Roof*, a fantasy reminiscent of Kaiser's *From Morn to Midnight*, Rice's *The Adding Machine* and Lawson's *Roger Bloomer*" (378). She sees *The Glass Menagerie* and other Williams plays as influenced by the *Stationendrama* ("drama of stations"). Such a play, typical of Expressionism, is structured in a series of short scenes, each of which represents a significant station in the protagonist's intense quest—a quest that tends to invite failure.[2] *From Morn to Midnight*, like *The Glass Menagerie*, organizes the quest into seven stations. The Cashier escapes from his imprisoning environment only to learn during the stations of his quest that money cannot buy self-fulfillment. In analogous fashion, as Corrigan observes, "[t]he episodes of *The Glass Menagerie* reveal Tom's gradually moving toward a break with his family that only years later he recognizes as a futile gesture" (379).

Corrigan's observation pinpoints a crucial difference between Tom and the Cashier: in his role as narrator, Tom is remembering the events leading up to his escape, whereas the Cashier experiences his escape and its consequences during the play. Moreover, the age of each character determines the kind of escape he seeks. Tom's youth in the "memory play" (Williams 7) makes him anticipate an expansive future in which he can find himself as an artist, whereas the Cashier's middle age makes him gamble on the possibility of experiencing in the present a series of thrilling moments—at a velodrome, a cabaret, and a Salvation Army hall. Furthermore, the time-span in which each character can come to terms with his quest also varies. Tom's "memory play" allows him to set the past in perspective, albeit a somewhat ironic one.[3] The Cashier has only the final seconds of the play to find some meaning in his quest.

The most significant difference between Tom and the Cashier inheres in the fact that Tom's drama is overwhelmingly personal and family-oriented, although there is some reason to believe that Williams intends the Wingfields' problems with reality to be typical of those of the human race in general. The Cashier's drama, however, is representative of the common experience of "any man who is condemned by social conditions and his passive acceptance of them to the monotonous drudgery of competitive bread-winning" (Kenworthy 25). The fact that Kaiser's characters—identified by role, not by name—are generalized types rather than individuals in the way that the Wingfields are individuals underscores the representative mode of the drama. The Cashier's quest takes him beyond his job and family circle to meet disillusionment and betrayal in various spheres of society, which cumulatively come to stand for society as a whole. Although Tom places his "memory play" in the perspective of a troubled world-picture, this perspective does not inform the texture of the play to the extent that the various societal stations structure the drama of the Cashier.

The spine of Tom's character is indicated in the description of him in the cast of characters: "A poet with a job in a warehouse. His nature is not remorseless, but to escape from a trap he has to act without pity" (5). The aspects of his character relevant to this discussion are developed primarily in scenes 3 and 4 of *The Glass Menagerie*. The quarrel between Tom and Amanda, his mother, begins in scene 3 when Amanda tries to impose her genteel standards on Tom and he rebels. On the day before the quarrel, Amanda confiscated his books, particularly one by D. H. Lawrence. In anger, Tom blurts out that, although he pays the bills, he isn't free to be himself: "House, house! Who pays the rent on it, who makes a slave of himself to—" (39). Tom feels that his growth has been stunted by his having to fulfill family obligations at the expense of self-discovery. The Expressionistic dimension of the scene—from Tom's point of view—is evident in the following stage direction: *"The dining-room area is lit with a turgid smoky red glow."* Significantly, *"[t]he quarrel was probably precipitated by Amanda's interruption of Tom's creative labor"* at the typewriter, a symbol of his attempt to assert his independence (40). To avoid Amanda's questions and remarks, Tom threatens to go to the movies, his characteristic way of dealing—or not dealing—with unwanted responsibilities. The movies are an escape from the grind at the shoe warehouse where he works and the problems at the apartment; both environments seem like prisons to Tom—prisons shutting him away from his true destiny as an artist.[4] "For sixty-five dollars a month I give up all that

I dream of doing and being *ever*. And you [Amanda] say self—*self's* all I ever think of" (41). Tom's description of the secret life he leads when he goes to the movies is only in part a joke. It is also a deeply felt fantasy of escape, expressed in terms of imagery drawn from the movies. Tom is taunting Amanda when he conjures up his B-movie fantasies, but he is also indulging his drive for adventure, which he can satisfy in no other way in his present situation:

> I'm going to opium dens! Yes, opium dens, dens of vice and criminals' hangouts, Mother. I've joined the Hogan Gang; I'm a hired assassin; I carry a tommy gun in a violin case! I run a string of cat houses in the Valley! They call me Killer, Killer Wingfield; I'm leading a double-life, a simple, honest warehouse worker by day, by night a dynamic *czar* of the *underworld*, Mother. (42)

Later, in scene 6, Tom articulates the same drive for adventure to Jim O'Connor, the gentleman caller:

> People go to the *movies* instead of *moving*! Hollywood characters are supposed to have all the adventures for everybody in America, while everybody in America sits in a dark room and watches them have them! Yes, until there's a war. That's when adventure becomes available to the masses! Everyone's dish, not only Gable's.... But I'm not patient. I don't want to wait till then. I'm tired of the movies and I am *about* to *move*! (79)

Through such adventures as a merchant sailor, he hopes to find freedom in all its manifestations.

After his altercation with Amanda in scene 3, Tom makes an awkward attempt to leave the apartment:

> *He goes through a series of violent, clumsy movements, seizing his overcoat, lunging to the door, pulling it fiercely open.... His arm catches in the sleeve of the coat as he struggles to pull it on. For a moment he is pinioned by the bulky garment. With an outraged groan he tears the coat off again, splitting the shoulder of it, and hurls it across the room. It strikes against Laura's [his sister's] glass collection, and there is a tinkle of shattering glass. Laura cries out as if wounded.* (42)

Gilbert Debusscher states that this episode—and the struggle with the overcoat in particular—"exemplifies Amanda's mothering role and Tom's growing impatience with it.... The whole action shows the confinement of Tom's life and his mother's active role in it, foreshadowing the cruel action of escape that will later become necessary. Tom's helpless kneeling beside the scattered debris [of the broken glass animals] also hints at the remorse which will haunt him after his departure, a remorse which he acknowledges in his last speech as narrator ..." (50). Obviously, he can't escape from his present situation without hurting someone he loves. Although Tom's will to escape from the family circle is an emotion he shares with his long-absent father (and the Cashier), such an escape is also a necessary first step in establishing his own sense of self—a primary consideration. John Gassner comments on "the validity of the instinct of self-preservation that made him [Tom] leave them [Amanda and Laura]" (1077). The weight of family obligations is something Tom must cast aside, but he cannot do so unscathed; after he has left, the memory of the past, which is the very substance of the play, leads him into an emotional impasse.

In scene 4 the prison becomes a coffin when Tom tells Laura about a stage show he saw in which Malvolio the Magician performed "the wonderfullest trick of all": "We nailed him into a coffin and he got out of the coffin without removing one nail.... There is a trick that would come in handy for me—get me out of this two-by-four situation!" (45). If he can escape, he plans to live life on his own terms. As he explains to Amanda, "Man is by instinct a lover, a hunter, a fighter, and none of those instincts are given much play at the warehouse!" Amanda, the outspoken enemy of instinct and adventure, thinks that Tom is simply rationalizing his selfishness: "Self, self, self is all that you ever think of!" (52–53). She returns to this point in her climactic argument with Tom: "Don't let anything interfere with your selfish pleasure!" (114).

If Tom's decision to leave home is motivated by "self-preservation," Gassner's term, the Cashier's act of embezzlement and subsequent desertion of his family are motivated by a drive to escape from relentless routine in order to discover whether money and the power it wields can buy self-fulfillment.[5] The Cashier has no instinctual life or sense of self in scene I of *From Morn to Midnight*. He is literally in a cage at the provincial bank where he works;[6] his situation is comparable to Tom's at the warehouse, although we never see Tom in that setting. The Cashier only goes through the motions of living; he is not jolted into life until his encounter at the bank with the Lady, whom he mistakenly suspects of being a smooth confidence artist because that is the way the Bank Manager and the Stout Gentleman see her. Unlike Tom, the Cashier is not alive until his libido is stimulated by an external event, specifically, his response to the Lady. As B. J. Kenworthy notes, "the sudden impact of the unusual breaks down the barrier of habit, and converts the machine into a man. The Lady ... inflames his senses" (25). In contrast, before the action of *The Glass Menagerie* begins, Tom's creative urge has already proven itself to be a powerful stimulus, impelling him to claim his freedom, and of course that stimulus comes from within rather than without. Because the Lady "inflames his senses," the Cashier embezzles 60,000 marks from the bank to finance the underworld adventures he thinks he and the Lady, who is actually the picture of probity, would share after he has escaped from the cage at the bank and his domestic prison. Although Tom neglects his duties at the warehouse and is ultimately fired as a consequence, he does not commit a crime as the price of his freedom. In a significant development, the Cashier's personality, along with his capacity to express himself orally, begins to emerge only after he has committed a crime and escaped from the cage at the bank.[7] For his part, Tom anticipates that his true vocation as an artist will become a reality only after he has jettisoned his present way of life. Indeed, it will emerge only if he does so. In both cases, the act of escaping is presented as potentially humanizing. Moreover, once the Cashier is aware of his imprisoned state, he, like Tom, prepares mentally for his anticipated freedom by developing fantasies of exotic adventure—in scene 3—comparable to Tom's B-movie fantasies, and by facing the fact that he must spurn family responsibility in order to achieve his goal. Both fantasies of liberating adventure lead to disillusionment that has a different consequence for each protagonist. After the Cashier has learned the true identity of the Lady and is left to his own devices, he moves from station to station with disastrous results, whereas Tom sinks into the spiritual limbo evident as the play concludes.[8]

    A further significant difference between the Cashier and Tom is apparent in the fact that the Cashier looks for self-fulfillment in terms of materialistic pursuits—as his monologue in scene 3 indicates (63–64)—and is clearly misguided, while Tom sees self-fulfillment in terms of an intricate web of human emotion and in terms of his evolution as an artist. As Leroy R. Shaw points out, the Cashier "has been selfishly motivated; he has mistaken the chance to find his identity as a creator. Instead of serving the ideal, he usurps power for ends that might enhance his self-esteem" (92). In the final moments of *From Morn to Midnight*, after the Cashier has been disillusioned with and betrayed by the Salvation Lass, he seems to be on the threshold of perceiving that he has been looking for rebirth in the wrong places and in the wrong way. However, his insight comes too late; he represents one of the many false starts in the attempt of society to evolve the New Man, "a symbol of a confession of faith in the possibility of man's moral regeneration" (Kenworthy 34).[9] Other more effective protagonists will follow and perhaps be more regenerate.[10] Tom's attempt at self-fulfillment, while no more successful than that of the Cashier, defines the terms of its own limitations and is not seen as one of many failed evolutionary experiments.

Scene 4 of *From Morn to Midnight* is the central one in which the relation between the Cashier and Tom may be explored. First, a dissimilarity: in order to try on his old familiar role one more time, the Cashier returns to his home after he has walked out of his cage at the bank.[11] He hopes to prove to himself by going home that he was justified in shattering the bars of his occupational cage and that he would be equally justified in shattering the bars of his domestic prison. Playing the family role one more time—in this one station of his quest—confirms his urge to kick over the traces in the pursuit of power and thrills. Many years after the event, Tom remembers—in each station of his quest—the experience of quitting his prisons; by so doing, he returns to the period before he walked out of each prison, the warehouse and the apartment, and he spends most of the play reinforcing the belief that both prisons, especially the domestic one, were unacceptable.

Scene 4 reveals another dissimilarity between the Cashier and Tom. Throughout this episode the Cashier's family remain passive observers of his crazy mood, which they think is due to alcohol, whereas Amanda always actively engages Tom in disputatious give-and-take. In spite of his resistance to Amanda's interference in his life, Tom tries to make concessions, particularly in regard to finding a gentleman caller for Laura. He leaves home only after a slow painful process, which shapes the plot. In contrast, the Cashier is enveloped by a controlling fantasy; there is little or no probing give-and-take between him and his family. When he leaves home, he does so precipitantly with a minimum of forethought or preparation. Furthermore, at the moment of departure, he rushes away without familial emotion, but Tom, at the same moment, rushes away with familial emotion. In spite of such differences between the two characters, the Cashier and Tom have certain points of contact that emerge in scene 4 of *From Morn to Midnight*.

The Cashier enters his parlor immediately after his liberating episode with the tree-as-skeleton (scene 3). During that episode his old self died, and he is about to experiment with a new, problematic identity, even though he senses that his adventure is doomed and that he will ultimately return to the tree-as-skeleton. The activities he encounters in his parlor seem typical of a dead world rather than the reborn world he imagines he is ready to experience. The sterile bourgeois life in his parlor is presented Expressionistically. (The tone is established immediately by the "blown geraniums" in the window-box.[12]) Each member of his household—Mother, Wife, First Daughter, Second Daughter—is close to a caricature; the demands each one makes on him are like the bars in a prison. The household rhythms and routines lack vitality. Collectively and individually, the members of his household are as relentlessly the enemies of instinct and adventure as Amanda is in her efforts to impose gentility on Tom. In the Cashier's initial conversation with his Wife, his thoughts are still with the tree-as-skeleton, and he speaks of his death and rebirth during that episode equivocally and in staccato rhythms, as he tells his Wife that he has just come "[o]ut of the grave" (6.5).[13] Some of the energy of these speeches is comparable to Tom's energy as he evokes the world of B-movies to Amanda. Here is the Cashier: "Thawed. Shaken by storms, like the spring. The wind whistled and roared; it plucked the flesh from me, and my bones sat naked, knuckles and ribs—bleached in a twinkling. A rattling boneyard! At last the sun melted me together again; from the soles of my feet upward. And here I stand" (65–66). Particularly in the tone of Tom's B-movie fantasies is the following answer the Cashier gives his Mother when she asks where he has been: "In deep dungeons, Mother! In bottomless pits beneath monstrous towers, deafened by clanking chains, blinded by darkness!" (66). As the Cashier transforms the imagery of imprisonment into a vision of adventure, his Wife and Mother assume that he is merely drunk. The Cashier projects some of his animation onto the Bank Manager, who is assumed by the Wife to have participated in the drunken escapade: "He [the Bank Manager] has his eye on a new mistress [the Lady]. An Italian beauty, in silks and furs—from the land of orange blossoms. Wrists like polished ivory. Black tresses—olive complexion. Diamonds. Real ... all real" (66). The headlong dialogue conveys a sense of release which indicates how caged the Cashier feels at the bank: "prisons are never closed. The procession of customers is endless. One at a time they hop through the open door, like sheep into a shambles. Inside they stand closely wedged together. There is no escaping, unless you make a saucy jump over all the backs!" That's what the Cashier has done: "But one jump for dear life, and you're out of the sweating, jostling crowd. One bold stroke—and here I am. Behind me nothing and before me—what?" (66).

The Cashier orders his family to fetch the props that identify his role as head of the household, so he can try on that role again and see how it feels. His jacket, slippers, cap, and pipe are brought to him, but when he is duly dressed, that role does not satisfy him; for one thing, his pipe is clogged and draws with difficulty—a clear indication of how his being is obstructed by domesticity. The various articles of clothing he puts on are comparable to the woolen muffler that Amanda insists Tom wear in scene 4 of *The Glass Menagerie*; in one sense that muffler is protective, but in another sense it is confining (Debusscher 50). The Cashier has a similar reaction to the clothing that goes with his domestic role. As he surveys the genteel activity in the parlor, he is convinced that his home is a prison:

Grandmother nodding in an armchair. Daughters: one busy with embroidery, the other playing the piano. Wife at cooking-range. Build four walls about this scene, and you have a family life.— Comfortable, cosy, contented.... Then one day—on your back, stiff and white. The table pushed back against the wall—cake and wine. In the middle a slanting yellow coffin.... A band of crepe hangs round the lamp—the piano stands untouched for a year—. (67)

The coffin is the symbol of the Cashier's domestic way of life. In a similar way, Tom compares his "two-by-four situation" at the apartment to the coffin in Malvolio the Magician's stage show (45). In order to live their lives, Tom and the Cashier must try to elude the coffin of domesticity. As he surveys the activities in his parlor, the Cashier comes to this conclusion: "Warm and cosy, this nest of yours; I won't deny its good points; but it doesn't stand the final test. No! The answer is clear. This is not a halting-place, but a signpost; the road leads further on" (68). Ignoring the protests of his Wife and Mother, the Cashier shatters the routine of mealtime; by doing so, he precipitates his Mother's death. He comments on this event with bitter humor: "She dies because a man goes out of the house before a meal" (68). Tom might almost be commenting on one of the genteel standards Amanda imposes on him, many of which are related to meals and eating. However, in spite of her limitations, Amanda is strong and resilient; she would never be done in by a breach of routine, as the Mother is. The Cashier wonders if he should allow his Mother's death to deflect him from his primary purpose—to escape—and he decides to pay for his desertion in cash from his salary and, without guilt, go on his way with the embezzled funds: "Pain brings no paralysis. The eyes are dry, but the mind runs on" (68). Tom does not escape so easily; the emotional scars he will bear as a result of deserting his family could be the making of him as an artist (Presley 72). While the Cashier wants to use all of the embezzled funds to search for the ultimate experience that money can buy, Tom is not driven by a materialistic obsession; his anticipated growth as a human being and an artist determines his actions to a great extent.

At the end of *The Glass Menagerie*, Tom is in a position to use his pain and guilt as a measure of his emerging maturity as a human being and an artist. However, the fact that years have gone by and he is still wandering about in a spiritual limbo seems to make his quest a lost cause. His experience as a merchant sailor have been a dead end, not a beginning. As previously indicated, Mary Ann Corrigan describes Tom's quest as "a futile gesture" (379); the same phrase is appropriate for the Cashier's quest, but for reasons very characteristic of Kaiser's world-view.[14] The futility of

Tom's quest should be placed in a particular context, as should that of the Cashier. Benjamin Nelson observes that "[t]he underlying belief in *The Glass Menagerie* is that there is very little, if any, reason for living. Man is by nature incomplete because his universe is fragmented. There is nothing to be done about this condition because nothing can be done about it. Human guilt becomes a corollary of universal guilt and man's life is an atonement for the human condition" (112). As background for this assessment, Nelson cites a seminal statement on human "incompletion" in Williams's short story "Desire and the Black Masseur," written in 1946. Nelson believes that one passage in particular from that story "emanates from the core of [Williams's] thought and is perhaps his most illuminating commentary about himself and his work. It represents a philosophy, or let us say an attitude toward man in the universe, which is to manifest itself in all his work." Here is part of the passage quoted by Nelson:

> The nature of man is full of such makeshift arrangements, devised by himself to cover his incompletion. He feels a part of himself to be like a missing wall or a room left unfurnished and he tries as well as he can to make up for it. The use of the imagination, resorting to dreams or the loftier purpose of art, is a mask he devises to cover his incompletion. (111)[15]

For Williams, self-fulfillment is impossible not because one is always outgrowing old selves and therefore the process can never be completed; instead, self-fulfillment is impossible because failure is built into the very process of striving. Tom's struggle for self-fulfillment is natural but bound to fail because "incompletion" is the very nature of human destiny, however hard one may struggle against that destiny.[16] Moreover, that struggle leads Tom ironically into another kind of prison and a species of self-obliterating guilt (Debusscher 52 and Durham 63, 71). In a sensitive analysis of Tom's dilemma, C. W. E. Bigsby discusses this vicious circle:

> The self becomes its own source of authority against an imprisoning world. But it is an inherently ambiguous refuge ... for the self may be a prison. This is the haunting menace of [Williams's] world. The desperate devices employed by his protagonists drive them further into an isolation which is itself the ultimate terror. (*Tennessee Williams, Arthur Miller, Edward Albee* 44)

The whole action of *The Glass Menagerie* allows Tom the scope he needs to decide to desert his family, whereas the Cashier decides on the same action in minutes. At the end of *From Morn to Midnight*, in a Salvation Army hall, the Cashier tries to come to terms with the futility of the quest he has pursued since he stole the money from the bank and left his family. Participating in the Army's confession ritual, the Cashier sees his quest as a series of stations—with heavy Christian overtones—leading erratically to spiritual insight.[17] "I confess! You can buy nothing worth having, even with all the money of all the banks in the world.... Money's the meanest of the paltry swindles in this world!" To show that, as a result of his confessing his sins, money means nothing to him, "*he scatters banknotes broadcast into the hall*" (85). Although his fervor is quickly dissipated when the crowd turns into a greedy mob, skirmishing for the banknotes, his greatest disillusionment comes when he is betrayed by the Salvation Lass, who, earlier in the day, appeared periodically as a sort of guardian angel, beckoning to his soul to give up the mad pursuit of money and power. The Cashier even envisaged himself and the Salvation Lass as a new Adam and Eve. Such a possibility is destroyed during the mob chaos; she turns him over to the Policeman for a cash reward after he made himself vulnerable as a result of his elated confession ritual. He is surrounded and tricked by a society as misguided and mercenary as he has been. Perhaps they are, collectively, his dark double. Instead of moving forward spiritually, he realizes that another prison is closing in on him: "From morning to midnight I run raging in a circle...." The earlier vision of the tree-as-skeleton becomes a skeleton of tangled wires, the gaping image of his soul-defeating materialism. Without thinking, he grabs a trumpet and blows a "fanfare" to the illuminated skeleton, thereby acknowledging his kinship with the spiritual void. Seconds later, he shoots himself in the breast and dies "*with arms outstretched against the Cross on the back wall. His husky gasp is like an Ecce, his heavy sigh is like a Homo*" (86). Although his quest, unlike Tom's, ends in a *coup de théâtre*, ambiguity drains his final moments of positive significance. The Cashier alludes to the words of Pilate—in John 19.5—who declares that he finds no fault in Jesus; in a matter of minutes, Pilate, fully intimidated, turns Jesus over to the mob to be crucified. "But the Cashier, who is trying to achieve self-realization without regard for others, cannot be compared to Christ who died for all mankind" (Schürer 85). Therefore, the Cashier's "*Ecce Homo*" could be either his belated affirmation of the rebirth he has been looking for in the wrong places and in the wrong way or an expression of self-mockery because, in his quest, he failed to behave like the New Man. However, it is difficult to imagine that he could behave like the New Man because, as William R. Elwood notes, the Cashier "has little or no potential for growth and hardly an inclination to attempt to change his life. He is unaware that external changes do not create internal ones" (36). "Only when he sees [in his final moments] how he has done wrong does he demonstrate potential for self-realization and growth" (38). In a sustained dialectical analysis of the Cashier's *Stationendrama*, Leroy R. Shaw finds a "link between the [C]ashier's conscious search for value and his unconscious need to save his soul" (73). In this light, the Cashier's materialism and his delight in the power he thinks money can buy are essentially a displacement of the spiritual impulse that should have impelled him and that may be adumbrated in his death throes. Nevertheless, throughout the play his "vitality" has been totally "misdirected," says B. J. Kenworthy (42). Also emphasizing "misdirected" activity, H. F. Garten isolates "the ultimate guilt" of the Cashier: "... his quest aims at self-fulfillment only, without regard to others. It is only in his later plays that Kaiser gives a positive answer: he finds it in man's moral obligations to his fellowmen" (xv).

Ernst Schürer considers the possibility that the Cashier's "*Ecce Homo*" alludes to Nietzsche's autobiographical work of that title, in which "the philosopher contrasts the Christian ideals with his own philosophy of the superman" (85). This critic gives a balanced commentary on the relevance of such a possible allusion:

> By attempting to reach Dionysiac ecstacy and a full life, the Cashier certainly approaches Nietzsche's ideal much closer than he does the Christian one. But he does not achieve an inner rebirth, a spiritual regeneration; he remains imprisoned by his past. He follows his accustomed thought patterns by trying to buy pleasure instead of completely rejecting this kind of society. When he finally recognizes that he has been chasing illusions all along, he takes his own life; he is faced by nothingness and sees no other way of escape. He never catches a glimpse of a better life. (85–86)

The Cashier never makes his potential self a value in itself in order to transcend his present self and the instincts of the unregenerate. His sense of self is complacent and unexamined.[18] "The truly powerful are not concerned with others but act out of a fullness and an overflow" (Kaufmann 194). This kind of enlightened, self-critical selfishness never motivates the Cashier. Because he is not committed to the "[r]evaluation of all values"—a phrase from Nietzsche's *Ecce Homo* (326)—his show of energy is indistinguishable from weakness.[19] Consequently, any resemblance between the Cashier and a true "revaluer of values" (Kaufmann 107) is an illusion; the only thing the two have in common is a consuming desire for freedom and power, but the Cashier's consuming desire is self-defeating.

Of course, despite his lifelong enthusiasm for Nietzsche, Kaiser is not recommending without reservation the Nietzschean superman as a model to be emulated; in fact, the superman is a dangerous example of potentially destructive individualism that can separate a man from his fellowmen. Commenting on the fate of the Cashier, Douglas Kellner feels that "Kaiser criticizes here the excessive individualism in certain Nietzschean-expressionist concepts of the New Man, showing that unrestrained individualism inevitably leads to the destruction of self and others" (180). Ernst Schürer points out that, throughout his life, Kaiser was bent on combining the Nietzschean superman with an enlightened humanitarian: he wanted "to fuse them into a coherent whole; but he never succeeded" (150).[20] *From Morn to Midnight* stages the misadventures of a pseudo-Nietzschean, who has no compensating humanitarian impulses. As a result of his quest, the Cashier, like Tom, has merely exchanged physical prisons for a psychological prison from which there is no possible escape. Although Tom has a lifetime to endure the prison of prisons that the Cashier endures for only minutes, the achievement of true selfhood—either long-range in Tom's case or short-range in the Cashier's case—is an impossibility in each instance. Therefore, an air of futility hangs over both quests—a futility that has roots in quite divergent world-views.

Certain aspects of the curtain scene of each play epitomize the divergent worldviews of each playwright. Tom's concluding thoughts reveal his sense of guilt about abandoning Laura in particular. The drama ends on a subdued defeatist note. Laura blows out her candles as Tom asks her to do, while Tom observes that "... nowadays the world is lit by lightning" (115). "Nowadays" is both a reference to a world at war and a sadly joking way of indicating that at all times reality decimates human aspirations. Twas ever thus and ever will be thus. Laura's candelabrum, in the words of Amanda (early in scene 7), "used to be on the altar at the Church of the Heavenly Rest. It was melted a little out of shape when the church burnt down. Lightning struck it one spring" (87–88).[21] Lightning must be reckoned with in human affairs; it strikes the sacred and the profane. Because this is the case, the damaged candelabrum refers to Laura's damaged spirit, which is thwarted by reality, and to Tom's pained memory of his sister, which even her love and forgiveness—her blowing out her candles as he asks her to do—cannot assuage.[22] The lightning—a symbol of "incompletion"—is the *eiron* mocking all human attempts at self-fulfillment and underscoring the futility of human endeavor. As Judith J. Thompson indicates, "[t]he play closes in darkness, all three characters confined in the prisons of self once more in a reality unrelieved by dreams of deliverance" (23).

From Morn to Midnight also ends in darkness: "... *all the lamps [in the Salvation Army hall] explode with a loud report.* "On the dark stage the Policeman says, anticlimactically, "There must be a short circuit in the main" (86). This observation suggests that dark disorder permeates the society that produced the Cashier and all those who are driven by his kind of obsession.[23] The "short circuit in the main" objectifies the relation between the fate of the Cashier and the "false values" of the society of a particular time and place. In B. J. Kenworthy's opinion, "... this society imposes its values—and it is the false values which Kaiser is concerned to expose—upon the individual, thus turning him from the course he should best follow." Kenworthy supports this statement with a translated quotation from Kaiser's essay *Dichtung und Energie* (*The Energetics of Poetry*), written in 1922: "Man is perfect from the very beginning..... The limitations to which he finally succumbs are not part of his inner nature—no, these limitations and inhibitions are imposed upon him from without, as a result of the distorted forms to which his destiny is subjected (43). This situation demands the authentic New Man. On the one hand, Kaiser is suggesting that the "short circuit in the main" is a tragicomic circumstance that might be amenable to solution with the emergence of the New Man. There is reason for qualified hope. On the other hand, as Laura blows out her candles, Williams is expressing his sadness about the ineluctability of the human condition.[24] His world-view is more pessimistic than Kaiser's. For Williams, human "incompletion" and the impulse to resist "an imprisoning world" (Bigsby, *Tennessee Williams, Arthur Miller, Edward Albee* 44) end in guilt and defeat—prisons absolute and impervious to challenge or evolutionary change. For Kaiser, there is always the remote possibility that someone who shows real potential as the New Man—someone whose "vitality" is not "misdirected" (Kenworthy 42)—will appear and prove more regenerate than the Cashier.

NOTES

1. R.S. Furness, David F. Kuhns, Michael Patterson, J. M. Ritchie, Walter H. Sokol, J. L. Styan, and John Willett offer comprehensive discussions of Expressionism; Peter Bauland, J. L. Styan, and Mardi Valgemae survey the presence of Expressionism in American Drama.

2. According to Michael Patterson, the *Stationendrama* was "probably named after the stations of the [C]ross.... In place of the analytic structure of the typical Naturalist play, [the *Stationendrama*] portrays events synthetically, the progression dictated not by the inner necessity of any plot but only by the writer/protagonist's search for self-realization" (52).

3. Delma E. Presley notes that Tom "has gained a perspective provided by his extensive travels in the world and, even more, by his longer journey through time" (28).

4. For a discussion of prisons, cages, and confinement in Tom's situation, see Debusscher 49–51.

5. Leroy R. Shaw evaluates the impact of routine on the Cashier (68, 77–78) and is perceptive about the connection between money and power in the spurious values of the Cashier (88–89, 100).

6. Discussing the 1920 German film of Kaiser's play, directed by Karl Heinz Martin and designed by Robert Neppach, Michael Patterson notes that in the scene in the provin-

cial bank "the Cashier was framed by a construction of luminescent chickenwire: he was literally cooped up at his Counter ..." (64–65).

7. As Leroy R. Shaw observes, "... crime has freed him [the Cashier] from a routine existence and brought him his first chance to experience life" (67). The same point could be made about Mr. Zero, the wage-slave who murders his boss in Elmer Rice's *The Adding Machine* (1923). As in the case of the Cashier, Mr. Zero's *Stationendrama* begins with a potentially liberating act that leads to another series of prisons. See Rowe 206–07, Styan 111–14, and Valgemae 62–65.

8. See Bigsby, *Modern American Drama* 41; *Tennessee Williams, Arthur Miller, Edward Albee* 48; Debusscher 52; Durham 71.

9. Characterizing the period between 1910 and 1914, Ernst Schürer comments that "writers revolted against the cultural and political manifestations of their age and ... envisioned a regeneration of mankind and the building of a new world" (81). Walter H. Sokel places the New Man in the complex intellectual context of "anthropocentric humanism" (175). For a detailed discussion of the New Man, see Kellner 166–200 and Sokel 158, 173–91.

10. Renate Benson believes that, in Kaiser's opinion, the appearance of a "regenerate" man is less than probable:

> *Von morgens bis mitternachts* sets the tone of most of Kaiser's Expressionist dramas, whose major theme is man's disillusionment and loss of values. Indeed, there are only two of Kaiser's plays which dramatise the triumph of the New Man, namely *Die Bürger von Calais* (*The Citizens of Calais*) and *Holle Weg Erde* (*Hell Way Earth*). The others display in various settings the unwillingness or the inability of mankind to become regenerate no matter how persuasive the examples offered to them by the regenerate. (112)

11. Leroy R. Shaw analyzes the function of role-playing in the Cashier's behavior (82).

12. Michael Patterson indicates that these geraniums symbolize "the Cashier's disillusionment with his bourgeois existence" (68).

13. "When the [C]ashier enters [the parlor], he tries to convey his new experience of spiritual rebirth, but he is met with complete incomprehension" (Garten xvii).

14. Although Leroy R. Shaw describes the Cashier's activity as "futile," this critic stresses a positive dialectic at work behind the whole process (99, 105, 116). Most critics, however, feel that "futile" is still the operative word at the end of the play. For example, in the opinion of Haskell M. Block and Robert G. Shedd, "[t]he Cashier ends a martyr to the futility of life, yet his protest lends dignity and purpose to his crude assertion of individuality" (487).

15. In a 1961 interview with Studs Terkel, Williams airs some of his views on "incompletion" (Terkel 82, 89–90). See Bigsby, *Modern American Drama* 35–36.

16. Elaine Borges Berutti expatiates on Tom's failed attempt to overcome his "incompletion" (81–87). She studies *The Glass Menagerie* "as a play in which the characters seek for escapism in order to try to compensate for their own fragmentation" (87).

17. "Just before tossing his money to the crowd, he refers to the various steps in his search as *Stationen*, a clear echo of the stations of the [C]ross, and Kaiser supports this suggestion by his staging of the [C]ashier's death" (Shaw 72).

18. Walter Kaufmann points out that for Nietzsche, "the will to power is conceived of as the will to overcome oneself" (200). See Kaufmann 111, 200–07, 251.

19. Nietzsche agreed with Goethe's definition of romanticism as "egoism coupled with weakness" (Kaufmann 380). The Cashier's quest is vulnerable to criticism by the

terms of this definition. Because of his admiration for Nietzsche, Kaiser would probably see the appositeness of this definition to the quest in *From Morn to Midnight*, in spite of his fundamental disagreement with Goethe's point of view. See Schürer 78.

20. Kaiser created his most humanitarian protagonist, Eustache de Saint-Pierre, in *Die Burgher von Calais* (*The Citizens of Calais*), written in 1914. However, he continued to search for the fusion of the superman and the humanitarian, alluded to by Ernst Schürer. In discussing *Die Erneuerung* (*Regeneration*), a 1919 "outline for a drama," Schürer makes the following comments about the protagonist: "Although the Individual feels himself superior to the rest [the people], he begs them not to erect walls between him and themselves. He pleads with the people not to send him into the desert of isolation but to admit him into their community" (94). Some of this material influenced *Holle Weg Erde* (*Hell Way Earth*), an unwieldy *Stationendrama*, culminating in the humanitarian regeneration of the protagonist.

21. Roger B. Stein, in a study of the religious substratum of *The Glass Menagerie*, sees a connection between the effects of lightning on the candelabrum and the allusion to lightning in Tom's final thoughts (16). This critic stresses the pessimistic implications of the play: "The church has been struck by lightning, and all hope of resurrection has been lost in this damned universe where belief turns into metaphor, where man seems abandoned by his God, and where the echoes of prayer are heard only in blasphemy or irony. The bleakness of Williams's vision in *The Glass Menagerie* is complete" (20).

22. Pebworth and Summers consider the possibility that Laura's blowing out her candles is an act of "forgiveness" (113).

23. Kaiser's symbolic words from the Policeman ... suggest that a universal ill afflicts the core of society" (Eben 272). Commenting on the same lines, H.F. Garten feels that "... the 'short circuit' has no doubt wider implications, signifying the lack of communication and frustration of man in the modern world" (xix).

24. Speaking of the plight of the Wingfields, Gilbert Debusscher states that "[t]heir flight ... is a desperate fending off of the inevitable, more often than not a retreat before an ineluctable fate" (66–67).

WORKS CITED

Bauland, Peter. *The Hooded Eagle: Modern German Drama on the New York Stage.* Syracuse: Syracuse UP, 1968.

Benson, Renate. *German Expressionist Drama: Ernst Toller and Georg Kaiser.* Macmillan Modern Dramatists. London: Macmillan, 1984.

Berutti, Elaine Borges. "*The Glass Menagerie*: Escapism as a Way Out of Fragmentation." *Estudos Anglo-Americanos* 12–13 (1988–89): 78–89.

Bigsby, C. W. E. *Modern American Drama*, 1945–1990. Cambridge: Cambridge UP, 1992.

————. *Tennessee Williams, Arthur Miller, Edward Albee.* Cambridge: Cambridge UP, 1984. Vol. 2 of *A Critical Introduction to Twentieth-Century American Drama.* 3 vols. 1982–85.

Block, Haskell M., and Robert G. Shedd. Introduction. *From Morn to Midnight.* By Georg Kaiser. Trans. Ashley Dukes [Theatre Guild version]. *Masters of Modern Drama.* Ed. Haskell M. Block and Robert G. Shedd. New York: Random, 1962. 487–88.

Bloom, Harold, ed. *Tennessee Williams's* The Glass Menagerie. Modern Critical Interpretations. New York: Chelsea, 1988.

Corrigan, Mary Ann. "Beyond Verisimilitude: Echoes of Expressionism in Williams' Plays." *Tennessee Williams: A Tribute*. Ed. Jac Tharpe. Jackson: UP of Mississippi, 1977. 375–412.

Debusscher, Gilbert. *Tennessee Williams: The Glass Menagerie*. York Notes. London: Longman, 1982.

Durham, Frank. "Tennessee Williams, Theatre Poet in Prose." Bloom 59–73.

Eben, Michael C. "Georg Kaiser's *Von morgens bis mitternachts* and Eugene O'Neill's *[The] Emperor Jones*: Affinities in Flight." *Georg Kaiser: eine Aufsatzsammlung nach einem Symposium in Edmonton, Kanada*. Ed. Holger A. Pausch and Ernest Reinhold. Berlin: Agora, 1980. 263–76.

Elwood, William R. "Kaiser's *Von Morgens bis Mitternachts* as a Metaphor for Chaos." *The Many Forms of Drama*. Ed. Karelisa V. Hartigan. The University of Florida Department of Classics Comparative Drama Conference Papers 5. Lanham: UP of America, 1985. 31–39.

Furness, R. S. *Expressionism*. The Critical Idiom 29. London: Methuen, 1973.

Garten, H. F. Introduction. *Von morgens bis mitternachts*. By Georg Kaiser. Ed. H. F. Garten. London: Methuen, 1968. vii–xvii.

Gassner, John. Introduction. *The Glass Menagerie*. By Tennessee Williams. *A Treasury of the Theatre Volume 2: From Henrik Ibsen to Robert Lowell*. Ed. John Gassner and Bernard F. Dukore. 4th ed., New York: Simon, 1970. 1076–77.

Kaiser, Georg. *From Morn to Midnight*. Trans. Ashley Dukes. *Expressionist Texts*. Ed. Mel Gordon. New York: PAJ, 1986. 50–86.

Kaufmann, Walter. *Nietzsche: Philosopher, Psychologist, Antichrist*. 4th ed. Princeton: Princeton UP, 1974.

Kellner, Douglas. "Expressionist Literature and the Dream of the 'New Man.'" *Passion and Rebellion: The Expressionist Heritage*. Ed. Stephen Eric Bronner and Douglas Kellner. New York: Columbia UP, 1988. 166–200.

Kenworthy, B.J. *Georg Kaiser*. Oxford: Blackwell, 1957.

Kuhns, David F. *German Expressionist Theatre: The Actor and the Stage*. Cambridge: Cambridge UP, 1997.

Nelson, Benjamin. *Tennessee Williams: The Man and His Work*. New York: Obolensky, 1961.

Nietzsche, Friedrich. *On the Genealogy of Morals and Ecce Homo*. Ed. and trans. Walter Kaufmann. New York: Vintage, 1969.

Patterson, Michael. *The Revolution in German Theatre, 1900–1933*. Boston: Routledge, 1981.

Pebworth, Ted-Larry, and Jay Claude Summers. *Williams' The Glass Menagerie*. Bar-Notes. New York: Barrister, 1966.

Presley, Delma E. The Glass Menagerie: *An American Memory*. Twayne's Masterwork Studies 43. Boston: Twayne, 1990.

Ritchie, J. M. *German Expressionist Drama*. Twayne's World's Authors 421. Boston: Twayne, 1976.

Rowe, Kenneth Thorpe. *A Theater in Your Head*. New York: Funk, 1960.

Schürer, Ernst. *Georg Kaiser*. Twayne's World Authors 196. Boston: Twayne, 1971.

Shaw, Leroy R. *The Playwright and Historical Change: Dramatic Strategies in Brecht, Hauptmann, Kaiser, and Wedekind*. Madison: U of Wisconsin P, 1970.

Sokel, Walter H. *The Writer in Extremis: Expressionism in Twentieth-Century German Literature*. Stanford: Stanford UP, 1959.

Stein, Roger B. "*The Glass Menagerie* Revisited: Catastrophe Without Violence." Bloom 7–20.

Styan, J. L. *Expressionism and Epic Theatre*. Cambridge: Cambridge UP, 1981. Vol. 3 of *Modern Drama in Theory and Practice*. 3 vols.

Terkel, Studs. "Studs Terkel Talks with Tennessee Williams." *Conversations with Tennessee Williams*. Ed. Albert J. Devlin. Jackson: UP of Mississippi, 1986. 78–96.

Thompson, Judith J. *Tennessee Williams' Plays: Memory, Myth, and Symbol*. University of Kansas Humanistic Studies 54. New York: Lang, 1987.

Valgemae, Mardi. *Accelerated Grimace: Expressionism in the American Drama of the 1920s*. Carbondale: Southern Illinois UP, 1972.

Willett, John. *Expressionism*. World University Library. London: Weidenfeld, 1970.

Williams, Tennessee. *The Glass Menagerie*. Rev. ed. New York: New Directions, 1970.

LORI LEATHERS SINGLE

Flying the Jolly Roger:
Images of Escape and Selfhood in
Tennessee Williams's The Glass Menagerie

One of the more interesting aspects in Williams's concept of a new "plastic theatre" is a metatheatrical technique known as the screen device. According to Esther Merle Jackson, and, more recently, Thomas P. Adler, Tennessee Williams's 1945 preface to *The Glass Menagerie* merits our attention as an important "manifesto" in the history of modern American drama (Jackson 90, Adler 137). In these "Production Notes," Williams called for a "new, plastic theatre 'to replace' the exhausted theatre of realistic conventions" (131).[1] To this end, Williams proposed the use of such non-realistic elements as theme music, unusual lighting, and "a screen on which were projected magic-lantern slides bearing images or titles" (132–134). Although these projections that Williams collectively called "The Screen Device" (132) have been for the most part critically neglected, a closer study of them as they operate in Williams's play supports a new psychological interpretation of *The Glass Menagerie*.

Included in the original script, this device calls for forty three separate "legends" and images to be projected onto the wall between the dining room and the front room of the set during the performance (132). Although Williams's use of projected images is generally assumed to have been influenced by the German director Erwin Piscator, founder and director of The Dramatic Workshop of the New School of Social Research in New

---

From *The Tennessee Williams Annual Review* (1999): pp. 69–85. © 1999 by *The Tennessee Williams Annual Review*.

York where Williams studied as a young man, actually he first encountered this innovation while a student at the State University of Iowa. In fact, Williams had experimented with the use of projected images as early as 1938 in *Not About Nightingales*. Nevertheless, any discussion of Williams's screen device needs to be contextualized in light of Piscator's work. As John Willett notes "no other director used film so extensively or thought about it so systematically as Piscator, who came to employ front projection, back projection, and simultaneous or overlapping projection from more than one source" (Willett 113). In one Berlin production, Piscator used four projection screens, which makes Williams's proposed use of a single screen, "indistinguishable from the rest when not in use" (132), seem conservative by comparison.

In addition, Williams's use of the projected legends and images in *The Glass Menagerie* differs from that of the two great German practitioners Piscator and Brecht, whose interests in the development of non-realist or "epic theatre" were primarily political (Esslin 23). Instead, Williams was more interested in private issues than public ones. In focusing on the social and political backdrop of the play, C. W. E. Bigsby has convincingly argued that "*The Glass Menagerie* is no more a play of purely private emotions and concerns than Chekhov's *The Cherry Orchard*" (36). Certainly, the harsh economic and political realities of 1930's America are a driving force in the action of the play. However, private emotions were the driving force within the playwright himself. In an 1981 interview with Dotson Rader, Williams recalled that "*Menagerie* grew out of the intense emotions I felt seeing my sister's mind begin to go" (qtd. in Devlin 331). Not only is *The Glass Menagerie* his most autobiographical work, but it is also a public form of personal expiation. Just as Tom's memory play may be interpreted as his way of exorcising his guilt, Adler believes that Williams wrote the play in order to come to terms with his own sense of culpability over his failure "to do anything to prevent the prefrontal lobotomy performed on his schizophrenic sister, Rose" (Adler 139). Williams suffered guilt for having survived the familial tensions that ultimately destroyed Rose. Like Tom in the play, remorse was the price he paid for his escape. So, where Piscator used projected images to create a public language for addressing political issues, Williams used projected images to create a private language for coping with personal tensions.

Williams was striving toward a style he called "personal lyricism" (qtd. in Jackson 29), a poetic dramatic form that Adler suggests is capable of "delineating and probing character psychology" (126). In his "Production Notes," Williams wrote:

> Expressionism and all other unconventional techniques in drama
> have only one valid aim, and that is a closer approach to truth ...
> a more penetrating and vivid expression of things as they are ...
> which the poetic imagination can represent or suggest, in essence,
> only through transformation, through changing into other forms
> than those which were merely present in appearance. (131)

In other words, he wanted to create a poetic dramatic language capable of revealing the reality beyond what on the surface appears to be real.

This was his original artistic vision; however, because of the collaborative nature of theatrical production, many of the unconventional techniques were cut from Eddie Dowling's original production (1944 Chicago, 1945 New York), resulting in two different published versions of the play. The Acting Edition caters to the American preference for realistic theatre "that asks its audience to make believe they are not making believe by accepting the illusion for the real thing" (Adler 136–7), or theatre in which illusion "has the appearance of truth" (144). In contrast, the Reading Edition with the original didascalia calls for the use of the metatheatrical screen device to break the illusion of reality which is so popular in the realistic tradition of American theatre. These projections are part of Williams's strategy to reveal the truth behind the mere "appearance" of reality (131).

The Dowling production and the Acting Edition have set the standard for performances of this play, while the more widely published Reading Edition is used as a literary text by students, teachers, and scholars. Although some controversy regarding reading theatrical texts as literature remains, Mary Ann Frese Witt and others have presented convincing arguments for reading the "voice in the didascaliae" (Wilt 105).[2] In fact, Williams invites such practice by including in the Reading Edition a wealth of paratextual information. In addition to the stage directions concerning the screen device, he provides an epigraph from E. E. Cummings, a brief production background, an abbreviated outline of the play, character descriptions, "The Production Notes," and an essay called "The Catastrophe of Success" (123–41). In fact, he claims to have included the screen device in this edition because it might "be of some interest to some readers to see how this device was conceived" (132). No doubt the most compelling reason for studying the screen device as a written text is that performances using this technique are rare. In brief, Williams's screen device survives almost exclusively as a written rather than a performed text.

In this written text, the Reading Edition, Williams describes the two-fold function of the screen device as having both a "structural" and an "emotional" value (132). It serves "to give accent to certain values in each scene," thereby clarifying the narrative line and providing "a definite emotional appeal, less definable but just as important" (132). Actually, the screen device is more complex than Williams's notes would indicate. According to Pfister's dramatic theory, both the non-verbal "images" and the verbal "legends," which make up the screen device, are "epic communication structures" and as such function in the following way:

> As far as the aesthetics of reception is concerned, these epic elements have an anti-illusionist function which is intended to counter any identification or empathy on the part of the audience with the figures and situations within the internal communication system, thereby encouraging a posture of critical distance. (71)

In other words, in addition to the structural and emotional values that Williams cites, the screen device by its very nature also functions as a Brechtian distancing technique. It disturbs the illusion of reality and keeps the audience from readily identifying with the characters in the play. As Borny suggests, this critical distance is important because it keeps the audience from reading the play as a "soap-opera" or melodrama (112). Because the play is about familial dysfunction, there are no heroes or villains in *The Glass Menagerie*. In order to understand the truth beneath the surface, the audience needs to maintain its objectivity. Tom's escape must be viewed as a necessary evil. Williams positions his audience for this perception in the character description; Tom's "nature is not remorseless, but to escape from a trap he has to act without pity" (129).

   In addition to creating a critical distance between the audience and the play, metatheatrical techniques have other characteristics that make them particularly suitable to this play. In his assessment of metatheatrical reception aesthetics, Lionel Abel suggests a number of qualities that underline the appropriateness of Williams's use of these techniques. According to Abel, metatheatre "glorifies the unwillingness of the imagination to regard any image of the world as ultimate" (113). Given the fact that Williams believes reality to be an "organic thing" (131), mutable and illusive, something that only the poetic imagination can come close to representing, it is fitting that he makes metatheatrical techniques part of his poetic vocabulary. Abel also claims that metatheatre creates the "sense that the world is a projection of human consciousness" (113). In the case of *The Glass Menagerie*, the world is a projection of Tom's consciousness. Rather than standing as a record of what has actually happened, the play represents what happened as Tom remembers it. And memory, as Williams tells us, "takes a lot of poetic license.

It omits some details; others are exaggerated" (143); it is subjective and "not realistic" (145). In other words, Williams warns his audience from the beginning that Tom may be an unreliable narrator. As George W. Crandell notes, the "imperfections" of Tom's memory are highlighted by the fact that Tom "remembers scenes he could not possibly have witnessed" (5). For example, Crandell cites Tom's description of the beginning of scene 6, a scene that occurs while Tom is still at work. Once again, Abel's assessment of metatheatre seems to fit nicely with what Williams says he wants to accomplish in this play. Moreover, the subjective nature of Tom's world is all the more reason for the audience to be objective, to maintain a critical distance.

In short, the screen device and other metatheatrical elements that Williams proposed in his original script were suited to the kind of play he wished to present. Nevertheless, the screen device has been controversial from the beginning. Although the use of projected images had been used in opera houses since before World War I, mainstream audiences of the mid-1940s seemed unready for this particular metatheatrical technique. As Brian Parker suggests, "American audiences were familiar with realism and theatricalism separately," but not when used in conjunction as Williams proposed to do in *The Glass Menagerie* (417). At any rate, Eddie Dowling, the original Broadway producer, "considered this device superfluous" (qtd. in Tischler 38), and the success of his production (561 performances) certainly helped to justify his opinion of the screen device.

Jo Mielziner, the set designer, thought that the screen device would be both distracting and redundant. Ironically, these are two of the screen device's intended functions. It distracts the audience's sense of reality within the play by calling their attention to its own theatricality; in so doing, it creates critical distance. The verbal legends are often redundant in that many of them either foreshadow or repeat lines from the dialogue of the play, thereby accentuating specific aspects of each scene. Despite the fact that Mielziner, like Williams, was interested in the renunciation of realism, apparently, he did not like the screen device as Williams conceived it.[3]

Even more surprising is John Gassner's negative critique of the screen device. Because he taught playwriting at The Dramatic Workshop (1940–1941) while it was under the direction of Piscator, the champion of projection devices, one would expect him to have been more receptive to the screen device. Instead, Gassner, Williams's former teacher, said *"The Glass Menagerie* was marred only by some preciosity [sic], mainly in the form of stage directions, most of which were eliminated in Eddie Dowling's memorable Broadway production" (qtd. in Borny 103). Nancy M. Tischler reports that Gassner "considered the screen device 'redundant and rather precious.' Williams is 'straining for effect not knowing that his simple tale, so hauntingly self-sufficient, needs no adornments'" (39). Perhaps he felt that the use of epic communication structures was inappropriate in a play that is more concerned with private tensions than public issues.

Since this initial negative reception, critics have voiced a variety of complaints about the screen device. These generally fall into one of three categories: 1) the screen device reflects the playwright's distrust of the performance aspect of the play; 2) it reflects the playwright's distrust of the reception aspect of the play; and 3) it is distracting. Roger B. Stein's comments invoke the first type of complaint when he writes that the "awkwardness" of the screen device is one case "where Williams has failed to develop and then rely upon the dramatic situation" (11). The second and third complaints are voiced by Lester A. Beaurline, who claims the "weakness of the device lies in the author's anxiousness and small confidence in his audience.... I suspect that if the screen device has ever been tried, it distracted the audience from the actors" (29). John Styan, author of *Modern Drama in Theory and Practice*, said that "the screen device got in the way of the direct impact of the play's action, and was wisely abandoned" (119).

There is, of course, validity in all three complaints. Williams did intend for the legends and images to "strengthen the effect" of both the written and the spoken lines in order to augment the dramatic situation (132). He also sought to guide the audience's attention by accenting "certain values in each scene" (132). The only aspect that he did not mention in regard to the screen device was the distancing effect. Significantly, all three complaints are directed at standard uses for metatheatrical techniques which suggests a general privileging of realistic over non-realistic techniques. As Borny discovered in his brief survey of the play's critical reception, "critics who prefer the Acting Edition usually do so because that version is more realistic" (106).

However, some critics who take their clue from the "Production Notes" in the Reading Edition argue for the importance of this device on the basis of its non-realistic or metatheatrical functions. As a Brechtian distancing device, it has been championed by Borny and R. B. Parker. According to these two critics, the ironic commentary provided by the screen device creates an important critical distance. Borny says that the device effectively prevents the audience "from empathising too readily with the characters from Tom's past" (113) and that this distance positions the audience to receive the "symbolic truth" of the play (108). Without this irony, he says, "all we have is soap-opera" (112). Parker, in his psychological reading, says the "device achieves more than reducing the sentimental 'nostalgia'" of the play (529); it also sheds light on Tom's "ironic, self-defensive distancing" from the grief and guilt he feels (529). Moreover, it adds to the sense of ambiguity that, according to Parker, is the key to understanding this play (531). Thomas P. Adler has suggested that the screen device "might also function to replicate how memory works by association as well as to diminish any excessively sentimental response in the manner of a Brechtian distantian device" (138). Delma E. Presley echoes Adler's observation, saying that the screen device recaptures "the impressionistic qualities of the human memory—Tom's and ours" (80). Others, like Jackson and Frank Durham, value the device for its symbolic qualities. Durham makes the interesting claim that "the motion picture serves as the symbol determining the overall form of the play" while the screen device operates as subtitles in a silent movie (63). Jackson, an early advocate of the screen device, is mostly concerned with the device's poetic aspects as part of Williams's symbolic language for the plastic theatre (90–94).

Although each of these critics has a different interpretation of *The Glass Menagerie*, they all agree that the screen device adds richness and complexity to the play. Borny is "convinced" that rejection of the non-realistic elements "results in a trivialization of the play" (102). Parker says that to "insist, as most critics do, that the projection device is jejune or pretentious is to do Williams and his play a grave injustice" (416). Williams himself claims to have proposed the use of non-realistic techniques, including the screen device, in order to "find a closer approach, a more penetrating and vivid expression of things as they are" (131), and what he achieved was a realistic psychological portrait of a dysfunctional family. Interestingly, only in the last thirty years has the psychiatric community developed the theory and terminology that allows us to discuss Williams's play in terms of the dynamics of familial dysfunction.

If Tennessee Williams intended *The Glass Menagerie* to hold "its audience through the revelation of quiet and ordinary truths," as he said in an interview with R. C. Lewis in 1947 (qtd. in Devlin 28), then any interpretation of this work must first begin by asking, "What are the quiet and ordinary truths that *The Glass Menagerie* reveals?" As the play opens, Tom, a narrator who has tricks in his pocket, promises to give us "truth in the pleasant disguise of illusion" (144), and part of the illusion he weaves are the forty-three legends and images known as the screen device. As mentioned above, this device as metatheatrical technique may function in a number of ways; however, of particular interest is the way it functions as part of Tom's subjective memory. From a more objective perspective, the non-verbal projection images associated with Amanda, Laura, and Tom function symbolically to reveal the psychological underpinnings of the dysfunctional Wingfield family. In doing so, these projections help Williams position his audience to receive the difficult, but unavoidable truths about such family situations.

Before examining these particular screen images, it is important to establish the familial context that makes them so meaningful. According to Irene and Herbert Goldenberg, co-authors of *Family Therapy: An Overview*, in "families that produce dysfunctional behavior—one or both adults and any of the children may be assigned roles inappropriately or be treated as if they have only a single personality characteristic ... instead of a wide range of human feelings and attitudes" (73). Within the dynamics of the Wingfield household, Tom, Amanda, and Laura have assumed certain roles; each character's role is "a rigid and constricted set of solutions to the problem of whom to be and how to act" (Gurman II 450). As in all dysfunctional families, a kind of stasis exists that appears to work as long as everyone stays within their prescribed roles. The roles in this Wingfield family drama/ memory play consist of the "rejected parent," the "identified-patient," and the "parentified-child" (Goldenberg 74, 330, 333).

Amanda is the "rejected parent," whose husband abandoned her sixteen years before and who, consequently, "seeks gratification" through her children (Goldenberg 74) and her idealized past. The physically and emotionally crippled Laura assumes the role of "scapegoat ... the identified-patient who is carrying the pathology for the entire family" (Goldenberg 76). As the one who most clearly has a problem, Laura is the "symptom bearer ... expressing a family's 'disequilibrium'" (Goldenberg 7). Finally, just as one might expect in a single parent dysfunctional family, the void left by the absent parent is filled by the "parentified-child" (Gurman II 449). In the Wingfield family, the parentified-child is Tom. Although parentification of a child may occur in a number of situations, the Goldenbergs report that more and more frequently they "see the phenomenon when a parent deserts the family ... [and] the child is expected to fill the parent role, physically as well as psychologically" (Goldenberg 73n2). When the father left, Tom apparently became "the little man of the house." Typical of the conflictual nature of child parentification, Tom is forced to assume the responsibilities that his father abandoned sixteen years ago while never being granted the autonomy that normally accompanies these adult responsibilities.

Ironically, within this stasis of rigidly assigned roles, there is typically a perpetual dance of mask swapping, with each character taking turns at playing the persecutor, the victim, and the rescuer.[4] In a dysfunctional family system, things appear to happen through the action of the dance, but nothing ever really changes, as illustrated in the discussion of scene 3 below. Amanda will continue reciting the story of the seventeen gentlemen callers:

TOM: I know what's coming!
LAURA: Yes. But let her tell it.
TOM: Again?
LAURA: She loves to tell it. (147)

Laura will continue to polish her glass collection, lost in whatever secret solace it affords her. As she says, "My glass collection takes up a good deal of time. Glass is something you have to take good care of" (220). And Tom will continue going to the movies and writing poems; "Nobody in their right minds goes to the movies as often as you pretend to" (163); "Shakespeare probably wrote a poem on that light bill, Mrs. Wingfield" (209). There will be small rebellions, accusations, recriminations, and acts of contrition, but nothing will ever change. The Wingfield family system is a sort of dance of death, "a nailed-up coffin" (167). In order for Tom to escape from this trap, Williams tells us that he will have "to act without pity" (129).

Given the dysfunctional context I have briefly outlined, Tom, author and narrator of his memory play, is also the "parentified-child" trying to make a clean break from his assigned familial role. At the beginning of the play, he has managed to escape from this role physically, but he remains bound to it by the guilt he feels over rejected parental responsibilities that should have never been his in the first place. His need to lay his past to rest, to exorcise his guilt, affects his choice of the non-verbal screen images linked to Amanda, Laura, and himself. Assuming the play is Tom's public form of personal expiation and by extension Williams's as well, it becomes important to look at how these images function symbolically to reveal the psychological truths about the Wingfield family—truths that might at last set Tom free.

As the single parent in the Wingfield household, Tom's mother represents the cornerstone of this family's dysfunction. Therefore, it is fitting to begin this discussion with Amanda. After Mr. Wingfield deserts her, she becomes the rejected parent. In order to compensate for the damage her ego sustains by this rejection, she has been, as Williams tells us, "clinging frantically to another time and place," one that is significantly populated by her younger self and her seventeen gentlemen callers (129). When she is not working at Famous-Barr demonstrating brassieres, she is busy selling subscriptions to a magazine that caters to female visions of romance. Consequently, the images Tom chooses to associate with his mother have to do with Amanda's idealized past, two slightly different images of her as a young girl (148, 203), and the romantic fantasies, two images of a glamour magazine cover (159, 179), that he correctly senses to be at the core of the family's dysfunction. In her failed adjustment to her new position as a single parent, she has victimized both of her children in different ways.

She victimizes Tom by assigning to him the inappropriate role of parent/partner. In the parentification of a child, "the child comes to feel responsible for the well-being of the parent(s)," while the parent shows a lack of empathy for the parentified-child (Gurman II 450–51). The larger-than-life photograph of the absent Mr. Wingfield and Amanda's frequent allusions to "your father" are constant reminders of the role Tom is expected to fill. When Tom apologizes after their big fight, Amanda takes advantage of his remorse to focus immediate attention on her role as the rejected parent.

> AMANDA: I've had to put up a solitary battle all these years. But you're my right-hand bower! Don't fall down, don't fail!
> TOM [gently]: I try, Mother. (171)

More than just a simple bid for his sympathy; this is an effort to reposition Tom into his role as the parentified-child, the role he temporarily escapes when he defies her parental authority the previous night. To pull him back into his role, she repeats the theme of us against the world, telling him, "all we have to cling to is—each other" (171). Once back in his role of parent/child, she quickly heaps parental responsibility on his shoulders. Although he is two years younger than his sister, Amanda tries to make Tom feel responsible for Laura's future while his own needs and dreams remain on hold (174–76).

In addition, the implicit incestuous aspect to this parent/child relationship need not be actual for it to work its damage on the child (Goldenberg 74). Without having actually replaced his father in Amanda's bed, he has been forced to be her partner in other equally inappropriate ways. That Amanda, in her accepted role as the rejected parent, has come to depend on Tom to shore up her image of herself as young and desirable is evidenced by the fact that in his anger he knows exactly what button to push. He ends their fight by delivering the *coup de grâce*, "You ugly—babbling old—witch ..." (164). Williams's stage directions emphasize her self-absorption by pointing out that she is so "*stunned and stupefied by the 'ugly witch'*" ... that she hardly notices the damage to Laura's glass collection (165). From Tom's perspective as the parentified-child, the screen image of Amanda as a young girl reflects the seductive nature of their parent/child relationship. He is more than her child. As her confidante, her husband substitute, Tom assumes the role of her "right-hand bower" in every area but her bower.

The screen images associated with Amanda also relate to her victimization of Laura. In her role as the rejected parent, Amanda persistently needs to have her own desirability affirmed. One of the ways she reinforces her own self-image is to accentuate Laura's difference. Despite the fact that Laura's handicap "need not be more than suggested on the stage" (129), Amanda has exaggerated its ugliness by making it an unmentionable in their house: "Nonsense! Laura, I've told you never, never to use that word" (157). Typically in dysfunctional families, "some chance characteristic that distinguishes the child from other family members ... is singled out and focused on by the others" in a process called "scapegoating" (Goldenberg 74–75). Once the role of the identified-patient becomes fixed, "the basis for chronic behavioral disturbance is established" (Goldenberg 75). By the time of the memory play, Laura's difference has developed into a serious problem, as evidenced by her emotional breakdown at the Rubicam Business College. She has become so withdrawn from the real world that Williams says, "she is like a piece of her own glass collection, too exquisitely fragile to move from the shelf" (129).

Years of listening to her mother's story of the seventeen gentlemen callers has slowly eroded her self confidence. Amanda tells her laconic daughter that it is not enough to have a "pretty face and a graceful figure— although I wasn't slighted in either respect." One must also understand the "art of conversation" (148). If her mother, who had all the qualities of a "pretty trap" (192), could not hold her man, how is Laura supposed to have any hope of trapping and holding a man? Convinced that she cannot hope to compete in the romantic arena, she concedes her failure: "I'm just not popular like you" (150). While Amanda speaks of "our gentlemen callers," and "flounces girlishly," Tom groans twice and Laura, with a catch in her voice, pronounces the dreaded truth: "Mother's afraid I'm going to be an old maid" (150).

In fact, the mother has to some extent set Laura up to be an "old maid" by providing a competitive rather than nurturing environment. Even on the night of Laura's gentleman caller, Amanda jealously tries to upstage her daughter. Just before she enters wearing the same "*girlish frock*" that she has worn for her own gentlemen callers, she announces, "I'm going to make a spectacular appearance!" (193). Significantly, the stage directions state that "*the legend of her youth is nearly revived*" (193). Tom is naturally "*embarrassed*" by his mother's inappropriate dress and demeanor, but Jim "*is altogether won over*" (203). Immediately, the screen image of Amanda as a girl appears; although the seventeen gentlemen callers are missing this time, the image still recalls the seductive powers of his mother in her youth.

Like the images associated with Amanda, Laura's non-verbal screen images also highlight her own failure to adjust to the adult role expected of a person her age, but they do so from a more sympathetic perspective. The depth and complexity of Tom's feelings for Laura are reflected in the fact that most of the non-verbal screen images are associated with her. Although he feels a tremendous amount of love for his sister, he also feels some justifiable resentment. Ultimately, she becomes the one who haunts his memory, the one he cannot completely leave behind. Consequently, the images associated with Laura point out her dysfunction, but they do so more gently and with more forgiveness than the images associated with Amanda.

All three non-verbal screen images associated with Laura are introduced in scene 2, in which Amanda uncovers Laura's "deception" (151), the situation that Tom refers to as "the fiasco at Rubicam's Business College" (159). This stands out as the turning point in the play, because in this scene Amanda begins to realize that Laura cannot cope with the world outside. The screen image of a bee-like "swarm of typewriters" precedes Amanda's revelation of the truth: "you had dropped out of school" (153). Tom's choice of a threatening mechanical screen image is an attempt to see things from Laura's perspective. At the same time, the surrealism of the image highlights her mental instability.

The second image associated with Laura is a "Winter scene in a park" (155). Her crippling shyness caused her to drop out of school, so she has spent the time alone "mostly in the park" (154) visiting the penguins and "the Jewel Box, that big glass house where they raise the tropical flowers" (155). This screen image and the solitary activities associated with it suggest a coldness about Laura. Like the image, Laura is lovely but cold and frozen in time. As Tom says, "She lives in a world of her own—a world of—little glass ornaments" (188). Even the glass of her menagerie and the big glass house seem to suggest ice. Like the penguins in the park and the tropical flowers in the big glass house, she is as "peculiar" as a flightless bird and incapable of surviving in the world outside as a hot-house plant (188).

Similarly, the screen image of blue roses symbolizes Laura's peculiarity and is the most important of the three non-verbal screen images associated with Laura. In addition to Laura and Amanda's dialogue concerning this nick-name and Jim and Laura's dialogue concerning the same, this image gets projected three times in the course of Tom's memory play (151, 157, 227). Just as red is a hot color, blue is a cold color. If red roses are the traditional symbol for romantic love, then blue roses must symbolize Laura's lack of passion or, as Bert Cardullo has suggested, her desire to transcend this world (82). Although blue is the wrong color for roses, it is the right color for Laura (228). She has no passion for life. She has dropped out of high school, out of business school, and out of life. In order for Tom to exorcise his guilt, he must reject the role of parentified-child and acknowledge the fact that he cannot be responsible for Laura's future. The coldness of the images associated with her correctly places some of the blame for her condition on Laura. Her withdrawal from life, to a large extent, remains her own choice.

As George W. Crandell observes, "Laura actively resists both the role that society prescribes for women as well as Amanda's insistence that she conform to it" (9). Although the nick-name was originally linked to a physical illness, the screen image becomes linked to a psychological illness.

Whereas Laura's screen images reflect the complexity of Tom's feelings for the sister he has abandoned, the one image he associates with his escape reflects the ambiguity he feels for having made that choice. On one hand, the sailing vessel represents the freedom and movement of the open sea and the Union of Merchant Seamen. On the other hand, the vessel is a pirate ship whose Jolly Roger, the skull and cross bones, symbolizes criminality and death. As Cardullo notes, Merchant Marine ships became primary targets when World War II broke out (91), and may be represented as the lightning that Tom refers to at the end of the play. Since the memory play is Tom's attempt to lay the past to rest, the most telling of screen images is the one he chooses for himself. "A sailing vessel with the Jolly Roger" (173, 200).[5]

On one level, the ship image represents Tom's desire to move from the claustrophobic confines of the Wingfield's tiny apartment to the vast open spaces of the ocean. Indeed, Williams establishes the motif of claustrophobia from the very first sentence of the opening stage directions: "The Wingfield apartment is in the rear of the building, one of those vast hive-like conglomerations of cellular living-units that flower as warty growths in overcrowded urban centers" (143). Significantly, it "is entered by a fire escape, a structure whose name is a touch of accidental poetic truth" (143).

For Tom, the claustrophobia is both physical and psychological. There are not enough bedrooms; Laura has to sleep in the living room. In addition to the absence of personal space, the real sense of claustrophobia comes from the way their lives are enmeshed, another common symptom of dysfunctional families (Gurman 449).[6] This problem is both voiced and demonstrated in the course of Tom's fight with Amanda.

> AMANDA: What is the matter with you, you—big—big—
> IDIOT!
> TOM: Look!—I've got no thing, no single thing—
> AMANDA: Lower your voice!
> TOM: —in my life here that I can call my OWN! (161)

They both interrupt each other throughout the argument so that even their voices become enmeshed. Only when Tom becomes physically threatening does she back off (164).

Typical of their dance of death, they switch masks at this point. Tom becomes the persecutor, and Amanda becomes the victim of his rage.

However, when he is "pinioned" by his coat, he rips it off and throws it across the room, accidentally breaking part of Laura's glass collection (164). "Laura cries out as if wounded" (164); Tom gets down on his knees and begins his act of contrition (165). So the scene ends with Tom back in his prescribed role as care-giver to Laura, the identified-patient, as he begins to collect the fallen glass. Given the fact that this family system allows Tom no space to take care of himself, to have a life of his own, it is no wonder that he dreams of wide open spaces and oceans of freedom.

In contrast to this stifling world of female domination, the manly world of the Union of Merchant Seamen represented by the image of a sailing ship seems like a breath of fresh air. Just before Tom confides in Jim about his plans to leave home via the merchant marines, the screen image of a sailing vessel with the Jolly Roger appears for the second time (200), and the stage directions tell us that Tom "looks like a voyager" (201). One can almost imagine the breeze in his hair.

In addition, Tom's decision to escape into an exclusively masculine world highlights an important gender issue in the play. In the Wingfield household, Tom's sexuality must be held in check. Amanda will not allow Tom even vicarious access into the world of adult sexuality. She will not allow the "filth" of that "insane Mr. Lawrence" in her house (161). Her outrage over Lawrence masks the genuine fear that Tom's sexual interests could result in his growing up and leaving home to create his own family. In short, her prudish outrage is not really about sex, but about Tom's independence.

Lawrence may be banned; however, when it comes down to trapping a man for Laura, Amanda openly peddles *The Homemaker's Companion*, with its female sexuality couched in terms such as "delicate cuplike breasts," "creamy thighs," and "bodies as powerful as Etruscan sculpture" (159). Appropriately, in this way Amanda earns the extra money "needed to properly feather the nest and plume the bird" (159). When the long awaited night of the gentleman caller arrives, Amanda transforms her daughter into a "pretty trap" (192) with a new dress (191) and a bra stuffed with "'Gay Deceivers'" (192). "All pretty girls are a trap, a pretty trap, and men expect them to be" (192). Ironically, the "tragic mistake" in Amanda's personal life was falling for a pretty trap in the form of the now absent Mr. Wingfield (186): "No girl can do worse than put herself at the mercy of a handsome appearance! I hope that Mr. O'Connor is not too good-looking" (186). As the rejected parent and victim of her own sexuality, Amanda views sex as a dangerous force that must be either suppressed or properly manipulated toward the goal of marriage. Tom's sexuality, having no place in Amanda's plans for Laura, must be suppressed, while Jim's sexuality, having everything to do with Amanda's plans, must be manipulated. Understandably, Tom associates escape with a masculine world.

Significantly, the sailing vessel that symbolizes Tom's escape is a pirate ship, a symbol rich in ambiguity. It represents a special species of ruthless thieves and murderers who are as often knighted as hung for their actions. Our culture's love/hate relationship with the pirate parallels Tom's love/hate relationship with himself and with the sister he has tried unsuccessfully to leave behind. The brutality and criminality generally associated with pirates represent Tom's uneasy conscience, the motivating force behind this memory play. Tom in the present is trying to lay his past to rest, to break the bond of guilt that still hampers his development as an adult.

The boyish naiveté implicit in the pirate ship image is also indicative of Tom's arrested growth. It links him to Jim, the high school star of *The Pirates of Penzance*, an operetta in which a group of unsuccessful pirates fall in love. It also links him to the romanticized pirates and adventures he experiences in the movies. He thinks he longs for adventure, but he really longs for the childhood he was never allowed to have. As the parentified-child, he has been unfairly forced into being a father to his sister by a mother who assumed that Laura was their shared responsibility. As if she were their child, Amanda tells Tom, "We have to be making some plans and provisions for her" (174). Ironically, the parentified-child can never grow up until he/she gives up the responsibilities unjustly placed upon him/her as a child. Tom has to renounce his adult responsibilities toward his family in order to become an adult in his own right.

Consequently, Tom, the narrator, sees himself as both hero and villain for having left home. Although leaving home is the natural step into adulthood from a normal childhood, Tom's experience as the parentified-child, as a stand-in for the husband of his mother and father of himself and his sister, has made this move toward selfhood almost impossible. It has taken him a long time to muster the pirate-like sense of villainy and daring necessary for him to make his move. As he prepares himself to follow in his father's footsteps, Tom tells Jim "I'm like my father. The bastard son of a bastard! Did you notice how he's grinning in his picture in there? And he's been absent going on sixteen years!" (202). This simultaneous announcement/denouncement of self occurs in scene 6 some time after the morning his father's photograph lights up in response to Tom's question about the nailed-up coffin: "You know it don't take much intelligence to get yourself into a nailed-up coffin, Laura. But who in hell ever got himself out of one without removing one nail? [As if in answer, the father's grinning photograph lights up. The scene dims out]" (167–68).

It takes Tom a great deal of time to work up his anger about his victimization. His explosive speech in scene 3 is the culmination of years of frustration: "You think I'm in love with the Continental Shoemakers? Look! I'd rather somebody picked up a crowbar and battered out my brains—than go back there mornings! ... If self is what I thought of, Mother, I'd be where he is—GONE!" (163). What finally pushes Tom over the edge is Amanda's failure to acknowledge the extent of his sacrifice. Amanda cannot face this truth without also acknowledging the injustice of Tom's prescribed role as parentified-child. Her accusations of selfishness are more than he can bear: "The more you shout about my selfishness to me the quicker I'll go, and I won't go to the movies!" (236).

The power and poignancy of *The Glass Menagerie* lie in the revelation of two difficult truths about the Wingfield family. First, Laura is not going to awaken suddenly and begin to participate in the real world. Jim's kiss was just a human kiss and not the magic kiss of a fairy tale prince. The dynamics of this dysfunctional family inhibit self-development and discourage autonomy. Sometimes, as in Laura's case, individual growth is forever arrested; as with the delicate creatures in her glass collection, she remains frozen in time. In the end she lifts her head and smiles at her mother, completely resigned to her role as identified-patient: "Amanda's gestures are slow and graceful, almost dancelike, as she comforts her daughter" (236). Laura has renounced all responsibility for making a life for herself.

Secondly, Tom's decision to leave becomes a matter of self-preservation, a necessary evil. If he stays, he will have to sacrifice his identity in favor of a role imposed on him by the familial dynamics. Tom realizes that his identity and dreams are unimportant to Amanda, the rejected parent, and incomprehensible to Laura, the identified-patient. As the parentified-child, he must sacrifice his self for the financial security of the family. "For sixty-five dollars a month I give up all that I dream of doing and being *ever*!" (64). Tom repeatedly associates his role as bread winner with a living death, a nailed-up coffin, because for him to remain is to commit psychic suicide. As he tells Amanda, "Every time you come in yelling that God damn '*Rise and Shine*!' '*Rise and Shine*!'" I say to myself, "'How *lucky dead* people are!' But I get up. I *go*!" (164).

So in the Wingfield family, as with many dysfunctional families, the natural process of leaving the nest, which should be a life-affirming celebration of a person's independence, has been perverted into a sort of exorcism of all family ties. Tom wants a total disassociation with his past, not because he does not love his mother and sister, but because of the pain that love causes him. He wants more than forgiveness; he wants forgetfulness; he wants to wish it all away. This, of course, is no more possible for Tom than it was for Williams himself.

Perhaps the most one can hope for is to make peace with oneself by recognizing the necessity of one's actions. As Adler has suggested, it is possible to view Tom's remembering as a therapeutic process, a way of working through the pain and guilt he feels for having escaped the nailed coffin, for having abandoned his mother and sister (139). In Tom's memory play, as in real life, the process of recovery involves recognizing the dysfunctional familial roles, accepting responsibility for one's own life, and learning to lay the past to rest. If one imagines that through the ritual of this process, Tom will be able to get on with his life, then Laura's final gesture of blowing out the candles can be interpreted as a release. This play is very much about what Williams called "the fragile, delicate ties that must be broken, that you inevitably break, when you try to fulfill yourself" (qtd. in Devlin 10).

NOTES

1. All future references to *The Glass Menagerie* will be noted by page number only.

2. For more on the current discourse concerning didascalia, see Michael Issacharoff and Robin F. Jones, ed., *Performing Texts* (Philadelphia: U of Pennsylvania P, 1988).

3. This does not mean that Mielziner was completely opposed to the use of projected images as is evidenced by his use of projections to leaf out the house and surrounding area in *Death of a Salesman* (1949).

4. In transactional analysis, this configuration is called the Karpman Triangle. It is discussed in *Born to Win: Transactional Analysis with Gestalt Experiments* by Muriel James and Dorothy Jongeward in the unit called "The Drama of Life Scripts" as being "illegitimate" when used for the purpose of manipulation (Reading, Ma: Addison-Wesley, 1973. 84–89).

5. In Cardullo's romanticized reading of the play, the pirate ship both mocks "Tom's fantasy of high adventure" and "augurs his own demise" (91).

6. The Goldenbergs define enmeshment as "an extreme form of proximity and intensity in family interactions in which members are overconnected and overinvolved in each others lives" (329).

WORKS CITED

Abel, Lionel. *Metatheatre: A View of Dramatic Form*. New York: Hill and Wang, 1963.

Adler, Thomas P. *American Drama, 1940–1960: A Critical History*. New York: Twayne, 1994.

Bigsby, C. W. E. "Entering *The Glass Menagerie*." The Cambridge Companion to Tennessee Williams. Ed. Matthew C. Roudane. Boston: Cambridge U P, 1997. 29–44.

Borny, Geoffrey. "The Two Glass Menageries: Reading Edition and Acting Edition." *Modern Critical Interpretations: Tennessee Williams's The Glass Menagerie*. Ed. Harold Bloom. New York: Chelsea House, 1988.

Cardullo, Bert. "The Blue Rose of St. Louis: Laura, Romanticism, and *The Glass Menagerie*." *The Tennessee Williams Annual Review* (1998): 81–92.

Crandell, W. George. "The Cinematic Eye in Tennessee Williams's *The Glass Menagerie*."

The Tennessee Williams Annual Review (1998): 1–11.

Devlin, Albert, ed. *Conversations with Tennessee Williams*. Jackson: U P of Mississippi, 1986.

Durham, Frank. "Tennessee Williams, Theatre Poet in Prose." *Modern Critical Interpretations: Tennessee Williams's The Glass Menagerie*. Ed. Harold Bloom. New York: Chelsea House, 1988. 59–73.

Esslin, Martin. *Brecht: A Choice of Evils: A Critical Study of the Man, His Work and His Opinions*. 4th ed. London: Methuen, 1984.

Goldenberg, Irene and Herbert Goldenberg. *Family Therapy: An Overview*. 2nd ed. Pacific Grove, CA: Brooks/Cole, 1985.

Gurman, Alan S. and David P. Kniskem, eds. *Handbook of Family Therapy*. Vol. 1. New York: Brunner/Mazel, 1991.

Jackson, Esther Merle. *The Broken World of Tennessee Williams*. Madison: U of Wisconsin P, 1965.

Parker, Brian (R. B. Parker). "The Composition of *The Glass Menagerie*: An Argument for Complexity." *Modern Drama* 25 (1982): 409–422.

Pfister, Manfred. *The Theory and Analysis of Drama*. Trans. John Halliday. Cambridge: Cambridge UP, 1988.

Presley, Delma E. *The Glass Menagerie: An American Memory*. Boston: Twayne, 1990.

Styan, J. L. *Modern Drama in Theory and Practice*. Vol. 3. Cambridge: Cambridge UP, 1981. 3 vols.

Tischler, Nancy M. "The Glass Menagerie: The Revelation of Quiet Truth." *Modern Critical Interpretations: Tennessee Williams's The Glass Menagerie*. Ed. Harold Bloom. New York: Chelsea House, 1988. 31–41.

Williams, Tennessee. *The Glass Menagerie*. 1945. *The Theatre of Tennessee Williams*. Vol. 1. New York: Peter Lang, 1989.

Willett, John. *The Theatre of Erwin Piscator: Half a Century of Politics in the Theatre*. London: Methuen, 1978.

Witt, Mary Ann Frese. "Reading Modern Drama: Voice in the Didascaliae." *Studies in the Literary Imagination*. 25.1 (1992): 103–112.

Chronology

1911	Thomas Lanier Williams is born in Columbus, Mississippi on March 26 to Cornelius Coffin Williams and Edwina Dakin, the daughter of Walter Edwin Dakin an ordained minister. He also has a sister, Rose Isobel, born November 17, 1909. Having just lost his job at the telephone company, Cornelius works as a shoe salesman.
1913	The Williams family moves to Nashville, Tennessee.
1915	The Williams family moves to Clarksdale, in western Mississippi.
1916	Tom's diphtheria develops into Bright's Disease according to the diagnosis of the local doctor. Tom is left paralyzed and unable to use his legs for about two years.
1918	Tom and Rose are separated from their grandparents, moving with their parents to St. Louis, where Cornelius is given an office job.
1919	A third child, Dakin, is born on February 21.
1920	Tom's friendship with Hazel Kramer begins.
1921	Edwina has a miscarriage.
1923	Tom starts at Ben Blewett Junior High School.
1924	Tom publishes a ghost story in the school magazine.
1925	Tom writes essay on factory fumes for the school yearbook. He moves to Soldan High School, where he writes movie reviews for the school newspaper.

1927	Tom moves to University City High School and wins third prize ($5) from the magazine *Smart Set* answering the question: "Can a good wife be a good sport?"
1928	His story "The Vengeance of Nitocris" is published in the magazine *Weird Tales*. Tom sails to Europe with Reverend Dakin and a party of female parishioners. In Paris he has what he called a "nearly psychotic crisis."
1929	Tom attends the University of Missouri at Columbia.
1930	Tom earns money during summer vacation by selling *Pictorial Review*. He falls in love with a boy during the autumn term, but the relationship remains unconsummated.
1931	Cornelius punishes Tom for his low grades by making him work through the summer vacation in a clerical job. Back at the university in the autumn, he enters the School of Journalism.
1932	Cornelius withdraws Tom from college. Tom studies shorthand and typing in night classes, doing menial work during the day for the International Shoe Company.
1933	Tom writes verse and stories. "Stella for Star," his twenty-third submission to the magazine *Story*, wins him $10 when he is awarded first prize in the Winifred Irwin competition.
1934	In June, Tom begins ten months of working in a warehouse for the shoe company.
1935	In the spring, Tom has what he claims is a heart attack, and recuperates at his grandparents' home in Memphis, where he writes a one-act play, *Cairo! Shanghai! Bombay!* which is staged by amateurs on July 12. In the fall, he attends Washington University in St. Louis and writes plays for an amateur group, the Mummers.
1936	Tom's story, "27 Wagons Full of Cotton" is published in *Manuscript*.
1937	*Candles to the Sun* is staged in St. Louis. Tom takes a playwriting class at the University of Iowa. A lobotomy is performed on Rose. Tom has what is probably his only heterosexual affair.
1938	Tom graduates with a degree in English literature. He goes to Chicago and in December to New Orleans, where he gets a series of part-time jobs.
1939	Tom moves into an attic apartment at 722 Toulouse Street in the old French Quarter. He sends out scripts under the name "Tennessee." In February, by subtracting three years

from his age, he enters some of his plays in a contest orga-
nized by the Group Theatre. He travels to California, wanting to try his luck as a Hollywood scriptwriter. Williams is
awarded a prize of $100 by the Group Theatre, and his
plays are sent to the agent, Audrey Wood. He travels to
Taos in New Mexico, where he visits Frieda Lawrence, and
returns to St. Louis, where he works on his play, *Battle of
Angels*. In September, he has his first meeting with Audrey
Wood in New York and stays for several weeks before
returning to St. Louis. Williams is awarded a Rockefeller
Foundation grant of $1,000.

1940 In January, Williams moves back to New York, where
he lives in a YMCA. He meets Donald Windham and
joins a playwriting seminar run by John Gassner at the
New School for Social Research, where students put on
his one-act play, *The Long Goodbye*. Classified 4F, he is
exempt from war service. Williams leaves New York for
spells in Memphis, and in Provincetown, Cape Cod. On
December 30, *Battle of Angels* is staged by the Theatre
Guild in Boston.

1941 On January 11, the *Battle of Angels* run ends. Williams starts
the story, "Portrait of a Girl in Glass," which will be developed into *The Glass Menagerie*.

1942 Williams returns to New York, staying with various friends
and lovers while doing odd jobs, including one at the
Beggar's Bar in Greenwich Village. He collaborates with
Donald Windham on dramatizing the D.H. Lawrence's
story, "You Touched Me." In August, Williams goes to
Jacksonville and works for the War Department operating
a teletype machine on the night shift. In late November,
he returns to New York, doing another series of odd jobs,
including stints as an elevator operator in a hotel, a bellhop,
and an usher in a movie theater.

1943 In April, Audrey Wood secures for him a six-month contract with M-G-M as a scriptwriter. In May, he rents rooms
on Ocean Avenue, Santa Monica, and, while working on a
script for Lana Turner, develops "Portrait of a Girl in Glass"
into a screenplay, "The Gentleman Caller." In October,
Williams loses his Hollywood job. On October 13, *You
Touched Me* opens in Cleveland. At Christmas, he returns to
St. Louis, where his grandmother is dying.

1944	On January 6, his grandmother dies. Williams writes the story "Oriflamme." In April, he is awarded $1,000 by the American Academy of Arts and Letters. He leaves for Provincetown where he works on *The Glass Menagerie* (a reworking of "The Gentleman Caller"). On December 26, *The Glass Menagerie* opens in Chicago.
1945	In January or February, Williams starts work on *A Streetcar Named Desire*. On March 31, *The Glass Menagerie* opens in New York. In April, he leaves for Mexico, where he stays at a guest house near Guadalajara, working on *A Streetcar Named Desire*. In September, he returns to New York, where *You Touched Me* opens on September 25. In December, he leaves for New Orleans.
1946	In January or February, Tom starts living with Pancho Rodrigues y Gonzalez. By May, he is suffering from abdominal pain and is examined in Wichita, Kansas and goes on to Taos. Tom begins a friendship with Carson McCullers and works on *Summer and Smoke*. In September, suffering from gastric pains, he returns to New York for tests. In October, he settles with Pancho into an apartment in New Orleans, where he continues working on *Summer and Smoke*, as well as drafting *Camino Real*.
1947	In January, Reverend Dakin travels with Williams and Pancho to Key West. In March, Tennessee sends the script of *A Streetcar Named Desire* to Audrey Wood. In June, Tennessee and Pancho rent a cottage in Provincetown. He meets Frank Merlo. On July 8, *Summer and Smoke* opens at the Gulf Oil Playhouse in Dallas. On December 3, *A Streetcar Named Desire* opens in New York, where it wins the New York Drama Critics' Circle Award and the Pulitzer Prize.
1948	In January, Williams travels to Paris and in February to Naples, Calabria, Sicily and Rome. In the summer, he pays his first visit to London, where John Gielgud is preparing a production of *The Glass Menagerie*. In August, he returns to New York on the *Queen Mary*. On October 6, *Summer and Smoke* opens in New York. In October, Frank Merlo moves in with him. Williams arranges for Rose to be moved into a private clinic. In November, he and Frank leave for Tangier, going on to Fez and Casablanca.
1949	In April, Williams travels to London, where *A Streetcar Named Desire* is about to open. In the winter, he rents a cottage in Key West and works on *The Rose Tattoo*.

1950	*The Roman Spring of Mrs. Stone* is published and the film of *The Glass Menagerie* is released. In December, *The Rose Tattoo* opens in Chicago.
1951	On February 3, *The Rose Tattoo* opens in New York, where it wins a Tony award. In March, Tennessee's grandfather, mother and brother come to stay with him in Key West. In July, Williams goes to Venice, where he drafts the story "Three Players of a Summer Game." In December, the film version of *A Streetcar Named Desire* is released.
1952	In January, *A Streetcar Named Desire* wins the New York Film Critics' Award. From June to September, *Summer and Smoke* is revived in New York.
1953	On March 19, *Camino Real* opens in New York. Williams works on *Cat on a Hot Tin Roof*. In April, he directs *The Starless Air* by Donald Windham in Houston.
1954	In the spring Williams is still working on *Cat on a Hot Tin Roof*. In New York in May, Williams and Carson McCullers appear at "An Evening at the 92nd Street Y." In October, he starts filming *The Rose Tattoo* in Key West.
1955	Reverend Dakin dies on February 14. On March 24, *Cat on a Hot Tin Roof* opens in New York, where it runs for 694 performances, winning the Pulitzer Prize, the Drama Critics' Circle and Donaldson awards. This is followed by a period of restless movement during which time he is unable to write. Williams becomes increasingly dependent on drugs. In the autumn, he is back in New York, working on the screenplay for *Baby Doll*.
1956	In January, *A Streetcar Named Desire* is revived in Miami with Tallulah Bankhead, and in February, the production moves to New York. On April 16, *Sweet Bird of Youth* premieres in Miami. Williams' relationship with Frank Merlo is deteriorating during the spring, followed by a near nervous breakdown in Rome the following summer. Back in New York in September, he learns that his mother has been committed to a psychiatric ward, but he leaves for the Virgin Islands before trying to help her.
1957	In January, Williams takes his mother to Key West, where he is working on *Orpheus Descending*, and on March 21 it opens in New York. In May, Cornelius dies at the age of seventy-seven. In June, Williams starts psychoanalysis with Dr. Lawrence Kubie.

1958	On January 7, *Garden District (Suddenly Last Summer* and *Something Unspoken*) opens off-Broadway and on September 16 in London. On January 30, *Cat on a Hot Tin Roof* opens in London. The film of *Cat on a Hot Tin Roof* is released. In early June, Williams breaks off analysis with Dr. Kubie and leaves for Europe. In the autumn, he works on *Period Adjustment*, which opens in Miami on December 29.
1959	On January 15, *The Rose Tattoo* opens in London. On March 10, *Sweet Bird of Youth* opens in New York. In April, Williams goes to Cuba, where he meets Ernest Hemingway and Fidel Castro. On April 14, *I Rise in Flame, Cried the Phoenix* opens in New York. In May, Williams goes to London for the British premiere of *Orpheus Descending*. On July 2, a one-act version of *The Night of the Iguana* is staged at the Spoleto Festival, directed by Frank Corsaro.
1960	In January, Corsaro arrives in Key West to work with Williams on *The Night of the Iguana*. On November 10, *Period of Adjustment* opens in New York. *Fugitive Kind* (the movie of *Orpheus Descending*) is released.
1961	In January, Williams leaves for Europe with Marion Vaccarro. On December 28, *The Night of the Iguana* opens in New York.
1962	*The Night of the Iguana* wins the New York Drama Critics' Circle Award. On July 11, *The Milk Train Doesn't Stop Here Anymore* opens at the Spoleto Festival.
1963	On January 16, *The Milk Train Doesn't Stop Here Anymore* opens in New York. In August, Frank Merlo is hospitalized and dies in September. From September to October, Williams is in Mexico where John Huston is filming *The Night of the Iguana*.
1964	On January 1, *The Milk Train Doesn't Stop Here Anymore* opens on Broadway, but closes after four performances. The film of *The Night of the Iguana* is released.
1966	On February 23, *Slapstick Tragedy* opens in New York.
1967	In January, Williams goes to Virgin Islands and works on screenplay for *Milk Train*. On September 29, Carson McCullers dies. In December, Williams goes to London for the world premiere of *The Two-Character Play* at the Hampstead Theatre Club.
1968	In February, *Kingdom of Earth* opens in Philadelphia, and on March 27, on Broadway.

1969   In January, Williams' brother, Dakin, arrives in Key West and organizes Williams' conversion to Catholicism. Williams is baptized on January 10. In February, he is hospitalized in Miami with the flu. After discharging himself, he takes an overdose of sleeping pills. On May 11, *In the Bar of a Tokyo Hotel* opens in New York. On June 21, Williams arrives in Tokyo for a production of *Streetcar*.

1971   In July, *The Two Character Play* is revived under the title *Out Cry* in Chicago, where he quarrels with Audrey Wood.

1972   In April, *Small Craft Warnings* opens at the Truck and Warehouse Theatre and transfers to the New Theatre on June 6.

1973   On March 1, *Out Cry* premiers in New York. In July, Williams spends two weeks in Tangier with Tom Field, and works on *The Red Devil Battery Sign*.

1974   In March, Williams travels to London for a new production of *Streetcar*. In May, *The Latter Days of a Celebrated Soubrette*, a reworking of the *Gnädiges Fräulein*, opens and closes after one off-Broadway performance. In June, *Out Cry* is produced unsuccessfully off-Broadway. In July, *Cat on a Hot Tin Roof* is revived in Stratford, Connecticut and, in September, on Broadway.

1975   In May, *The Glass Menagerie* is revived at the Brooks Atkinson Theatre. In the Spring, Edwin Sherin goes to Key West to work with Williams on *The Red Devil Battery Sign*, which Sherin will direct. In June, it opens disastrously in Boston. On September 16, *Summer and Smoke* is revived in New York. In October, *Sweet Bird of Youth* opens in Washington and transfers to Broadway and *The Glass Menagerie* is revived at Circle in the Square. On December 16, *Summer and Smoke* is revived at Circle in the Square.

1976   On January 16, *This Is (An Entertainment)* is staged by the American Conservatory Theatre in San Francisco. In May, Williams serves as president of the jury at Cannes. In October, Williams is ejected from a hotel in San Francisco; in December, he is initiated as life member of the American Academy of Arts and Letters.

1977   In April, *Vieux Carré* is staged on Broadway. In June, Williams is in London for *The Red Devil Battery Sign*, which opens at the Roundhouse.

1978	In January, *Tiger Tail*, a stage version of *Baby Doll*, is tried out unsuccessfully in Atlanta. In June, *Creve Coeur* is staged in Charleston. In August, Williams goes to London for the West End production of *Vieux Carré*. In the autumn, he leases a new apartment at Manhattan Plaza, employs a new secretary, Jay Leo Colt, and transfers to a new agent at International Creative Management, Mitch Douglas.
1979	On January 10, *Creve Coeur* opens in New York at the Hudson Guild Theatre.
1980	On March 26, *Clothes for a Summer Hotel* opens at the Cort Theatre. In June, Edwina dies at the age of ninety-five. In the autumn, Williams accepts an invitation to be Distinguished Writer in Residence at the University of British Columbia in Vancouver.
1981	On August 24, *Something Cloudy, Something Clear* is staged at the Bouwerie Theatre, New York.
1982	On April 27, *A House Not Meant to Stand* opens in Chicago at the Goodman Theatre.
1983	Williams dies on February 24 in New York.

Contributors

HAROLD BLOOM is Sterling Professor of the Humanities at Yale University. He is the author of 30 books, including *Shelley's Mythmaking* (1959), *The Visionary Company* (1961), *Blake's Apocalypse* (1963), *Yeats* (1970), *A Map of Misreading* (1975), *Kabbalah and Criticism* (1975), *Agon: Toward a Theory of Revisionism* (1982), *The American Religion* (1992), *The Western Canon* (1994), and *Omens of Millennium: The Gnosis of Angels, Dreams, and Resurrection* (1996). *The Anxiety of Influence* (1973) sets forth Professor Bloom's provocative theory of the literary relationships between the great writers and their predecessors. His most recent books include *Shakespeare: The Invention of the Human* (1998), a 1998 National Book Award finalist, *How to Read and Why* (2000), *Genius: A Mosaic of One Hundred Exemplary Creative Minds* (2002), *Hamlet: Poem Unlimited* (2003), *Where Shall Wisdom Be Found?* (2004), and *Jesus and Yahweh: The Names Divine* (2005). In 1999, Professor Bloom received the prestigious American Academy of Arts and Letters Gold Medal for Criticism. He has also received the International Prize of Catalonia, the Alfonso Reyes Prize of Mexico, and the Hans Christian Andersen Bicentennial Prize of Denmark.

NANCY M. TISCHLER has been a professor of English and Humanitites at the Pennsylvania State University and Director of Summer Sessions. She has also taught at the University of Arkansas, George Washington University and Susquehanna University. She is the author of *Dorothy L. Sayers*, *A Pilgrim Soul* (1979), *Student Companion to Tennessee Williams* (2000) and editor of *The Selected Letters of Tennessee Williams* (2000).

FRANK DURHAM has been a professor of English at the University of South Carolina. He is the author of *Elmer Rice* (1970), "Tennessee Williams: Theatre Poet in Prose" (1971), and *Dubose Heyward: The Man Who Wrote Porgy* (1954).

THOMAS E. SCHEYE has been a professor of English at Loyola College in Maryland. He is the author of "Two Gentlemen of Milan" (1974).

BRIAN PARKER is a professor emeritus of English at Trinity College, University of Toronto, where he served as founding director of the Graduate Drama Center, Head of Graduate English Studies, and Vice Provost of Trinity College. He is the author of "Documentary Sources for *Camino Real*" (1998), "Bringing Back Big Daddy" (2000), and editor of *Coriolanus* for the Oxford Shakespeare Series (1994).

ROGER BOXILL is a professor emeritus, Graduate English Department at City College of New York. He is the author of *Shaw and the Doctors* (1969) and an author of "Theatre Reviews" (*Shakespeare Quarterly*) (1984).

DREWEY WAYNE GUNN has been a professor of English at Texas A & I University. He is the author of *The Gay Male Sleuth in Print and Film: A History and Annotated Bibliography* (2005), *Tennessee William: A Bibliography* (1991), and *American and British Writers in Mexico, 1556–1973* (1974).

C. W. E. BIGSBY has been a professor of American Studies at the University of East Anglia. He is the author of *Staging Gay Lives* (1996), *Modern American Drama, 1945–1990* (1992), and editor of *The Cambridge Companion to Arthur Miller* (1997).

GILBERT DEBUSSCHER has been a professor of English and American Literature at the University of Brussels in Belgium. He is the author of *American Literature in Belgium* (1988), "Creative Rewriting: European and American Influences on the Dramas of Tennessee Williams" (1997) and an editor of *New Essays on American Drama* (1989).

BERT CARDULLO has been an associate professor of Theater and Drama at the University of Michigan. He is the author of *Theatrical Reflections: Notes on the Form and Practice of Drama* (2005), *In Search of Cinema: Writings on International Film Art* (2004), and *Indelible Images: New Perspectives on Classic Films* (1987).

LORI LEATHERS SINGLE has been a doctoral student in English at Georgia State University. She is the author of "*Alice Moore Dunbar-Nelson (1875–1935)*" (2000) and "Reading Against the Grain: The U.S. Reception of Branagh's Mary Shelley's *Frankenstein*" (1998).

Bibliography

Adler, Thomas P. "The Search for God in the Plays of Tennessee Williams." *Renascence* 26 (1973): 48–56.

———. "Tennessee William's 'Personal Lyricism': Toward an Androgynous Form." From *Realism and the American Dramatic Tradition*. Edited by William Demastes. Tuscaloosa: University of Alabama Press (1996): 172–188.

Bigsby, C. W. E. *A Critical Introduction to Twentieth-Century American Drama*, Vol. 2; Tennessee Williams, Arthur Miller, Edward Albee. Cambridge: Cambridge University Press, 1984.

Bloom, Harold, ed. *Modern Critical Views: Tennessee Williams*. New Haven, Conn.: Chelsea House, 1987.

———. *Tennessee Williams's "The Glass Menagerie."* Edited by Harold Bloom. New York: Chelsea House Publishers, 1988.

Bluefarb, Sam. "*The Glass Menagerie*: Three Visions of Time." *College English* 24 (April 1963): 513–518.

Brooks, Charles B. "The Comic Tennessee Williams." *The Quarterly Journal of Speech* 44 (1958): 275–281.

Broussard, Louis. *American Drama: Contemporary Allegory from Eugene O'Neill to Tennessee Williams*. Norman: University of Oklahoma Press, 1962.

Cate, Hollis L., and Delma E. Presley. "Beyond Stereotype: Ambiguity in Amanda Wingfield." *Notes on Mississippi Writers* 3, no. 3 (1971): 91–100.

Clayton, John Strother. "The Sister Figure in the Plays of Tennessee Williams." *Carolina Quarterly* 12 (1960): 47–60.

Cluck, Nancy Anne. "Showing or Telling: Narrators in the Drama of Tennessee Williams." *American Literature* 51 (1979): 94–93.

Clurman, Harold. *The Divine Pastime*. New York: Macmillan, 1974.

Cohn, Ruby. "The Garrulous Grotesques of Tennessee Williams." *Dialogue in American Drama*. Bloomington: Indiana University Press, 1971.

Colanzi, Rita. "Caged Birds: Bad Faith in Tennessee Williams's Drama. *Modern Drama* 35, no. 3 (September 1992): 451–465.

Corrigan, Mary Ann. "Memory, Dream and Myth in the Plays of Tennessee Williams." *Renascence* 28, no. 3 (Spring 1976): 155–167.

Crandell, George W. "The Cinematic Eye in Tennessee Williams's *The Glass Menagerie*." *The Tennessee Williams Annual Review* 1 (1998): 1–11.

DaPonte, Durant. "Tennessee Williams' Gallery of Feminine Characters." *Tennessee Studies in Literature* 10 (1965): 7–26.

Dervin, Daniel A. "The Spook in the Rainforest: The Incestuous Structure of Tennessee Williams's Plays." *Psychocultural Review* 3, no. 2 (Summer/Fall 1979): 153–183.

Falk, Signi Lenea. *Tennessee Williams*. Boston: Twayne Publishers, 2d edition, 1978.

Hale, Allean. "Tennessee Williams's St. Louis Blues." *Mississippi Quarterly* 48, no. 4 (Fall 1995): 609–625.

Hayman, Ronald. *Tennessee Williams: Everyone Else Is an Audience*. New Haven: Yale University Press, 1993.

Jackson, Esther Merle. *The Broken World of Tennessee Williams*. Madison: University of Wisconsin Press, 1965.

King, Kimball. "Tennessee Williams: A Southern Writer." *Mississippi Quarterly* 48, no. 4 (Fall 1995): 627–647.

Konas, Gary. "Tennessee Williams and Lanford Wilson at the Missouri Crossroads." *Studies in American Drama, 1945–Present* 5 (1990): 23–41.

Londre, Felicia Hardison. *Tennessee Williams*. New York: Frederick Ungar Publishers, 1979.

Lumley, Frederick. *Trends in 20th Century Drama*. New York: Oxford University Press, 1960.

McGlinn, Jeanne M. "Tennessee Williams' Women: Illusion and Reality, Sexuality and Love." From *Tennessee Williams: A Tribute*. Jackson: University Press of Mississippi (1977): 510–524.

O'Connor, Jacqueline. *Dramatizing Dementia: Madness in the Plays of Tennessee Williams.* Bowling Green, Ohio: Bowling Green State University Popular Press, 1997.

Parker, R.B., ed. *Twentieth Century Interpretations of the "The Glass Menagerie."* Englewood Cliffs, NJ: Prentice-Hall, 1983.

Reynolds, James. "The Failure of Technology in *The Glass Menagerie.*" *Modern Drama* vol,. 34, No. 4 (December 1991): 522–527.

Sievers, W. David. "Tennessee Williams and Arthur Miller." *Freud on Broadway: A History of Psychoanalysis and the American Drama.* New York: Hermitage (1955): 370–399.

Siebold, Thomas, ed. *Readings on The Glass Menagerie.* San Diego: Greenhaven Press, 1998.

Spoto, Donald. *The Kindness of Strangers: The Life of Tennessee Williams.* New York: Da Capo Press, 1997.

Thompson, Judith J. *Tennessee Williams' Plays: Memory, Myth, and Symbol.* Rev. ed. New York: Peter Lang, 2002.

Van Antwerp, Margaret A., and Sally Johns, eds. *Tennessee Williams.* Detroit: Gale (1984): 58–74.

Weales, Gerald. "Tennessee Williams's Fugitive Kind." *American Drama Since World War II.* New York: Harcourt, Brace and World (1962): 18–39.

Williams, Tennessee. *Memoirs.* Garden City, New York: Doubleday, 1975.

Acknowledgments

"*The Glass Menagerie*" by Nancy M. Tischler. From *Tennessee Williams: Rebellious Puritan*. New York: The Citadel Press (1961): 91–116. © 1961 by The Citadel Press. All rights reserved. Reprinted by arrangement with Kensington Publishing Corp. www.kensingtonbooks.com.

"Tennessee Williams, Theatre Poet in Prose" by Frank Durham. From *South Atlantic Bulletin*, vol. XXXVI, no. 2 (March 1971): 3–16. © 1971 by the South Atlantic Modern Language Association. Reprinted by permission.

"*The Glass Menagerie*: 'It's no tragedy, Freckles'" by Thomas E. Scheye. From *Tennessee Williams: A Tribute*. Jackson: University Press of Mississippi (1977): 207–213. © 1977 by the University Press of Mississippi. Reprinted by permission.

Parker, Brian. "The Composition of *The Glass Menagerie*: An Argument for Complexity." From *Modern Drama*, vol. XXV, no. 3 (September 1982): 409–422. © 1982 by the University of Toronto. Reprinted by permission from the Graduate Centre for the Study of Drama at the University of Toronto and the University of Toronto Press Incorporated. www.utpjournals.com.

"'The Glass Menagerie' (1944)" by Roger Boxill. From *Tennessee Williams*. New York: St. Martin's Press (1987): 61–75. © 1987 by Roger Boxill. Reprinted with permission of Palgrave Macmillan.

"'More than Just a Little Chekhovian': *The Sea Gull* as a Source for the Characters in *The Glass Menagerie*" by Drewey Wayne Gunn. From *Modern Drama*, vol. XXXIII, no. 3 (September 1990): 313–321. © 1990 by the University of Toronto. Reprinted by permission.

"Entering *The Glass Menagerie*" by C. W. E. Bigsby. From *The Cambridge Companion to Tennessee Williams*. Edited by Matthew C. Roudané. Cambridge and New York: Cambridge University Press (1997): 29–44. © 1997 by Cambridge University Press. Reprinted by permission.

"'Where Memory Begins': New Texas Light on *The Glass Menagerie*" by Gilbert Debusscher. From *The Tennessee Williams Annual Review* (1998): 53–62. © 1998 by *The Tennessee Williams Annual Review*. Reprinted by permission.

"The Blue Rose of St. Louis: Laura, Romanticism, and *The Glass Menagerie*" by Bert Cardullo. From *The Tennessee Williams Annual Review* (1998): 81–92. © 1998 by *The Tennessee Williams Annual Review*. Reprinted by permission.

"Tennessee Williams's Tom Wingfield and Georg Kaiser's Cashier: A Contextual Comparison" by William Fordyce. From *Papers on Language & Literature*, vol. 34, no. 3 (Summer 1998): 250–272. © 1998 by the Board of Trustees Southern Illinois University. Reprinted by permission.

"Flying the Jolly Roger: Images of Escape and Selfhood in Tennessee Williams's *The Glass Menagerie* by Lori Leathers Single. From *The Tennessee Williams Annual Review* (1999): 69–85. © 1999 by *The Tennessee Williams Annual Review*. Reprinted by permission.

Every effort has been made to contact the owners of copyrighted material and secure copyright permission. Articles appearing in this volume generally appear much as they did in their original publication with few or no editorial changes. In some cases foreign language text has been removed from the original essay. Those interested in locating the original source will find bibliographic information in the bibliography and acknowledgments sections of this volume.

Index